Motor Racing

gettyimages

Motor Racing

The Early Years
Die Anfänge des Motorsports
Les Débuts de la Course Automobile

Text by Brian Laban

Picture research by
Alex Linghorn

KÖNEMANN

Right: Demogeot and his Darracq, with which he finished third in the Coppa della Velocità in Brescia in 1907.

Rechts: Demogeot und sein Darracq, mit dem er beim Coppa della Velocità in Brescia 1907 den dritten Platz erreichte.

À droite : Demogeot et sa Darracq avec laquelle il a obtenu la troisième place lors de la Coppa della Velocità à Brescia en 1907.

This edition © Tandem Verlag GmbH
KÖNEMANN is a trademark and an imprint of Tandem Verlag GmbH
Photographs © 2001 Getty Images

This book was produced by Book Projects Department at Getty Images.
Please refer all editorial queries to this department at Getty Images,
Unique House, 21–31 Woodfield Road, London W9 2BA

For KÖNEMANN: For Getty Images:
Managing editor: Sally Bald   Art director: Alex Linghorn
Assistant editors: Lucile Bas, Meike Hilbring   Design: Tea McAleer
Translation into German: Manfred Allié   Editor: Richard Collins
Translation into French: Arnaud Dupin de Beyssat   Proof reader: Liz Ihre
                                  Special thanks to: Getty Images
                                  scanning department, Brian Doherty, Leon Meyer

Printed in China

ISBN-10: 3-8331-1354-5
ISBN-13: 978-3-8331-1354-3

10 9 8 7 6 5 4 3 2
X IX VIII VII VI V IV III II I

Frontispiece: Mike Hawthorn, the 1959 World Champion, sits in his Ferrari in the Monaco pits during practice for
the 1957 Monaco Grand Prix, where he crashed during the race.

Frontispiz: Mike Hawthorn, der Weltmeister von 1959 sitzt in seinem Ferrari beim Boxenstopp während des Trainings
für den Großen Preis von Monaco, 1957, bei dem er während des Rennens einen Unfall hatte.

Frontispice : Mike Hawthorn, le champion du monde en 1959, dans sa Ferrari, au stand lors des essais
pour le Grand Prix de Monaco en 1957, au cours duquel il eut un accident durant la course.

Contents

Inhalt

Sommaire

Prologue

Motor sport, in its many guises, is one of the most glamorous sports in the world and one of the most widely watched, by people in virtually every country all over the globe. It is also one of the most complex of sports, with its interdependence of man (or woman) and machine, its modern reliance on commercial sponsorship and its high levels of technology. But behind the glamour, the money and the science, motor racing in the 21st century is fundamentally the same pure sport that it was throughout the 20th century, the same sport that it was from its late 19th-century origins. Now, as then, nothing can be taken for granted. Speed is nothing without reliability and intelligence and tactics can still overcome apparently impossible odds, while to win involves an indefinable combination of car, driver, behind-the-scenes team work and, not least, good fortune. It is that uncertainty, as much as the glamour and power, which makes motor racing fascinating.

The sport was a natural consequence of the second car: as soon as there were two cars in one arena, it was inevitable that they would want to race against each other. Fundamentally, it represents the need to prove one design's superiority over another, and the ability of the driver to contribute to that superiority. To the manufacturers of motor cars, and not only sporting cars but also by extension even the most ordinary family saloon, motor racing is a place where ideas are tried out, lessons are learned and reputations are made and lost. From the earliest days of the sport, manufacturers and sponsors alike have known the truth of the saying 'win on Sunday, sell on Monday'. To the spectator and enthusiast, motor sport provides a glimpse of what is possible, and what to aspire to.

Motoring competition began before the end of the 19th century with motoring trials, whose primary purpose was to demonstrate that the new automobiles were capable of practical, everyday use. These trials quickly developed into head-to-head contests on which the sport has been based ever since. It has taken many forms, the popularity of different disciplines or types of motor racing ebbing and flowing over the years. Drivers have raced on public roads, on artificial road circuits, on banked tracks, on dirt ovals, up and down rural hillsides and through the great mountain passes of Europe, along beaches, on ice and on forest tracks. They have raced wheel to wheel against each other, against the clock, against the handicapper and the points judge. They have raced, rallied, trialed and hillclimbed everything from the standard family saloon car to the multimillion pound, 1,000hp Grand Prix car, but always with the same goal of going as quickly as whatever piece of machinery involved will allow. At its outer limits, that also included the quest to be the fastest of all, as the world's land speed record evolved, at least in its early days, in parallel with the fastest racing cars.

At its roots, motor sport has been contested on a shoestring by back garden innovators who have experimented with other people's hardware and their own ideas, and very occasionally given the big guns something to think about. At the upper levels, it has been funded by the manufacturers, by wealthy individuals, by oil companies, tyre makers, engine builders and component suppliers. In the 1930s, in Germany at least, it was funded by the government itself, ostensibly in pursuit of technical excellence but in reality to make a political point, that of national superiority. Latterly, the sport has been massively subsidised by commercial sponsors, many of which may have no connections with the motor industry beyond their racing connections, but who nevertheless become household names because of those connections, whether they are a cigarette maker, a clothing manufacturer, a computer company or a bank. But whatever the name on the car, the sport itself does not at heart change.

Motor racing has always been dangerous and, as such, a sport for heroes. It claimed its first fatalities long before the turn of its first decade, and sadly the element of driver mortality has been an intrinsic part of the sport ever since; but it has learned lessons from that, and so have the car makers whose everyday products have moved those lessons further down the line. They have learned technical lessons from success, too, as the high-pressure development of brakes, tyres, suspension systems, fuels, engine aerodynamics and electronics have filtered down from racing to the road. Racing most certainly *does* improve the breed.

But that is not its main purpose. Fundamentally, motor racing is show business and the vast majority of the people who are in it are only there because spectators, either on the spot or via the world's television networks, ultimately attract the sponsors, the car makers and the myriad other participants who make the sport possible. Motor racing needs its outside income, but the people who provide that income need motor racing just as badly. Ultimately, it is a case of each feeding off the other.

It has evolved in quite well-defined eras. The earliest days were the 'empirical' era, where the car makers in effect went their own way, piling on the size and power in pursuit of speed before the people who controlled the sport created a framework of technical regulations which gave it the infrastructure to develop more practically. The 1920s became a golden age, drawing on the technical lessons of wartime, as well as a new, wider acceptance of the car itself. In the 1930s national rivalries reflected the world's political direction, and in the 1940s and 1950s the sport revived and grew.

Early race series pitted country against country as well as make against make, and until the coming of commercial sponsorship in the late 1960s the red of Italy, the Racing Green of Britain, the blue of France and the silver of Germany were as recognisable as any football strip to the sport's enthusiasts, and even to the wider world. The colours were a symbol of great rivalries, from the battles between Bentley and Bugatti at Le Mans in the 1920s and early 1930s to the national contests between Mercedes-Benz and Auto Union before the Second World War, and Alfa Romeo, Maserati and Ferrari after it. Throughout the sport's history the dominant marques have

changed, and never more spectacularly than in the period encompassed by this book. Domination started with the French, passed to Germany, back to France with occasional incursions from the English in the 1920s, then to Italy, back to Germany, to Italy again, to Germany as Mercedes-Benz returned to the scene in the mid-1950s, and ultimately began to shift back towards Britain at the end of the 1950s as the UK led the latest technical revolution which put the engine behind the driver instead of in front.

That move in itself marked the beginning of the end of a broader era – the early days of the sport. The changes gained pace in the 1960s, both technically and commercially, and motor racing, while retaining its fundamental philosophies, took on a different character. For some people it lost something in the transition, but that is an arguable point. What is seldom disputed is that the period covered by this book was a notable age for motor sport, one filled (even given the overuse of the adjective) with great names and great events that are still remembered with awe and affection. The face of motor racing today may have changed, but the drama and romance have always been there in equal measure.

Der Motorsport in seinen vielen Erscheinungsformen gehört zu den spektakulärsten Sportarten der Welt und hat Anhänger rund um den Erdball. Und kaum ein Sport ist komplexer, mit seiner engen Verbindung von Mensch und Maschine, der aufwändigen Technik und der großen Rolle, die Sponsoren aus der Wirtschaft heute spielen. Doch trotz Glamour, Geld und High Tech ist der Motorsport auch im 21. Jahrhundert das geblieben, was er seit seinen Anfängen im späten 19. und das ganze 20. Jahrhundert hindurch war – ein reiner Sport. Heute wie damals ist nichts daran selbstverständlich. Geschwindigkeit allein ist gar nichts, wenn es an der Zuverlässigkeit fehlt, Intelligenz und Taktik können auch heute noch den überlegensten Gegner bezwingen, während für einen Rennsieg das Zusammenspiel von Fahrer und Wagen, gute Teamarbeit hinter den Kulissen und nicht zuletzt eine Portion Glück erforderlich sind. Dass sich diese Faktoren nie berechnen lassen, das macht, neben Schnelligkeit und Spektakel, den Motorsport so faszinierend.

Als zum ersten Automobil ein zweites hinzukam, war der Sport geboren – sie mussten ihre Kräfte messen. Die Konstrukteure wollten zeigen, dass ihre Wagen überlegen waren, und die Fahrer, dass sie diese Überlegenheit zu nutzen verstanden. Für die Hersteller, ob nun von Sportwagen oder braven Limousinen, ist die Rennstrecke der Ort, an dem neue Ideen erprobt werden, an dem man aus Fehlern lernt, sich Ansehen verschafft oder es auch verspielt. Wer am Sonntag gewinnt, bei dem klingeln am Montag die Kassen – das wussten Fabrikanten und Sponsoren schon, als der Sport noch in den Kinderschuhen steckte. Für die Zuschauer zeigen die Rennen, was möglich ist und welche Ziele angestrebt werden.

Die früheste Form des Wettbewerbs waren am Ende des 19. Jahrhunderts die Versuchsfahrten, die in erster Linie unter Beweis stellen sollten, dass die Automobile im Alltag gebrauchstüchtig waren. Aus der Versuchs- wurde jedoch binnen kurzem eine Wettfahrt, und das ist der Motorsport bis heute geblieben. Sein Spektrum wurde breiter, und bald erfreute sich die eine, bald die andere Variante größerer Beliebtheit. Rennen sind auf öffentlichen Straßen gefahren worden, auf speziellen Rundstrecken, auf Rennkursen mit Steilkurven, auf Staubpisten, ländlichen Hügeln und den großen Bergpässen Europas, an Stränden, auf Eis und auf Waldwegen. Fahrer sind gegeneinander angetreten, gegen die Uhr, gegen Handicapper und Punktrichter. Rennen,

Rallyes, Test- und Bergfahrten sind mit Fahrzeugen aller Arten gefahren worden, vom Serienmodell bis zu millionenteuren 1000-PS-Grand-Prix-Wagen, aber stets mit derselben Absicht: so schnell zu sein wie nur möglich. Im Extremfall sogar der Schnellste überhaupt, denn zumindest zu Beginn entwickelten sich Weltrekordfahrten parallel zum übrigen Renngeschehen.

In seiner einfachsten Form wurde der Sport von Tüftlern betrieben, die mit minimalem Budget von einer Garage aus mit gekauften Wagen und viel Phantasie experimentierten, und dann und wann den Großen Denkanstöße gaben. Am anderen Ende des Spektrums haben die Automobilfirmen den Motorsport finanziert, Millionäre, Ölgesellschaften, Reifenhersteller, Zulieferer von Motoren und Komponenten. Einmal, in den dreißiger Jahren in Deutschland, wurde er zur Staatsangelegenheit, vorgeblich, um die Technik voranzutreiben, in Wirklichkeit jedoch, um nationale Überlegenheit zur Schau zu stellen. In den letzten Jahren sind Sponsoren aus der Wirtschaft immer mehr in den Vordergrund getreten – Firmen, die außer dieser kommerziellen oft keinerlei Verbindung zur Automobilindustrie haben, durch die Werbung jedoch ihren Bekanntheitsgrad in der Öffentlichkeit steigern, ob nun Zigaretten- oder Kleiderhersteller, Computerfirmen oder Banken. Aber ganz gleich, welcher Name auf dem Wagen steht, in seinem Innersten bleibt der Sport stets, was er immer war.

Von Anfang an ist der Motorsport gefährlich gewesen – er ist ein Sport für Helden. Lange bevor sein erstes Jahrzehnt um war, hatte er Todesopfer gefordert, und dass immer wieder Fahrer ihr Leben lassen, gehört leider bis heute dazu; aber Rennbetrieb und Hersteller lernen aus den Unfällen, und die Erkenntnisse kommen in den Serienmodellen allen zugute. Und auch vom Ringen um den Erfolg profitieren alle, denn er beschleunigt die Entwicklung von Bremsen, Reifen, Radaufhängungen, Treibstoffen, Motoren und Aerodynamik, die vom Sport aus Eingang in den Alltag finden. Rennsport dient dem Fortschritt, daran kann es keinen Zweifel geben.

Doch das ist nicht sein Haupt-Daseinszweck. Motorsport ist Showbusiness, und die große Mehrzahl derer, die für diesen Sport arbeiten, tun es letzten Endes, weil nur das Publikum, entweder an den Rennstrecken oder vor den Fernsehern, die Sponsoren, Autofirmen und unzählige andere anlockt, die den Sport erst möglich machen. Der Motorsport ist auf die Finanzierung von außen angewiesen, doch ebenso brauchen die Geldgeber den Motorsport als Werbeträger. Jeder profitiert dabei vom anderen.

Die Entwicklung lässt sich in recht eindeutig bestimmbare Etappen einteilen. Am Anfang stand die »empirische« Ära, als im Grunde jeder Hersteller tat, was er wollte, und mit immer größeren und stärkeren Wagen immer größere Geschwindigkeiten erreichte. Als nächstes kam durch technische Vorgaben der Organisatoren eine gewisse Ordnung in den Sport, und innerhalb dieses Rahmens entwickelten sich praktikablere Rennformen. In den zwanziger Jahren setzten sich die konstruktiven Neuerungen des Weltkriegs durch, und das erste goldene Zeitalter des Rennsports begann, zumal es das Jahrzehnt war, in dem das Automobil überall Einzug in den Alltag hielt. Die dreißiger Jahre waren, wie in der großen Politik, von nationalen Rivalitäten geprägt, doch nach dem Krieg stand wieder der Sport im Mittelpunkt und erreichte in den fünfziger Jahren ungeahnte Dimensionen.

In den frühen Rennen traten nicht nur die Marken, sondern auch die Nationen gegeneinander an, und bis sie Ende der sechziger Jahre von den Aufschriften der Sponsoren verdrängt wurden, waren das italienische Rot, das britische Dunkelgrün, Frankreichs Blau und Deutschlands Silber für den Rennbegeisterten und darüber hinaus in der Öffentlichkeit so unverwechselbar wie für den Fußballfreund die Farben der Trikots. So traten die Rivalen gegeneinander an, in Le Mans in den zwanziger und dreißiger Jahren Bentley und Bugatti, vor dem Zweiten Weltkrieg Mercedes-Benz und Auto Union, in den fünfziger Jahren Alfa Romeo, Maserati und Ferrari. Im Laufe der Jahre haben sich die Gewichte zwischen den Nationen verschoben, und besonders dramatisch in den Jahrzehnten, die unser Buch beschreibt. Die ersten Jahre waren von den Franzosen geprägt, dann herrschten die Deutschen vor, später wieder Frankreich mit einigen britischen Vorstößen in den zwanziger Jahren, dann rückten die Italiener in den Vordergrund, danach die Deutschen und wieder die Italiener, und in den fünfziger Jahren, als Mercedes-Benz ins Renngeschehen zurückkehrte, dominierten von neuem die Deutschen, bis am Ende des Jahrzehnts mit der revolutionären Verlagerung des Motors hinter den Fahrer wieder die Briten die Nase vorn hatten.

Diese Neuerung lässt sich als Wendepunkt in der Geschichte des Motorrennsports bezeichnen, als Abschluss seiner ersten Epoche. In der Technik und auch im nun vom Kommerz bestimmten Erscheinungsbild waren die sechziger Jahre ein Jahrzehnt der großen Veränderungen, und der ganze Charakter des Motorsports wandelte sich. Manche sagen, er habe etwas von seinen ursprünglichen Qualitäten verloren, aber darüber lässt sich streiten. Niemand wird jedoch bestreiten, dass die ersten Jahrzehnte des Sports, von denen unser Buch handelt, aufregende Jahre waren, auf deren große Fahrer und Rennen man heute mit Bewunderung zurückblickt. Und auch wenn der Motorsport nun ein anderes Gesicht hat, sind doch Drama und Abenteuer dieselben wie eh und je.

In the years before the Second World War, Grand Prix racing was dominated by the State-sponsored German teams, Mercedes-Benz, here at Donington in 1937, and Auto Union.

In den Jahren vor dem Zweiten Weltkrieg beherrschten die staatlich finanzierten deutschen Teams die Rennstrecken: Mercedes-Benz, hier 1937 in Donington, und Auto Union.

Avant la Seconde Guerre mondiale, la course en Grand Prix est dominée par les écuries allemandes, financées par le gouvernement, Auto Union et Mercedes-Benz (ici à Donington en 1937).

1

Of Trials and Road Races

When the motor car was invented in the mid-1880s, it was a relatively crude and unsophisticated creation whose design was not so much about speed as about mobility independent of the horse or the railway. But once the motor car's internal combustion horsepower started to take its passengers from A to B as quickly and as reliably as the more traditional kind of horse power, the next items on the wish list were to travel more quickly, more reliably and further afield than had been possible before. Not least, the new invention also had to establish itself with an initially sceptical, even hostile public. So automobiles improved rapidly, and either side of the turn of the century it was a natural thing to test their performance first against the elements and the landscape, and then, as production spread, against each other. Thus, the motor car gave rise to motoring trials, the trials became competitive, and the competition between rival makes and their drivers became a sport, with many different branches.

If Germany was the birthplace of the car, France was the country in which it first became established commercially. France also became motor sport's nursery, even before the 20th century dawned, and the headquarters of motor racing's organising body has remained in France ever since. The first organised competition that could genuinely be regarded as a race (although it was called a trial) took place on 22 July 1894, when some twenty-one machines of enormously variable provenance set out from Paris to Rouen, a distance of just under 80 miles. Count de Dion's steam car was the first to arrive, but the 5,000 franc first prize, presented by *Le Petit Journal* and starting a motor sport tradition of commercial sponsorship, was shared between the petrol-engined Panhards and Peugeots which followed him – starting another ongoing motor sport tradition of results occasionally being decided by the rule book some time after the event.

That pioneering event heralded a tradition of great road races that dominated the sport's formative years, and created its first heroes, but it also led to its first tragedies and inevitable conflicts with the establishment. The town-to-town era lasted less than ten years and, for the most part, the great races had Paris as either their starting-point, as in the Paris–Bordeaux races of 1899 and 1901 and the Paris–Vienna race of 1902, or occasionally as both start and finish point, as was the case in the Paris–Bordeaux–Paris of 1895 and Paris–Amsterdam–Paris of 1898. The unique demands of these races, often featuring the long, arrow-straight French Routes Nationales, shaped the early racing cars, with an emphasis on straight-line speed, from huge engines but still relatively simple technology. Such cars were built mainly on the front-engine, rear-drive layout established by Panhard et Levassor, and created considerable reputations for marques such as Peugeot, Renault, Fiat, Mercedes, Napier, Darracq and De Dietrich into the early days of the 20th century. But the great speeds on largely unprotected, unsurfaced roads were a recipe for disaster. Road racing's reputation spread worldwide but the format came to an abrupt end with the ill-fated Paris–Madrid race of 1903. The race was halted in Bordeaux (by order of the government) following the deaths of a number of spectators and the driver Marcel Renault, and the first era of motor racing died with them.

In the first instance, the alternative was still to run events on the public highway, but to create temporarily closed courses on which both competitors and spectators could be far better marshalled and better protected than they had ever been along the early inter-city routes. The first of these closed courses were again mostly in France, but were also now spreading to Germany, Italy, Ireland and eventually to America. They were usually roughly triangular in shape with towns and villages defining their extremes, and with lap distances typically of between 40 and 100 miles. By now, too, it was not uncommon for average speed to be more than 60mph, occasionally even 70mph, and for the fastest cars to travel considerably faster than that on the straight sections.

These new 'circuit' races were one aspect of an increasingly sophisticated structure for the sport, which introduced new technical regulations, new racing formats and what became a famous family of races bringing not only individual makes and drivers but also national representative teams head to head. Such races had many patrons, from the wealthy Italian sportsman Vincenzo Florio to the even wealthier American financier and pioneer racing motorist William K. Vanderbilt, and even the ruling classes in the German Kaiserpreis races. The Gordon Bennett Trophy races were perhaps the most famous of all. Promoted by the American sportsman and newspaper proprietor James Gordon Bennett, they saw teams of three cars from each invited country competing against each other not only for the handsome trophy but also for the honour of their country hosting the following year's event. Most importantly, they pitted America against Europe, but Europe came out on top. From 1900 to 1905, France won four times, Germany and Britain once each, with the German win in 1903 taken by a new, more scientific breed of car which launched Mercedes as the dominant racing car of its day. That win was taken by Camille Jenatzy, the Belgian driver who had also been the first man in the world to exceed 60mph in an automobile (the electrically powered Jamais Contente in 1899), in an era when motor racing and record breaking were still closely linked.

Britain had won the right to stage that 1903 Gordon Bennett race, but Jenatzy's win came on a public road circuit in Ireland, with the eliminating trials in the Isle of Man, because the British authorities, unlike their French, German or Italian counterparts, would not countenance racing on public roads on the mainland. It was one more example of Britain's class-ridden early resistance to motoring, which had already seen even the relatively gentle sport of hillclimbing forced off the public roads and on to closed venues on private land. But that official antipathy gave rise to another of the great developments of the first age of motor racing which would shape its whole future – the opening of the world's first purpose-built closed venue for motoring competitions, at Brooklands, near Weybridge in Surrey. That famous banked oval, built on his family estate by wealthy Surrey landowner Hugh Fortescue Locke King, was opened in June 1907 with various record runs, followed by its first race meeting in July. It was a place where motoring enthusiasts could bring their families and their picnics to enjoy spectacular racing, a garden party atmosphere, and even, if they wished, a flutter with the on-course bookmakers. But Brooklands played a much more important role; it was also a proving ground for the industry, a test track for anyone who wished to pay for the facility, and, until speeds escalated still further, a venue for setting outright world speed records.

Against this background of changing race formats and more structured competitions, the cars themselves, after a period of almost unrestricted design, continued to develop more scientifically, and now within some official frameworks – the first racing formulae. Now, brute force would not always win, as restrictions on engine size, weight or fuel consumption among other things created a level playing field for the contestants where science would become more important than simple muscle, while performance continued to improve all the time. The new formulae became the basis for a new kind of competition, again pioneered in France and known as

Grand Prix racing. The first of the many was the French Grand Prix of June 1906, run to the same technical regulations as the Gordon Bennett races over a triangular 65-mile course near the town of Le Mans. The 770-mile race, run over two days with the cars despatched at 90-second intervals rather than in one massed start, was won by the Hungarian Ferenc Szisz's Renault ahead of Felice Nazzaro's Fiat at an average speed of 63mph – with a fastest lap from Paul Baras in the Brasier at more than 73mph. That first race was a great success and it established a new racing format. In future, cars complying with a strict technical formula would race over a fixed number of laps on a closed circuit, the winner being the one to complete the course in the shortest time. The format would survive and become familiar, albeit with considerable changes, for many years to come

In barely a decade and a half, from the Paris–Rouen Trial of 1894 to the beginning of the 1910s, motor sport had been born, and had come through an interesting and often troubled infancy to reach a point of considerable maturity. It was already an entirely international sport, contested on both sides of the Atlantic; it had a huge following of both competitors and spectators; it had massive variety in its make-up, from trials and hillclimbs to Grands Prix and record breaking. And increasingly it was of great importance to the pioneering motor manufacturers, commercially, as a proving ground and as a crucible for new thinking. From this point, there was no looking back.

Als der Motorwagen Mitte der 1880er Jahre aufkam, war er zunächst ein recht grobes und unzuverlässiges Gefährt, das nicht dazu da war, schnell zu fahren, sondern dazu, Unabhängigkeit von Pferd und Eisenbahn zu schaffen. Doch als die Pferdestärken des Verbrennungsmotors die Reisenden erst einmal ebenso schnell und zuverlässig ans Ziel brachten wie das gute alte Pferd, stand der Sinn nach mehr Geschwindigkeit, noch größerer Zuverlässigkeit und weiter entfernten Zielen denn je. Und die neue Erfindung musste sich erst noch vor einer skeptischen, wenn nicht sogar feindseligen Öffentlichkeit bewähren. So ging die technische Entwicklung um die Jahrhundertwende rasch voran, und bald maßen die Automobile sich in ihrer Leistung nicht mehr nur am Auf und Ab der Landschaft und an den Elementen; aus den Test- wurden Wettfahrten, und aus dem Wettbewerb zwischen Marken und Fahrern entstand der Sport in all seinen Spielarten.

Die Geburtsstätte des Automobils stand in Deutschland, doch Frankreich war das Land, in dem es sich zuerst durchsetzte. Frankreich war auch, noch vor Anbruch des 20. Jahrhunderts, die Kinderstube des Motorsports, und das Hauptquartier seiner Organisationen ist bis heute dort geblieben. Die erste Veranstaltung, die als Rennen gelten kann (auch wenn sie als Testfahrt ausgeschrieben war), fand am 22. Juli 1894 statt, als etwa 21 Wagen höchst unterschiedlicher Bauart sich auf die Fahrt von Paris nach Rouen machten, eine Strecke von knapp 130 Kilometern. Der Dampfwagen des Grafen de Dion ging als erster ins Ziel. Der Preis von 5000 Francs, den *Le Petit Journal* gestiftet hatte – womit die Zeitung die Motorsporttradition des kommerziellen Sponsoring begründete –, ging gemeinschaftlich an die nachfolgenden benzinbetriebenen Panhards und Peugeots. Auch das war der Beginn einer Tradition: dass bisweilen die Regeln und nicht die Zielflagge entschieden, wer Sieger eines Rennens wird.

Diese Pionierfahrt stand am Anfang einer Reihe von klassischen Straßenrennen, wie sie typisch für die Anfangsjahre des Sports waren; diese Rennen schufen die ersten Helden, forderten aber auch die ersten Todesopfer und sorgten für die ersten Konflikte mit der Öffentlichkeit. Die Ära der Straßenrennen von Stadt zu Stadt dauerte nicht einmal zehn Jahre, wobei die meisten dieser Rennen von Paris ausgingen, etwa die Fahrten Paris–Bordeaux von 1899 und 1901 und Paris–Wien, 1902, und bisweilen auch wieder dort endeten,

wie 1895 die Fahrt Paris–Bordeaux–Paris und 1898 Paris–Amsterdam–Paris. Die Anforderungen dieser Rennen, die oft über die langen, pfeilgeraden französischen Routes nationales führten, bestimmten die frühen Wagen, die mit starken Motoren und einfachem Fahrwerk vor allem für Tempo auf geraden Strecken ausgelegt waren. Die meisten folgten dem Bauprinzip, das Panhard et Levassor als Standard etabliert hatten, mit Motor vorn und Hinterradantrieb, und zu den Firmen, die mit Rennsiegen ins neue Jahrhundert gingen, zählten Peugeot, Renault, Fiat, Mercedes, Napier, Darracq und De Dietrich. Doch die hohen Geschwindigkeiten auf den ungesicherten, großenteils unbefestigten Straßen forderten Unglücke geradezu heraus. Obwohl sie weltweit für Aufsehen sorgten, kam diese Art von Straßenrennen mit der tragischen Fahrt Paris–Madrid im Jahre 1903 zu einem abrupten Ende. Auf staatliche Anordnung hin wurde das Rennen in Bordeaux abgebrochen, nachdem der Fahrer Marcel Renault und eine Reihe von Zuschauern ums Leben gekommen waren, und mit ihnen wurde die erste Epoche des Motorsports zu Grabe getragen.

Als Ersatz kamen Rennen auf, die zwar nach wie vor auf öffentlichen Straßen stattfanden, jedoch auf Rundstrecken, die für die Zeit des Rennens abgesperrt waren, sodass Fahrer wie Zuschauer sich besser dirigieren und besser schützen ließen. Die ersten dieser Rundstrecken entstanden wiederum in Frankreich, doch bald breitete sich die Idee auch in Deutschland, Italien, Irland und schließlich sogar in Amerika aus. Meist bildete die Streckenführung eine Art Dreieck mit Städten oder Dörfern an den Eckpunkten, und die typische Länge lag zwischen etwa 60 und 160 Kilometern. Inzwischen waren auch Durchschnittsgeschwindigkeiten von 100 oder sogar 110 Stundenkilometern keine Seltenheit mehr, und die besten Wagen waren auf den Geraden noch weitaus schneller.

Diese neuen »Rennstrecken« waren ein Anzeichen dafür, dass der Sport allmählich eine Infrastruktur bekam; bald gab es technische Vorschriften, Regeln für bestimmte Rennformen, und die klassischen Rennen bildeten sich heraus, in denen nicht nur Marken und Fahrer gegeneinander antraten, sondern auch Teams, die ihre jeweilige Nation vertraten. Hinter den Rennen standen oft Gönner, etwa der wohlhabende italienische Sportsmann Vincenzo Florio oder der noch wohlhabendere amerikanische Finanzier und Rennpionier William K. Vanderbilt; bei den deutschen Kaiserpreis-Rennen war es sogar der Adel des Landes. Die Rennen um die

Gordon-Bennett-Trophäe waren wohl die berühmtesten. Aus jedem Land, das zur Teilnahme geladen wurde, traten drei Wagen an, die nicht nur um den stattlichen Pokal wetteiferten, den der sportbegeisterte amerikanische Zeitungsverleger James Gordon Bennett ausgesetzt hatte, sondern auch um die Ehre, im folgenden Jahr das Rennen auszurichten. Vor allem trat erstmals Europa gegen Amerika an, wobei anfangs die Europäer deutlich überlegen waren. Zwischen 1900 und 1905 konnten die Franzosen vier Siege verbuchen, Deutschland und Großbritannien je einen, wobei der siegreiche deutsche Wagen im Jahr 1903 ein Mercedes war – systematischer konstruiert als die Konkurrenz und deshalb überall erfolgreich. Am Steuer saß der Belgier Camille Jenatzy, der 1899 mit seinem Elektrowagen Jamais Contente als erster die 100-Stundenkilometer-Grenze überschritten hatte, in einer Zeit, in der Rennen und Rekordfahrten noch nicht so streng getrennt waren wie in späteren Jahren.

Das Recht auf das Gordon-Bennett-Rennen von 1903 hatte im Vorjahr Großbritannien gewonnen, doch Jenatzy errang seinen Sieg auf einem Straßenkurs in Irland (nach Vorentscheidungen auf der Isle of Man), denn anders als in Frankreich, Deutschland und Italien gestatteten die britischen Behörden auf der Hauptinsel keine Rennen auf öffentlichen Straßen. Es war ein weiteres Beispiel dafür, wie sehr in Großbritannien in den frühen Jahren die herrschenden konservativen Kreise die Ausbreitung des Automobils behinderten, und selbst der vergleichsweise harmlose Sport der Bergfahrten durfte nur auf abgezäuntem Privatland stattfinden. Doch die offizielle Antipathie gab den Anstoß zu einer weiteren wichtigen Entwicklung in der Frühzeit des Motorsports, die entscheidend für die Zukunft sein sollte – die Eröffnung der ersten speziell für Automobilrennen gebauten Rundstrecke in Brooklands bei Weybridge in Surrey. Zur Einweihung dieses legendären Ovals auf dem Familiensitz des Gutsherrn Hugh Fortescue Locke King im Juni 1907 fand eine Reihe von Rekordfahrten statt, und im Juli folgte das erste Rennen. Motorsportbegeisterte konnten mit ihren Familien zum Picknick kommen und den spektakulären Fahrten zusehen, es herrschte die Stimmung einer Gartenparty, und wer wollte, konnte auch sein Glück bei den fliegenden Buchmachern versuchen. Doch Brooklands hatte mehr zu bieten als das; es war auch eine Teststrecke für die Industrie und für jeden, der den Kurs für seine Zwecke mietete, und es wurden sogar Weltrekorde darauf gefahren, bis das Tempo für die Strecke zu hoch wurde.

Vor dem Hintergrund allmählich straffer strukturierter Rennen entwickelten sich die Fahrzeuge; auf die Phase des Experimentierens folgten systematischere Konstruktionen, für die auch bald Regeln festgelegt wurden – die ersten Rennformeln. Nun siegte nicht mehr automatisch die pure Kraft, denn Begrenzungen in Motorgröße, Gewicht oder Benzinverbrauch sorgten für gleiche Startbedingungen, sodass Verstand nun wichtiger war als Muskeln, wobei die Leistungen trotzdem ständig weiter stiegen. Die neuen Formeln ermöglichten eine neue Form von Rennen, die wiederum zuerst in Frankreich stattfanden und die unter dem Namen Grand-Prix-Rennen bekannt wurden. Der erste unter vielen war der Große Preis von Frankreich im Juni 1906, veranstaltet nach den gleichen Vorgaben wie die Gordon-Bennett-Rennen über einen 105 Kilometer langen Dreieckskurs bei Le Mans. 1240 Kilometer wurden in zwei Renntagen gefahren, und zwar nicht mit Massenstarts, sondern mit Wagen, die in anderthalbminütigem Abstand auf den Kurs gingen; Sieger war mit einer Durchschnittsgeschwindigkeit von 101,4 km/h der Ungar Ferenc Szisz auf Renault vor Felice Nazzaro auf Fiat, und die schnellste Runde fuhr Paul Barat auf seinem Brasier mit fast 120 Stundenkilometern. Dieses erste Rennen war ein großer Erfolg, und ein neuer Renntyp war geboren. Von da an traten in einem typischen Rennen Wagen an, für die bestimmte technische Spezifikationen vorgegeben waren, sie fuhren eine festgelegte Zahl von Runden auf einem geschlossenen Kurs, und Sieger war derjenige, der die Gesamtstrecke in kürzester Zeit zurückgelegt hatte. Trotz aller Veränderungen sollte sich dieses Grundmuster über viele Jahre hinweg durchsetzen.

Kaum anderthalb Jahrzehnte waren vergangen, doch in dieser Zeit von der Fahrt Paris–Rouen im Jahr 1894 bis etwa zum Jahr 1910 war der Motorsport zur Welt gekommen, hatte eine turbulente, oft gefährliche Kindheit überstanden und es zu einer gewissen Reife gebracht. Der Sport war längst international geworden, und Rennen fanden beiderseits des Atlantiks statt; die Zahl der Zuschauer wie die der Teilnehmer hatte sich vervielfacht, und Rennen wurden in allen erdenklichen Formen veranstaltet, von Vergleichs- und Bergfahrten bis zu den Grand Prix und Rekordfahrten. Die aufstrebende Motorindustrie hatte den Wert der Rennen für Test und Entwicklung erkannt. Von da an ging es nur noch voran.

With the 60hp Mercedes which won the 1903 Gordon Bennett race, Daimler-Benz reshaped the early racing car and the theme continued into this 1908 120hp model.

Mit dem im Gordon-Bennett-Rennen von 1903 siegreichen 60-PS-Mercedes schuf Daimler-Benz einen neuen Rennwagentyp, in dessen Nachfolge auch dieses 120-PS-Modell von 1908 steht.

Avec la Mercedes 60 ch, détentrice de la Coupe Gordon Bennett 1903, Daimler-Benz donne un nouveau visage à la voiture de course, qu'il conservera notamment pour cette 120 ch de 1908.

Fritz Erle's Benz had a troubled run in the 1907 Florio Cup (for cars conforming to Kaiserpreis rules), finishing tenth, behind winner Cav. Ferdinando Minoia's Isotta-Fraschini.

Fritz Erle trat 1907 mit seinem Benz beim Rennen um den Florio-Pokal (nach den Regeln des Kaiserpreises) an, kam aber nur mit Mühen als Zehnter ins Ziel; Sieger war Cav. Ferdinando Minoia auf Isotta-Fraschini.

La Benz de Fritz Erle connaît quelques malheurs lors de la Coupe Florio de 1907 (réservée aux voitures satisfaisant aux règles du Kaiserpreis) et finit dixième derrière l'Isotta-Fraschini du chevalier Ferdinando Minoia.

Le véhicule automobile inventé au milieu des années 1880 est en réalité une machine assez rudimentaire, créée non pas tant pour la vitesse que pour offrir une mobilité individuelle indépendante du cheval ou du chemin de fer. Toutefois, dès que la puissance du moteur à combustion interne permet de transporter des passagers de A à B aussi vite et avec autant de sécurité qu'un cheval, on souhaite alors voyager plus rapidement encore et dans de meilleures conditions. Il faut aussi que cette nouvelle invention se forge une réputation meilleure auprès d'un public au départ en majorité sceptique, voire hostile. Au tournant du XIXᵉ siècle, l'automobile ayant déjà énormément évolué, il paraît tout naturel d'éprouver ses qualités et de mesurer ses performances face aux éléments et sur des distances de plus en plus importantes puis, à mesure que leur nombre augmente, de faire concourir des voitures différentes les unes contre les autres. C'est ainsi que les concours automobiles se transforment petit à petit en compétitions, et que ces compétitions entre firmes rivales et leurs pilotes respectifs deviennent un sport organisé, comportant différents types d'épreuves.

Si l'Allemagne est le pays de naissance de l'automobile, la France devient, bien avant le début du XXᵉ siècle, non seulement celui où elle connaît son premier lancement commercial mais aussi le berceau du sport automobile ; c'est d'ailleurs à Paris que demeure le siège de sa principale organisation. Le 22 juillet 1894, la première compétition que l'on peut vraiment considérer comme une course (bien qu'elle se soit appelée concours) réunit près de vingt et une machines de provenances très diverses sur un parcours de tout juste 129 kilomètres entre Paris et Rouen. Alors que la voiture à vapeur du comte de Dion arrive première, le prix de 5000 francs offert au vainqueur par *Le Petit Journal* est toutefois partagé entre ses suivantes, une Panhard et une Peugeot équipées d'un moteur à pétrole. La détermination du classement par la réglementation et entériné sur le tapis vert un certain temps après l'épreuve et non en fonction des résultats obtenus sur le terrain, n'est pas en effet une notion moderne.

Ce premier concours marque la genèse du sport automobile et annonce la décennie de ces grandes épreuves sur route qui vont engendrer des héros de légende mais entraîner aussi les premières tragédies et des conflits inévitables avec les autorités. La plupart de ces courses de ville à ville ont alors Paris soit comme point de départ, comme dans les Paris–Bordeaux de 1899 et 1901 ou le Paris–Vienne de 1902, soit comme point de départ et d'arrivée, par exemple pour la course Paris–Bordeaux–Paris de 1895 et le Paris–Amsterdam–Paris de 1898. Le tracé particulier de ces épreuves et le règlement qui leur est appliqué influencent la conception des premières voitures de course en faisant porter les efforts sur la vitesse en ligne droite. Mues par d'énormes moteurs d'une technologie encore relativement simple, la plupart reprennent la conception à moteur avant et propulsion arrière définie par Panhard et Levassor qui fait la notoriété de marques comme Peugeot, Renault, Fiat, Mercedes, Napier, Darracq et De Dietrich dans les premières années du XXᵉ siècle. Toutefois, les vitesses atteintes sur des routes mal protégées et au revêtement souvent inexistant ne peuvent conduire qu'à la catastrophe. La formule du ville à ville s'achève ainsi brutalement avec l'accident survenu à Bordeaux dans le Paris–Madrid de 1903 qui, ayant provoqué la mort de plusieurs spectateurs et du pilote Marcel Renault, conduit le gouvernement français à interdire toute compétition ouverte. L'événement sonne ainsi le glas de la première ère de la course automobile.

La solution trouvée en premier ressort consiste à courir sur la voie publique mais sur un parcours en boucle temporairement neutralisé, ce qui permet de canaliser et de protéger plus facilement concurrents et spectateurs. Là encore, les premières épreuves disputées suivant cette nouvelle formule ont tout d'abord lieu en France, puis avant d'être organisées en Allemagne, en Italie, en Irlande et, enfin, aux États-Unis. Le circuit est généralement un vague triangle d'un périmètre compris entre 65 et 160 kilomètres, dont les sommets sont marqués par une ville ou un village. À cette époque déjà, il n'est pas rare que la vitesse moyenne dépasse les 96 km/h, voire 112 km/h, avec des pointes plus importantes en ligne droite pour les voitures les plus rapides.

La création de ces courses sur « circuit » n'est qu'une des manifestations d'une organisation de plus en plus sophistiquée, qui va introduire successivement une nouvelle réglementation technique, des types de compétition originaux et une formule de course grâce à laquelle vont pouvoir s'affronter entre eux non seulement des marques et des pilotes mais également des équipes nationales. De toutes les courses organisées par des mécènes, depuis le riche sportif italien Vincenzo Florio au richissime financier et motoriste pionnier américain William K. Vanderbilt en passant par l'aristocratie dirigeante allemande pour le Kaiserpreis, la plus célèbre est sans aucun doute la Coupe Gordon Bennett. Créé par le magnat de la presse américain James Gordon Bennett, ce tournoi oppose entre elles les nations représentées chacune par trois voitures, le pays vainqueur remportant non seulement le trophée mais également l'honneur d'accueillir l'épreuve l'année suivante. Si la coupe est l'occasion de confronter les automobiles américaines aux européennes, l'Europe sort finalement de l'épreuve à son avantage : entre 1900 et 1905, la France gagne quatre fois, la Grande-Bretagne et l'Allemagne une fois chacune. Cette dernière nation obtient la victoire en 1903 grâce au nouveau type de voiture de course, élaborée plus « scientifiquement », que lance Mercedes. Son volant est confié au pilote belge Camille Jenatzy, qui avait été déjà le premier homme au monde à dépasser les 96,50 km/h dans une automobile (la Jamais Contente, à moteur électrique, en 1899) à une époque où course automobile et tentatives de records de vitesse étaient deux activités étroitement liées.

Si c'est bien la Grande-Bretagne qui organise la coupe Gordon Bennett de 1903, Jenatzy obtient toutefois la victoire sur un tracé routier irlandais – les épreuves éliminatoires s'étant déroulées sur l'île de Man – car les autorités britanniques continuent d'interdire de fait les courses sur route ouverte, contrairement aux Français, aux Allemands ou aux Italiens. Il s'agit d'un exemple supplémentaire de la résistance obstinée du gouvernement britannique à l'automobile, qui a déjà contraint les amateurs de courses de côte à quitter la voie publique pour s'élancer sur des terrains privés. C'est cependant cette antipathie officielle qui entraîne une nouvelle évolution majeure de la course automobile : la création à Brooklands, près de Weybridge (Surrey), du premier véritable autodrome. Ce célèbre ovale à virages relevés, aménagé sur son domaine familial par Hugh Fortescue Locke King, un riche propriétaire terrien du Surrey, est inauguré en juin 1907 par plusieurs tentatives de record et, en juillet, par une première véritable course. Ce lieu offre l'occasion aux passionnés d'automobile de pique-niquer avec leur famille dans une atmosphère de garden-party tout en assistant à des courses spectaculaires et même, s'ils le désirent, d'engager des paris sur le résultat des courses avec les bookmakers. Brooklands joue cependant un rôle plus important pour la Grande-Bretagne en servant non seulement de piste d'essai pour l'industrie automobile et ceux qui ont les moyens de louer ses installations mais aussi, jusqu'à ce que les vitesses atteintes ne lui soient plus adaptées, de piste où établir les records du monde de vitesse.

Face à cette transformation du format des courses et à l'organisation plus pragmatique de la compétition, la conception des voitures elles-mêmes, après une période de quasi liberté, suit une évolution plus scientifique et s'inscrit désormais dans le cadre réglementaire officiel des « formules ». Les limitations que ces formules apportent, entre autres paramètres, à la cylindrée, au poids ou à la consommation du moteur, permettent désormais à tous les concurrents de s'affronter à armes égales et obligent les constructeurs à privilégier la technique à la puissance brute pour améliorer les performances des voitures. Une formule particulière est alors élaborée pour un nouveau type de compétition : le Grand Prix. La première épreuve du genre est le Grand Prix de l'Automobile Club de France, disputé en juin 1906 sur un tracé triangulaire de 106 km aménagé aux alentours du Mans ; la course, qui conserve le règlement technique de la coupe Gordon Bennett, se dispute en revanche sur 1240 km et se déroule sur deux jours, les voitures partant à 90 secondes d'intervalle et non toutes ensemble. Elle est remportée par la Renault du Hongrois Ferenc Szisz devant la Fiat de Felice Nazzaro à la moyenne de 101 km/h – Paul Baras et sa Brasier s'arrogeant le record du tour à plus de 117 km/h de moyenne. Le grand succès de ce premier Grand Prix définit un nouveau format de compétition, appelé à un grand avenir : les voitures, répondant à une formule technique stricte, doivent parcourir un nombre fixé de tours sur un circuit fermé, le vainqueur étant celui qui termine la course dans le temps le plus court. Cette formule, malgré divers et importants aménagements successifs, va perdurer de nombreuses années.

Le sport automobile est né, a connu une enfance intéressante mais souvent difficile et atteint sa maturité en quinze ans à peine, du concours Paris–Rouen de 1894 au début des années 1910. Il s'agit déjà d'un sport international aux disciplines très diverses – depuis les concours et les courses de côte jusqu'aux Grand Prix et aux tentatives de records – dont les épreuves sont disputées et suivies par un nombre croissant de concurrents et de spectateurs des deux côtés de l'Atlantique. Mais il se révèle avoir aussi, et de plus en plus, une importance considérable pour les motoristes, aussi bien en tant qu'argument commercial que comme terrain d'essai pour de nouveaux concepts. Désormais, l'automobile et le sport ne peuvent que progresser ensemble.

The progress of speed

The Paris–Rouen Trial of 22 July 1894 was
the world's first serious motoring competition, and set the scene for a generation of
road races. Twenty-one cars took part,
seventeen finished. They were led home
by a De Dion steam tractor, but the first
petrol car to finish was Adolphe Clément's
Peugeot (opposite, above left). In June 1895
Emile Levassor's Panhard (opposite, above
right) led the petrol cars in the 735-mile
Paris–Bordeaux–Paris race at an average of
just over 15mph. Only four years later, in
1899, Camille Jenatzy (right) became the
first man to travel at more than 60mph, and
in 1904, in Ostend, Louis Rigolly with the
100hp Gobron-Brillié (opposite, below)
became the first to exceed 100mph.

Mehr Tempo

Das Rennen Paris–Rouen vom 22. Juli 1894
war die weltweit erste wirkliche Automobil-
Wettfahrt und gab das Muster für eine
ganze Generation von Straßenrennen vor.
Einundzwanzig Wagen traten an, siebzehn
kamen ins Ziel. Das Feld führte ein Dampf-
traktor von De Dion an; der Schnellste mit
Verbrennungsmotor war Adolphe Cléments
Peugeot (gegenüber, oben links). Im Juni
1895 fuhr Émile Levassors Panhard (gegenüber, oben rechts) auf dem 1180 Kilometer
langen Rennen Paris–Bordeaux–Paris
mit einem Durchschnittstempo von gut
24 km/h allen anderen Benzinwagen
davon. Nur vier Jahre darauf, 1899, erreichte
der Belgier Camille Jenatzy (rechts) die
100-Stundenkilometer-Marke. 1904 fuhr
Louis Rigolly auf dem 100-PS-Gobron-
Brillié in Ostende (gegenüber, unten)
erstmals schneller als 100 Meilen die
Stunde (160 km/h).

Toujours plus vite

Le concours Paris–Rouen du 22 juillet 1894,
première véritable compétition automobile,
jette les bases de la course sur route.
21 voitures y participent et 17 la terminent.
Devancée par une traction à vapeur De Dion,
la première voiture à pétrole à franchir la
ligne d'arrivée est la Peugeot d'Adolphe
Clément (ci-contre, en haut à gauche). En
juin 1895, la Panhard d'Émile Levassor (ci-
contre, en haut à droite) prend la tête des
voitures à pétrole lors de la course Paris–
Bordeaux–Paris, 1180 km parcourus à la
moyenne de 24 km/h. Quatre ans plus tard,
Camille Jenatzy (à droite) devient le premier
homme à dépasser les 96 km/h et, en 1904 à
Ostende, Louis Rigolly le premier à dépasser
160 km/h au volant d'une Gobron-Brillié
100 ch (ci-contre en bas).

A proving ground for the sporting car

In 1905 Britain's Automobile Club instituted what became the longest running event in the history of motor sport, the Tourist Trophy. It originated in the Isle of Man, because Britain would not allow speed events on mainland roads. Percy Northey's Rolls-Royce (above) finished second to John Napier's Arrol-Johnston, after Charles Rolls' Rolls-Royce broke its gearbox.

Sportwagen zeigen, was sie können

1905 veranstaltete der britische Automobilclub erstmals ein Rennen, das das langlebigste des Motorsports werden sollte: die Tourist Trophy. Es fand auf der Isle of Man statt, denn auf der britischen Hauptinsel gestatteten die Behörden keine Straßenrennen. Nachdem Charles Rolls mit Getriebeschaden ausgefallen war, wurde Percy Northey, ebenfalls auf Rolls-Royce (oben), hinter John Napier auf Arrol-Johnston Zweiter.

Un terrain d'essai pour les voitures de sport

L'Automobile Club de Grande-Bretagne institue en 1905 ce qui va devenir la compétition la plus pérenne de l'histoire du sport automobile : le Tourist Trophy, organisé pour la 1ʳᵉ fois dans l'île de Man, la Grande-Bretagne n'autorisant pas les courses de vitesse sur route ouverte. L'Arrol-Johnston de John Napier termine première devant la Rolls-Royce de Percy Northey (ci-dessus) après que celle de Charles Rolls a cassé sa boîte de vitesses.

Great men with a love of speed

Henry Ford and the Hon. C.S. Rolls built very different kinds of car, but both had a passion for motor sport. Ford stands alongside his '999' racer (above), with novice driver Barney Oldfield, at the Grosse Point one-mile dirt oval in Michigan in December 1902. Charles Stewart Rolls (left) at the wheel of his 8hp Panhard of 1898, one of his earliest competition cars.

Die Schnellsten am Volant

Verschiedener als die Wagen von Henry Ford und C. S. Rolls konnten Automobile kaum sein, doch beiden gemeinsam war die Liebe zum Motorsport. Ford (oben) im Dezember 1902 auf dem unbefestigten Rundkurs von Grosse Point in Michigan am »999«-Rennwagen mit seinem jungen Fahrer Barney Oldfield. Charles Stewart Rolls (links) sitzt 1898 am Steuer des 8-PS-Panhard, einem der ersten Wagen, in denen er bei Rennen antrat.

Des hommes épris de vitesse

Henry Ford et Charles Stewart Rolls construisaient des voitures de types très différents mais partageaient une même passion pour le sport automobile. On voit ici Ford posant près de sa « 999 » de course (ci-dessus), avec le pilote débutant Barney Oldfield, sur l'ovale en terre de 1-mile de Grosse Point (Michigan), en décembre 1902. C. S. Rolls (à gauche) au volant de sa Panhard 8 ch de 1898, l'une de ses premières voitures de course.

Reliability as a prelude to speed

Speed and reliability trials of every description were at the heart of the early years of competition motoring. A 20hp Talbot attacks Dunmail Rise (above) during the 1908 RAC 2,000-mile trial. Prince Henry of Prussia (left), younger brother of Kaiser Wilhelm II, was a keen sporting motorist who competed in the 1906 Herkomer Trial in this Benz, and from 1908 lent his name to the Prince Henry Trial.

Zuerst die Zuverlässigkeit, dann das Tempo

In den ersten Jahren standen Geschwindigkeit und Zuverlässigkeit im Mittelpunkt der Vergleichsfahrten. Auf der 2000-Meilen-Fahrt des RAC von 1908 nimmt ein 20-PS-Talbot den Hügel Dunmail Rise in Angriff (oben). Prinz Heinrich von Preußen (links), der Bruder Kaiser Wilhelms II., war ein begeisterter Motorsportler und trat 1906 mit diesem Benz zur Herkomer-Fahrt an; der Prinz-Heinrich-Fahrt, die von 1908 an stattfand, gab er den Namen.

La fiabilité au service de la vitesse

Les concours de vitesse et de fiabilité, de tous les genres, furent l'essentiel des premières années de la compétition automobile. Une Talbot 20 ch attaque la pente de Dunmail Rise (ci-dessus) lors de l'épreuve des 2000 miles du RAC de 1908. Passionné de pilotage, le prince Henri de Prusse (à gauche), frère cadet de l'empereur Guillaume II, participa au concours Herkomer de 1906 sur une Benz et laissa son nom au Concours du Prince Henri à partir de 1908.

An American challenge

James Gordon Bennett was a flamboyant New Yorker, a wealthy newspaper publisher who sent H.M. Stanley to Africa to search for Livingstone. In 1900 he offered the Gordon Bennett Trophy (right) for a series of match races between American and European car makers. The 1903 Napier team (above) competed in Ireland, with drivers Stock, Jarrott and Edge, in a race won by Jenatzy for Mercedes.

Amerikanische Herausforderer

Der New Yorker Zeitungsbaron James Gordon Bennett war ein Mann mit Hang zum Ausgefallenen – seinerzeit hatte er H. M. Stanley nach Afrika auf die Suche nach Livingstone geschickt. Im Jahr 1900 stiftete er die Gordon-Bennett-Trophäe (rechts) für eine Reihe von Wettfahrten zwischen amerikanischen und europäischen Marken. Die Napier-Mannschaft (oben) kam 1903 mit den Fahrern Stock, Jarrott und Edge zum Rennen nach Irland, doch als Sieger ging Jenatzy auf Mercedes ins Ziel.

Le défi américain

New-yorkais extravagant, James Gordon Bennett était un riche propriétaire de journaux qui finança l'expédition africaine de H. M. Stanley à la recherche de Livingstone. En 1900, il crée le Trophée Gordon Bennett (à droite) offert au vainqueur d'un tournoi entre constructeurs américains et européens. L'équipe Napier, composée des pilotes Stock, Jarrott et Edge (ci-dessus), participe en 1903 en Irlande à une course remportée par Jenatzy sur Mercedes.

Crossing continents…

The Peking–Paris race of 1907 was proposed by the French newspaper *Le Matin* under the headline: 'Will anyone agree to go from Peking to Paris by motor car this summer?' Many parts of the route had little or no proper roads, but Prince Scipio Borghese (left) won the gruelling marathon in his 40hp Itala (above), entering Paris two months to the day after leaving Peking, and more than three weeks ahead of the next car.

Durch die Kontinente …

Das Rennen Peking–Paris hatte die Zeitung *Le Matin* 1907 mit der Schlagzeile ins Leben gerufen: »Wer wäre bereit, in diesem Sommer mit dem Motorwagen von Peking nach Paris zu fahren?« Weite Teile der Strecke waren unwegsam, vielfach gab es überhaupt keine Straßen, doch Fürst Scipio Borghese (links) nahm die Strapazen auf sich und gewann das Marathonrennen mit einem 40-PS-Itala (oben). Auf den Tag genau zwei Monate nach dem Start in Peking traf er in Paris ein, über drei Wochen vor dem ersten Konkurrenten.

Traverser des continents …

La course Paris–Pékin de 1907 fut proposée par le journal français *Le Matin* sous le titre : « Qui désire se rendre en voiture de Pékin à Paris en été ? ». Le prince Scipio Borghese (à gauche) remporte ce marathon difficile avec son Itala 40 ch, ici dans l'une des nombreuses étapes mal carrossées (ci-dessus), en arrivant à Paris deux mois jour pour jour après avoir quitté Pékin, et plus de trois semaines avant le second concurrent.

...and from west to east

An even more ambitious event began in New York, on 12 February 1908 (above), with Paris again the goal. The plan was for the cars (from left to right De Dion, Sizaire Naudin, Zust, Motobloc and Thomas Flyer, with Protos behind) to drive from Alaska over frozen rivers and lakes to the Bering Sea, over the frozen Bering Sea to Siberia and thence to Paris. The weather was so severe that the organisers resorted to calling the cars back and shipping them across the Pacific. The single-cylinder Sizaire Naudin (below) had given up on the first day, but, after 169 days and a long battle with the Protos, the Thomas Flyer arrived in Paris and was declared the winner.

... und von West nach Ost

Ein noch ehrgeizigeres Unternehmen startete am 12. Februar 1908 in New York (oben), wiederum mit Paris als Ziel. Die Wagen (von links nach rechts: De Dion, Sizaire Naudin, Zust, Motobloc und Thomas Flyer, mit Protos in der zweiten Reihe) sollten von Alaska über zugefrorene Flüsse und Seen zur Beringsee fahren, über das Eis nach Sibirien und von dort nach Paris. Das Wetter war so schlecht, dass die Teilnehmer schließlich zurückgerufen wurden und die Fahrzeuge per Schiff über den Pazifik gingen. Der Einzylinder von Sizaire Naudin (unten) gab schon am ersten Tag auf, doch Thomas Flyer kam nach 169 Tagen und zähem Ringen mit dem Protos tatsächlich in der französischen Hauptstadt an.

... et d'Ouest en Est

La nouvelle compétition qui part de New York le 12 février 1908 à destination de Paris est plus ambitieuse encore. Il est prévu que les voitures (en haut, de gauche à droite : De Dion, Sizaire Naudin, Zust, Motobloc et Thomas Flyer, avec des Protos derrière) traversent l'Alaska sur les fleuves et les lacs gelés avant de franchir la mer de Béring pour passer en Sibérie et continuer vers Paris. Les conditions météorologiques furent si épouvantables que les organisateurs durent rappeler les pilotes pour leur faire traverser le Pacifique en bateau. Si la monocylindre Sizaire Naudin (en bas) abandonne le premier jour, la Thomas Flyer arrive à Paris et remporte la victoire après 169 jours de course et une longue lutte contre les Protos.

From road to track

In 1909 America created the Indianapolis Motor Speedway, and in 1911 the track hosted the first of its Memorial Day 500-mile races. At the time it was traditional for each car to carry a riding mechanic, but Ray Harroun would win the inaugural 500 in his Marmon Wasp without one, but *with* the aid of a rear-view mirror.

Von der Straße zur Rennstrecke

1909 entstand in Amerika der Indianapolis Motor Speedway, und 1911 fand am Memorial Day das erste der berühmten 500-Meilen-Rennen statt. Damals war es noch üblich, dass jeder Wagen einen Mechaniker an Bord hatte, doch Ray Harroun gewann das erste 500-Meilen-Rennen in einem Marmon Wasp ohne Beifahrer – er hatte ihn durch einen Rückspiegel ersetzt.

De la route à la piste

Les États-Unis construisent en 1909 l'Indianapolis Motor Speedway et c'est en 1911, le jour du Memorial Day, que la piste accueille la première de ses célèbres courses de 500 Miles. À l'époque, il est de tradition que chaque voiture dispose d'un mécanicien « navigant » ; Ray Harroun, sur sa Marmon Wasp, s'est rendu célèbre en remportant cette course d'inauguration sans mécanicien mais avec un rétroviseur.

New York, New York

As well as being the starting- or finishing-point for many long-distance events, soon after the turn of the century New York had several race tracks, and Brooklyn had a record course on the Ocean Parkway, where Victor Hémery competed in November 1900. A year later, 25,000 spectators watched Henri Fournier's Mors reach almost 70mph here.

New York, New York

Um die Jahrhundertwende war New York nicht nur Start- oder Zielpunkt für viele Langstreckenrennen, sondern verfügte auch über mehrere Rennkurse, und auf dem Ocean Parkway in Brooklyn fanden Rekordfahrten statt. Victor Hémery trat im November 1900 dort an, und im Jahr darauf verfolgten fast 25 000 Zuschauer, wie Henri Fournier auf seinem Mors mehr als 110 Stundenkilometer erreichte.

New York, New York

Point de départ et d'arrivée de nombreuses compétitions d'endurance, New York dispose peu après le tournant du siècle de plusieurs circuits automobiles, notamment à Brooklyn, où Victor Hémery courut en novembre 1900 sur la piste de vitesse d'Ocean Parkway. Un an plus tard, 25 000 spectateurs voient la Mors de Henri Fournier atteindre près de .2 km/h.

Tragic end of a golden era
The end for the great inter-city road races came with the tragic Paris–Madrid race of May 1903. There were numerous accidents and several fatalities, including Marcel Renault of the famous French car-making family. Marcel's 30hp Renault was going well in the early stages (above left) but at Théry he met his end (above). His brother Louis was told of Marcel's death by their other brother, Fernand (left), in Bordeaux, where the race was stopped. Louis had been the first to arrive in Bordeaux, but later starter Fernand Gabriel's Mors was declared the winner.

Das tragische Ende einer goldenen Zeit
Das Ende der großen Straßenrennen von Stadt zu Stadt kam mit der von Unglücken gezeichneten Fahrt Paris–Madrid im Mai 1903. Es gab mehrere Todesopfer, darunter Marcel Renault aus der berühmten französischen Fabrikantenfamilie. Anfangs lag Marcel mit dem 30-PS-Renault gut im Rennen (oben links), bis zum tödlichen Unfall in Théry (oben). Sein Bruder Louis erfuhr in Bordeaux durch den dritten Bruder Fernand von Marcels Tod (links), und das Rennen wurde abgebrochen. Louis war als Erster in Bordeaux eingetroffen, doch Sieger wurde der später gestartete Fernand Gabriel auf Mors.

La fin tragique d'un âge d'or
La fin des grandes courses de ville à ville est provoquée par le tragique Paris–Madrid de mai 1903, théâtre de nombreux incidents et accidents mortels, dont celui de la Renault 30 ch de Marcel Renault, qui sort de la route à Théry (ci-dessus) après s'être bien comportée dans les premières étapes (en haut à gauche). Fernand Renault (en bas à gauche) apprend à Louis la mort de leur frère à Bordeaux, où la course est alors interrompue. Bien que Louis ait été le premier à arriver à Bordeaux, c'est Fernand Gabriel, sur Mors, qui fut déclaré vainqueur.

Controlling the risks

With inter-city racing outlawed, shorter 'circuits' were created, still on real roads but now with stricter controls and far better protection for both racers and spectators. This is Jules Goux's Peugeot en route to second place, behind team-mate Georges Boillot, in the 1913 Grand Prix of France, on the Amiens circuit.

Weniger Risiko

Nachdem die Städterennen nun verboten waren, entstanden kürzere Rundstrecken, weiterhin auf öffentlichen Straßen, doch mit strengeren Auflagen und besserem Schutz für Fahrer und Zuschauer. Auf diesem Bild vom Großen Preis von Frankreich, 1913 auf dem Kurs von Amiens ausgetragen, liegt Jules Goux auf Peugeot an zweiter Stelle hinter seinem Stallgefährten Georges Boillot, der das Rennen gewann.

Contrôler les risques

Puisque les courses de ville à ville sont désormais interdites, on construit alors des « circuits » sur route plus petits mais qui offrent désormais de bien meilleures protections pour les spectateurs et les coureurs et un contrôle plus strict du public. Le circuit d'Amiens, où la Peugeot de Jules Goux terminera à la seconde place, derrière son coéquipier Georges Boillot, lors du Grand Prix de France de 1913, en est un exemple.

Racing to improve the breed

When Brooklands opened in 1907, the Austin Motor Company had only recently built its first cars, but by 1908 Austin had also built its first racing car – the Grand Prix model, based on the company's 60hp tourer chassis and with a 9.7-litre 6-cylinder engine. Three lined up on the Brooklands grid on 8 June 1908 (right), and Dario Resta's machine (above) emerged as the race winner.

Alles für den Fortschritt

Als Brooklands 1907 eröffnete, baute die Austin Motor Company gerade erst ihre ersten Fahrzeuge, doch 1908 gab es bereits einen Austin-Rennwagen – das Grand-Prix-Modell auf dem Chassis des 60-PS-Tourers mit 9,7-Liter-Sechszylinder. Drei Exemplare starteten am 8. Juni 1908 in Brooklands (rechts), und Dario Resta (oben) kam als Erster ins Ziel.

La course améliore les voitures

L'Austin Motor Company vient juste de sortir ses premières unités lorsque l'autodrome de Brooklands ouvre en 1907. En 1908, Austin construit alors sa première voiture de course, le modèle Grand Prix, basé sur le châssis de la berline 60 ch et équipé d'un moteur 6 cylindres de 9,7 litres. Des trois exemplaires alignés sur la grille de départ de Brooklands le 8 juin 1908 (à droite), c'est celle de Dario Resta (ci-dessus) qui sortira victorieuse de l'épreuve.

Keeping the wheels turning

Refuelling at Brooklands in 1907 (top), and the crew of a Pope-Hartford changing tyres in an American race of around the same period (above). In the earliest days, the tyres and rims were removed from the wheels, before fully detachable wheels and tyres became the norm for much quicker changes.

Damit die Räder rollen

Auftanken in Brooklands 1907 (ganz oben) und Reifenwechsel bei einem amerikanischen Rennen zur gleichen Zeit (oben) mit den Pope-Hartford-Mechanikern in voller Aktion. Anfangs waren die Felgenkränze samt Reifen an den Speichen verschraubt, und erst später kamen abnehmbare Räder und Reifen auf, die einen weitaus schnelleren Wechsel ermöglichten.

La roue tourne

Ravitaillement à Brooklands en 1907 (en haut) tandis que des mécaniciens changent les roues d'une Pope-Hartford lors d'une épreuve américaine de la même période (ci-dessus). Alors qu'il fallait auparavant retirer le pneumatique de la jante lors des crevaisons, la roue entièrement amovible, qui permet un changement plus rapide, devient rapidement la norme.

The pits and the 'Brickyard'

When 'the pits' first appeared as a place from which to work at the side of the race track, they were literally that – shallow pits at the side of the road to provide space and protection for spare parts and mechanics, as here at Indianapolis, which was repaved with bricks soon after its opening, earning it the fond nickname the 'Brickyard'.

Die Boxen und der »Brickyard«

Als die »Boxen« am Rand der Rennbahn, von denen aus die Mechaniker arbeiteten, aufkamen, sahen sie wirklich aus wie Pferdeboxen – flache Gruben, die Ersatzteilen und Monteuren Platz und Sicherheit boten. Das Bild zeigt sie in Indianapolis – dem »Brickyard«, wie die Strecke mit Spitznamen hieß, seit sie kurz nach ihrer Eröffnung einen Straßenbelag aus Backsteinen bekommen hatte.

Les fosses et le « Brickyard »

Les premiers stands n'étaient rien moins que des fosses (pit en anglais) étroites construites en bord de piste, où les mécaniciens s'installaient avec les pièces détachées, comme ici à Indianapolis. Le circuit doit son surnom de « Brickyard » (champ de briques) à son pavement de briques, refait peu après son inauguration.

The well-dressed racing motorist
When bodywork was at best rudimentary and at worst non-existent, drivers wore whatever was appropriate to the conditions. The American driver in the 24-hour race at Point Breeze (left) and J. Gaal (centre) at the 1908 Tourist Trophy favour waterproofs, leather helmets and goggles; P.D. Sterling (right) sports tweeds before the same 1908 TT race.

Der zünftige Dress
Zu einer Zeit, in der Karosserien bestenfalls im Ansatz vorhanden waren und oft ganz fehlten, mussten die Fahrer sehen, dass sie sich mit ihrer Kleidung schützten, so gut es ging. Der amerikanische Fahrer (links), beim 24-Stunden-Rennen von Point Breeze, und J. Gaal (Mitte) bei der Tourist Trophy von 1908 bevorzugen Regenmantel, Lederhelm und Schutzbrille; P. D. Sterling (rechts) präsentiert sich auf derselben TT in Tweed.

Des pilotes bien habillés
À l'époque où la carrosserie reste rudimentaire, les pilotes portent des tenues appropriées aux conditions de conduite. Ce pilote américain, lors d'une course de 24 heures à Point Breeze (à gauche), et J. Gaal (au centre), lors du Tourist Trophy de 1908, sont équipés d'un poncho imperméable, d'un casque de cuir et de lunettes de motocycliste ; P. D. Sterling (à droite), plus sobre, a préféré revêtir un confortable costume de tweed.

A triumph for America

In 1904 William K. Vanderbilt, pioneer racing motorist and wealthy son of the Vanderbilt dynasty, created the Vanderbilt Cup races, with America challenging Europe's finest marques. In 1908 the event moved onto a closed circuit, the Long Island Motor Parkway in New York, and the race was won by George Robertson in a Locomobile. It was the first all-American victory.

Ein Triumph für Amerika

1904 rief William K. Vanderbilt, Rennpionier und Spross der Milionärsfamilie, das Rennen um den Vanderbilt-Pokal ins Leben, in dem Amerika die großen europäischen Marken herausforderte. 1908 wurde es erstmals auf einem geschlossenen Rundkurs ausgetragen, dem Long Island Motor Parkway in New York; Sieger war George Robertson auf Locomobile – das erste Mal, dass Fahrer und Wagen aus Amerika waren.

Un triomphe pour les États-Unis

C'est en 1904 que William K. Vanderbilt, pionnier de la course automobile, crée la Coupe Vanderbilt, une série d'épreuves au cours desquelles les États-Unis affrontent les meilleures marques européennes. En 1908, la compétition est organisée sur un circuit fermé, le Long Island Motor Parkway de New York, et remportée par George Robertson sur Locomobile. C'est la première victoire entièrement américaine.

The great Sicilian road race
In 1906, wealthy Italian Vincenzo Florio created one of Italy's greatest road races, the Targa Florio, run in mountainous Sicily, where his family lived. In 1907 Florio, in a De Dion-Bouton (above), competed in the voiturette race before the main event, and finished second. The main race was won by his friend and former chauffeur Felice Nazzaro in a Fiat.

Auf Siziliens Straßen
Der wohlhabende Italiener Vincenzo Florio stiftete eines der großen Rennen des Landes, die Targa Florio, die von 1906 an auf den Bergstraßen seiner sizilianischen Heimat stattfand. 1907 trat Florio selbst an und kam mit einem De Dion-Bouton auf den zweiten Rang der Voiturette-Klasse (oben). Das Hauptrennen gewann sein Freund und ehemaliger Chauffeur Felice Nazzaro auf Fiat.

La grande course sicilienne
Le riche Italien Vincenzo Florio crée en 1906 l'une des plus grandes épreuves sur route d'Italie, la Targa Florio, qui se court dans les montagnes de Sicile où vivait sa famille. En 1907, Florio et sa De Dion-Bouton (ci-dessus) terminent seconds de la course des voiturettes, organisée avant la principale épreuve, remportée cette année-là par son ami et ancien chauffeur Felice Nazzaro, sur Fiat.

Italy's Grand Prix road race

On mainland Italy there was also a tradition of road racing, including Vincenzo Florio's Coppa Florio, and the Coppa della Velocità, run parallel with the Coppa Florio in 1907, but for cars racing to the Grand Prix formula where the earlier race essentially followed Kaiserpreis rules. The race was run on a circuit based in Brescia and was won by Milanese Alessandro Cagno's Itala, seen (below) at speed on one of the dusty straight sections before rain fell, and (above) approaching the finish.

Der Große Preis von Italien

Auch auf dem italienischen Festland gab es Straßenrennen, darunter Vincenzo Florios Coppa Florio, veranstaltet nach den Regeln des Kaiserpreises; parallel dazu fand 1907 die Coppa della Velocità als Grand-Prix-Rennen statt. Veranstaltet wurden die Rennen auf einer Strecke rund um Brescia, Sieger war der Itala-Pilot Alessandro Cagno, den wir hier (unten) auf einer der staubigen langen Geraden sehen, bevor Regen einsetzte, und (oben) beim Einlauf ins Ziel.

Grand Prix en Italie

L'Italie a également ses courses sur route, dont la Coppa Florio de Vincenzo Florio et la Coppa della Velocità, courue en parallèle à la Coppa Florio de 1907 mais pour des voitures conformes à la formule Grand Prix alors que les précédentes compétitions adoptaient essentiellement les règles du Kaiserpreis. L'épreuve, organisée sur un circuit aménagé à Brescia, fut remportée par le Milanais Alessandro Cagno sur une Itala, à pleine vitesse dans l'une des lignes droites avant la pluie (en bas) et à proximité de l'arrivée (ci-dessus).

America and Europe cross over

Lewis Strang (above, driving an Isotta in 1908) worked as a chauffeur in Europe but returned to America as a racing driver. Numerous wins earned him a drive in the French Grand Prix, replacing fellow American Montague Roberts (opposite above, at wheel) in the Thomas, but he retired early. Frenchman Albert Clément was third in the 1906 Grand Prix in his Clément-Bayard (opposite below), and also raced in that year's Vanderbilt Cup.

Über den Ozean

Lewis Strang (oben, 1908 im Isotta) kam als Chauffeur nach Europa und kehrte als Rennfahrer in die USA zurück. Er startete beim Großen Preis von Frankreich, wo er für Montague Roberts (gegenüber, oben, am Steuer) im Thomas antrat und bald ausschied. Beim Großen Preis von 1906 war Albert Clément mit seinem Clément-Bayard Dritter (gegenüber, unten) und nahm im selben Jahr am Vanderbilt Cup teil.

Échanges Europe – États-Unis

Strang (ci-dessus, sur Isotta en 1908) fut chauffeur en Europe mais revint aux États-Unis comme pilote de course. Les victoires qu'il obtint lui permirent de conduire la Thomas lors du Grand Prix de France en remplacement de Roberts (ci-contre en haut, au volant), mais il dut abandonner dès le début de la course. Clément, 3ᵉ au Grand Prix de 1906 dans une Clément-Bayard (ci-contre en bas), participa à la Coupe Vanderbilt.

A different kind of racing venue
When the banked concrete speed bowl of Brooklands opened
in 1907, it was the world's first purpose-built motor racing track
– and also a proving ground for the motor industry. Cars on the
banking during the O'Gorman Trophy race in 1909 show different approaches in the quest for speed, including A.J. Hancock's
stripped Vauxhall (number 6), which won the race.

Eine Rennstrecke wie noch nie
Der 1907 fertiggestellte, aus Beton gegossene und mit Steilkurven
versehene Hochgeschwindigkeits-Rundkurs von Brooklands
war die erste für Rennen gebaute Strecke – und ein Testgelände
für die Industrie. Die Wagen im Wettstreit um den O'Gorman-
Pokal von 1909 zeigen, dass mit unterschiedlichsten Mitteln um
Tempo gerungen wurde; A. J. Hancock trat in einem Vauxhall
ohne Karosserie an (Nummer 6) und gewann das Rennen.

Un nouveau type de circuit
L'anneau de vitesse à virages relevés de Brooklands, construit
en 1907, est le premier autodrome destiné spécifiquement à la
course. Les voitures que l'on voit dans le virage relevé lors du
Trophée O'Gorman de 1909 montrent les différentes approches
de la recherche de la vitesse par les constructeurs, comme
cette Vauxhall à la carrosserie très dépouillée de A. J. Hancock
(numéro 6), qui remporta l'épreuve.

The right crowd

Brooklands, near Weybridge in Surrey and within an easy train ride or drive from London, was soon as famous for its sociable atmosphere as for its racing, and its motto became 'the right crowd with no crowding'. This is one corner of the paddock, by the finishing line just before the Members Banking, during the wet Easter meeting in April 1908.

In guter Gesellschaft

Brooklands bei Weybridge in Surrey war von London aus leicht mit Zug oder Wagen zu erreichen und bald als gesellschaftlicher Treffpunkt ebenso beliebt wie als Rennplatz. Sein Motto hieß »Geselligkeit ohne Gedränge«. Hier ein Blick auf die Mitte des Areals an Start und Ziel, aufgenommen beim verregneten Osterrennen im April 1908.

Une foule passionnée

L'autodrome de Brooklands, près de Weybridge (Surrey), facilement accessible en train ou en voiture depuis Londres, doit sa réputation autant à son atmosphère conviviale qu'aux courses qui s'y déroulent. Ce coin du paddock, près de la ligne d'arrivée juste avant le Members Banking, lors de la réunion de Pâques en avril 1908, illustre bien la devise du circuit : « la foule sans la bousculade ».

From the turf to the track

It was not long before Brooklands adopted the idea of putting numbers on competing cars, but in the very first Brooklands races the runners had adopted an idea from horse racing which saw the drivers wearing 'colours', just like a jockey. This is Scantlebury in a Sizaire in 1908, combining both numbers and colours.

Vom Rasen auf die Piste

Schon bald wurden in Brooklands die Fahrzeuge mit Nummern gekennzeichnet, doch zunächst traten die Fahrer in »Farben« an, wie Jockeys beim Pferderennen. Scantlebury in seinem Sizaire, aufgenommen 1908, zeigt beides.

Du turf à la piste

S'il ne fallut pas longtemps pour que Brooklands adopte l'idée d'apposer un numéro sur les voitures en compétition, dès les premières courses les pilotes ont imité les jockey des courses hippiques en portant la casaque de couleur. En 1908, Scantlebury, dans une Sizaire, combine à la fois casaque et numéro.

The cradle of speed
Brooklands, with its long straights, high banking and concrete surface, allowed sustained speeds that simply were not possible at other venues, and that made it a mecca for record-breakers as well as racers. Napiers excelled in both disciplines; this is Frank Newton's car winning the 90hp Stakes in June 1908.

Die Wiege der Geschwindigkeit
Mit seinen langen Geraden, den Steilkurven und der Betonpiste machte Brooklands Geschwindigkeiten möglich, die anderswo nicht zu erreichen waren, und so wurde es zum Mekka sowohl für Renn- als auch für Rekordfahrer. Die Wagen von Napier glänzten in beiden Disziplinen, hier mit dem siegreichen Frank Newton beim Rennen der 90-PS-Klasse vom Juni 1908.

Le berceau de la vitesse
Brooklands, avec ses longues lignes droites, ses grands virages relevés et son revêtement en béton, devient vite la Mecque des briseurs de records et des pilotes de course car on peut y atteindre des vitesses moyennes tout simplement inimaginables sur d'autres circuits. Les Napier excellaient dans les deux disciplines ; on voit ici la voiture de Frank Newton remporter le Prix des 90 ch en juin 1908.

On the beaches – a natural speed venue
As an alternative to both the public highway and the self-contained speed bowl of Brooklands, a suitably long stretch of firm, flat beach was a near-perfect speed venue and sand racing became a popular variant of motor sport for many years. This is Arthur Rawlinson at Portmarnock in his stripped 4-cylinder racer in September 1904.

Strandpisten – ein Geschenk der Natur
Als Alternative zu öffentlichen Straßen oder dem Rennkurs von Brooklands bot sich ein genügend langer, flacher und fester Streifen Sandstrand als beinahe perfekter Rennplatz an, und viele Jahre lang waren Sandrennen eine beliebte Form des Motorsports. Hier sehen wir Arthur Rawlinson in Portmarnock auf dem nackten Chassis eines Vierzylinder-Rennwagens, September 1904.

La plage – une piste de vitesse naturelle
Alternative aux grandes voies publiques et à l'autodrome de vitesse de Brooklands, la longue étendue de sable dur et plat d'une plage constitue une piste de vitesse presque parfaite et le théâtre populaire de compétitions automobiles pendant plusieurs années. On voit ici Arthur Rawlinson dans sa voiture sans carrosserie, à Portmarnock en septembre 1904.

On the American shoreline

Beach racing was as popular on the opposite side of the Atlantic as it was in Britain, and some famous venues were born on the sand long before tracks were built nearby. American legend Ralph de Palma (above right) raced his Fiat at Daytona in March 1909, and Guy Vaughan's White steamer sped to victory in a $500 match race at Atlantic City (below right).

An Amerikas Küsten

Sandrennen waren jenseits des Atlantiks genauso beliebt wie auf der britischen Seite, und manche berühmten Rennen fanden am Strand statt, bevor in der Nähe Pisten gebaut wurden. Die amerikanische Legende Ralph de Palma (rechts oben) sieht man im März 1909 am Strand von Daytona mit seinem Fiat, und Guy Vaughan errang in Atlantic City mit einem White-Dampfwagen den 500-Dollar-Preis (rechts unten).

Sur la côte américaine

La course sur plage est aussi appréciée de l'autre côté de l'Atlantique qu'en Grande-Bretagne ; certaines épreuves naquirent sur le sable bien avant qu'on ne construise une piste à proximité. Ralph de Palma, coureur américain de légende (en haut à droite), pilote sa Fiat à Daytona en mars 1909. La White de Guy Vaughan fonce vers la victoire dans une course primée de 500 $ à Atlantic City (en bas à droite).

As hot as pepper

A.J. Hancock was Vauxhall's star driver in the early years of Brooklands, and a prolific record-breaker. In 1909 he drove a streamlined version of his 3-litre Vauxhall racer (above) with a slim single-seater body and wind-cheating nose. The car was nicknamed 'KN', because it was said to be 'hotter than cayenne pepper' and by the end of the year Hancock had taken the flying half-mile class record to 88.6mph. Nicknames were popular at Brooklands: Frank Newton's race-winning Napier of 1908 (below) had been dubbed 'Firefly'.

Scharf wie Pfeffer

A. J. Hancock, Vauxhalls Fahrer-Ass in den ersten Jahren von Brooklands, brach zahlreiche Rekorde. 1909 war er (oben) mit dem 3-Liter-Renn-wagen, einem Einsitzer mit Stromlinienverkleidung und windschnittiger Nase, zu sehen. Der Wagen hörte auf den Spitznamen »KN«, weil er »schärfer als Cayennepfeffer« war, und Ende des Jahres stellte Hancock mit 88,6 mph (142,6 km/h) einen neuen Klassenrekord für die halbe Meile mit fliegendem Start auf. Spitznamen waren damals in Brooklands beliebt: Frank Newtons erfolgreicher Napier von 1908 (unten) hieß »Firefly« (Glühwürmchen).

Plus fort que le poivre

A. J. Hancock était non seulement le pilote vedette de Vauxhall dans les premières années d'existence de Brooklands mais aussi un fameux briseur de records. En 1909, il pilotait une version profilée de la Vauxhall 3 litres (en haut), à l'étroit châssis monoplace et un avant aérodynamique. Cette voiture fut surnommée « KN » (prononcer Caille-N) parce qu'on la disait « plus forte que du poivre de Cayenne ». À la fin de cette année, Hancock s'adjugeait le record de sa catégorie dans le demi mile, à la vitesse de 142,6 km/h. Les surnoms étaient d'ailleurs populaires à Brooklands : la Napier victorieuse de Franck Newton de 1908 (en bas) était ainsi appelée « Firefly » (la « luciole »).

A record-breaker returns

Shortly before Brooklands opened for racing, S.F. Edge proved its potential with a twenty-four-hour, single-handed record run in his Napier, averaging 65.9mph. Fifteen years later, in 1922, he attacked his own record (this time, because running at night was forbidden, in two twelve-hour stints) with this 6-cylinder Spyker – and set a new mark of 74.3mph.

Rekord zum zweiten

Kurz bevor Brooklands für den Rennbetrieb eröffnet wurde, zeigte S. F. Edge die Möglichkeiten der Strecke mit einer 24-Stunden-Einzelfahrt in seinem Napier, bei der er auf einen Schnitt von 106 km/h kam. Fünfzehn Jahre darauf, 1922, trat er mit diesem Spyker-Sechszylinder zur Jagd auf den eigenen Rekord an (nun in zwei 12-Stunden-Etappen, weil Nachtfahrten verboten waren) – und brachte die Höchstmarke auf 119,5 km/h.

Le retour d'un recordman

Peu avant l'ouverture de Brooklands à la compétition, S. F. Edge démontra tout le potentiel du circuit en pilotant 24 heures d'affilée sa Napier à la moyenne de 106 km/h. Quinze ans plus tard, en 1922, il battait son propre record (cette fois en deux étapes de 12 heures seulement car il était désormais interdit de rouler de nuit) avec cette Spyker 6-cylindres en réalisant une vitesse de 119,5 km/h.

When things go wrong

Motor racing was always a dangerous sport, and accidents a spectacular part of the scene. (Clockwise from top left) Moore-Brabazon's Minerva at Brooklands in 1907; Martin up-ended at Eu in the 1908 Grand Prix des Voiturettes; a warning too late for another Brooklands driver; an overturned car on the Brooklands test hill at the race track.

Nicht immer geht es gut

Autorennen sind stets ein gefährlicher Sport gewesen, und spektakuläre Unfälle gehören dazu. (Im Uhrzeigersinn von oben links) Moore-Brabazons Minerva in Brooklands, 1907, Martin am Boden beim Grand Prix des Voiturettes 1908 in Eu, ein Warnschild, das für einen weiteren Brooklands-Fahrer zu spät kam, und ein umgekipptes Auto auf dem Testhügel der Brookland-Strecke.

Quand tout va mal

La course automobile a toujours été un sport dangereux et les accidents de voitures spectaculaires. (Dans le sens des aiguilles d'une montre, à partir du haut) La Minerva de Moore-Brabazon à Brooklands en 1907 ; Martin dans le Grand Prix des Voiturettes de 1908 à Eu ; ce pilote a dû voir trop tard ce panneau de Brooklands ; une voiture renversée sur la colline du circuit de Brookland.

Saved by a helping hand

Arthur Duray's riding mechanic hangs on to a spare tyre and rim with their De Dietrich, while Duray holds on to mechanic and wheel, in the 1906 Vanderbilt Cup race on the Long Island road course. They survived to finish third in the 297-mile race, behind Louis Wagner's Darracq and Vincenzo Lancia's works Fiat, in an event marred by poor crowd control and one fatal accident.

Die helfende Hand

Long Island, Vanderbilt Cup 1906: Arthur Durays Mechaniker umklammert verzweifelt den Ersatzreifen in ihrem De Dietrich, und Duray hält Mechaniker und Lenkrad fest. Sie überstanden das 478 km lange, durch schlechte Abschirmung des Publikums gefährdete und von einem tödlichen Unfall überschattete Rennen und kamen auf den dritten Platz, hinter Louis Wagner auf Darracq und Vincenzo Lancia auf dem Werks-Fiat.

Sauvé par une main secourable

Arthur Duray retient et son mécanicien et la roue de secours de leur De Dietrich lors de l'épreuve de la Coupe Vanderbilt 1906 organisée à Long Island. Ils finirent troisième de cette course de 478 km, marquée par un accident mortel et des mouvements de foule incontrôlés, derrière la Darracq de Louis Wagner et la Fiat d'usine de Vincenzo Lancia.

Part of the supporting cast

On 1 October 1910, Harry Grant won the Vanderbilt Cup race in his Alco. He averaged 65.2mph on the controversial Long Island Motor Parkway, in a race marred by the deaths of two riding mechanics and several accidents involving spectators. On the same day, W. Endicott's Cole (above) won the supporting race, the Massapequa Sweepstakes, at an average of 55.0mph.

Teil des Rahmenprogramms

Am 1. Oktober 1910 gewann Harry Grant das Vanderbilt-Rennen auf seinem Alco mit einer Durchschnittsgeschwindigkeit von 104,9 km/h. Auf dem umstrittenen Straßenkurs auf Long Island verunglückten zwei Mechaniker und es gab mehrere Zwischen-fälle mit Zuschauern. Die Massapequa Sweepstakes, die am selben Tag stattfanden, entschied mit einem Durchschnitt von 88,5 km/h W. Endicott auf Cole für sich (oben).

Une partie des supporters

Le 1er octobre 1910, Harry Grant remporte la Coupe Vanderbilt avec son Alco. Il réalise une moyenne de 104,9 km/h sur le circuit controversé du Long Island Motor Parkway et dans une course endeuillée par la mort de deux mécaniciens navigants et plusieurs accidents impliquant des spectateurs. La Cole de W. Endicott (ci-dessus) remporte le Massapequa Sweepstakes, une course de second plan, à la moyenne de 88,5 km/h.

Time and money

Timekeepers studying the results at the Bexhill motor races on the sands of the Sussex seaside town in 1907 (above); and bookmakers (below) at the Easter race meeting at Brooklands in April 1908, where on-course betting was a popular feature in the paddock, and yet another link between the early days of motor racing and the old horse racing tradition.

Zeit und Geld

Zeitnehmer (oben) studieren die Ergebnisse des Rennens von Bexhill, das 1907 am Strand dieses Badeortes in Sussex stattfand, und Buchmacher (unten) hoffen beim Osterrennen 1908 in Brooklands auf Kunden. Buchmacher waren in der Arena von Brooklands allgegenwärtig – ein weiteres Bindeglied zwischen dem frühen Motorsport und der alten Tradition der Pferderennen.

Le temps et l'argent

Les chronométreurs contrôlent les résultats des épreuves organisées en 1907 sur les plages de Bexhill, une station balnéaire du Sussex (en haut). Les bookmakers, ici au paddock pendant la réunion de Pâques à Brooklands en avril 1908 (en bas), sont un élément indispensable du décor, où ils font la transition entre la tradition hippique ancienne et les débuts de la compétition automobile.

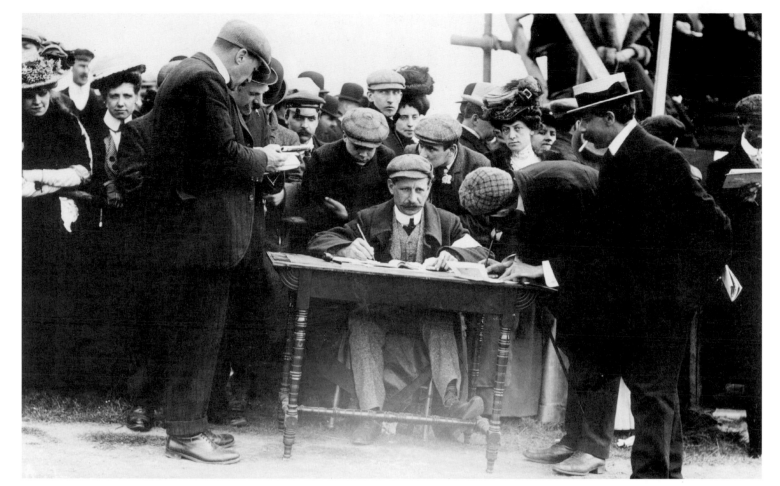

Gentlemen, start your engines

The first Vanderbilt Cup, in 1904, used a 28-mile course in Nassau County, New York.
Of the eighteen entries, five were American, the rest from Germany, Italy and France. The
race was won by expatriate American George Heath's 90hp Panhard (above).
Before its first 500-mile race in 1911, Indianapolis held events at many other distances,
including this 100-miler in around 1910 (right), and coined the instruction 'gentlemen,
start your engines'.

Meine Herren, starten Sie die Motoren

Das erste Rennen um den Vanderbilt Cup fand im Jahr 1904 auf einem 45 Kilometer
langen Rundkurs in Nassau County, New York, statt. Von den achtzehn Teilnehmern
waren fünf Amerikaner, die übrigen stammten aus Deutschland, Italien und Frankreich.
Sieger wurde der in Europa lebende Amerikaner George Heath auf einem 90-PS-Panhard
(oben). Vor dem ersten 500-Meilen-Rennen, 1911, fanden in Indianapolis zahlreiche
Veranstaltungen über andere Distanzen statt, hier (rechts, ca. 1910) über 100 Meilen,
und die Redewendung »Meine Herren, starten Sie die Motoren« wurde dort geprägt.

Messieurs, démarrez les moteurs

La première Coupe Vanderbilt fut disputée en 1904 sur un circuit de 45 km tracé dans
le comté de Nassau (New York). Cinq des dix-huit concurrents étaient Américains, les
autres venant d'Allemagne, d'Italie et de France. La course fut remportée par la Panhard
90 ch de l'Américain expatrié George Heath (ci-dessus). Avant la création des célèbres
500 Miles en 1911, Indianapolis organisait des épreuves sur bien d'autres distances, dont
une de 100 miles vers 1910 (à droite), au cours de laquelle fut donné l'ordre fameux :
« Messieurs, démarrez vos moteurs ».

The 'Four-Inch' race

In 1908 the Tourist Trophy was run to a formula which allowed a maximum of four cylinders each with a maximum bore of four inches – and it became known as the 'Four-Inch' race. It was run on an Isle of Man circuit controversially modified to make it 'safer', and won by W. Watson's Hutton – actually a modified Napier, here rounding Ramsey Hairpin.

Das »Vier Zoll«-Rennen

Für die Tourist Trophy von 1908 galt, dass die Motoren maximal vier Zylinder und die Zylinder maximal vier Zoll Bohrung haben durften – daher der Name »Vier Zoll«-Rennen. Es fand auf der Isle of Man statt, nach heftig diskutierten Sicherheitsmaß-nahmen an der Strecke, und endete mit dem Sieg W. Watsons auf einem Hutton – genau genommen einem modifizierten Napier, den wir hier in der Haarnadelkurve von Ramsey sehen.

La course des « Four-Inch »

En 1908, le Tourist Trophy se court suivant une formule réser-vée aux moteurs de quatre cylindres d'un alésage maximum de 4 pouces – d'où ce nom de course des « Four Inch ». Elle fut organisée sur le circuit de l'île de Man, aménagé pour le rendre plus « sûr », et remportée par la Hutton de W. Watson – en fait une Napier modifiée – que l'on voit ici négocier l'épingle de Ramsey.

Building on a promising start

After its successful debut in 1905, the Tourist Trophy would become established as the longest surviving of all the great motor races. In 1906 the event was ostensibly, as it had been in 1905, for 'touring' cars, with no outside mechanical assistance or stocks of spares. Girling's Darracq (above) retired at three-quarter distance; the Hon. C.S. Rolls won, in a Rolls-Royce.

Ein viel versprechender Anfang

Nach dem erfolgreichen Debüt 1905 wurde die Tourist Trophy zur festen Einrichtung und sollte das langlebigste der großen Autorennen werden. Wie im ersten Jahr war das Rennen auch 1906 nur für Tourenwagen ausgeschrieben, die keine Ersatzteile mit sich führen und keine Hilfe von fremden Mechanikern annehmen durften. Girlings Darracq (oben) fiel nach drei Vierteln der Strecke aus, Sieger wurde C. S. Rolls mit einem Rolls-Royce.

Un départ prometteur

Le Tourist Trophy, après le succès de la première édition de 1905, va devenir l'une des grandes compétitions automobiles qui a duré le plus longtemps. En 1906, l'épreuve est encore réservée aux voitures de «tourisme», sans assistance extérieure ni pièces de rechange. La Darracq de Girling (ci-dessus) ayant abandonné aux trois-quarts de la course, c'est la Rolls-Royce de C. S. Rolls qui termine victorieuse.

Proving the automobile, on real roads

T. Waite, with full complement of passengers in his 24hp Minerva (right), during the Cardiff Open Hillclimb in August 1907; competitors in the 1908 Royal Automobile Club and Scottish Automobile Club Trial in 1908 – a 12hp Shamrock passing through a town (opposite above); and a 25hp Deasy attacking a steep, muddy hairpin on the Rest-and-be-Thankful Hillclimb in Scotland (opposite below).

Zuverlässigkeitsfahrten

T. Waite im vollbesetzten 24-PS-Minerva bei der Bergprüfung von Cardiff, August 1907 (rechts); ein 12-PS-Shamrock, Teilnehmer am Trial des Royal Automobile Club und des Scottish Automobile Club, 1908, passiert eine Stadt (gegenüber, oben); und ein Deasy mit 25 PS meistert eine steile, schlammige Haarnadelkurve der »Rest and be Thankful«-Bergfahrt in Schottland (gegenüber, unten).

Essais sur route

T. Waite et sa Minerva 24 ch, chargée de passagers (à droite), lors de la Cardiff Open Hillclimb en août 1907 ; concurrente du Royal Automobile Club et du Scottish Automobile Club Trial de 1908, une Shamrock 12 ch traverse un village (ci-contre en haut) ; une Deasy 25 ch attaque une épingle à cheveu difficile et glissante de la course de côte Rest-and-be-Thankful organisée en Écosse (ci-contre en bas).

A problem of keeping control

The course for the first Vanderbilt Cup in 1904, around Nassau County, New York, and the Queens borough of New York City, should have been a fine racing venue, but the first race had minimal crowd control, one competitor died, and vandals threw nails and broken glass onto the road. Over the years the course was modified, the policing increased, but the crowd problems – and fatalities – continued. No race was held in 1907 but later races on the new Long Island Motor Parkway saw further deaths, and the end of the New York courses.

Schwer zu bändigen

Der Kurs für das erste Vanderbilt-Rennen von 1904 durch Nassau County im Staate New York und durch den Stadtteil Queens hätte eine gute Strecke sein können, doch es war kaum dafür gesorgt, die Zuschauer zurückzuhalten. Ein Fahrer kam um, und Vandalen warfen Nägel und Glasscherben auf die Straße. Im Laufe der Jahre wurden die Maßnahmen verstärkt, doch es kam immer wieder zu Schwierigkeiten mit Zuschauern – und zu Todesfällen. 1907 fiel das Rennen aus, doch spätere Läufe auf dem neuen Long Island Motor Parkway forderten weitere Opfer. Schließlich wurden Rennen in New York verboten.

Canaliser la foule

Le circuit tracé pour la première Coupe Vanderbilt de 1904 autour du comté de Nassau (État de New York) et du quartier de Queens, dans la banlieue de New York, aurait pu être l'occasion d'une belle compétition. On déplora malheureusement dès la première course la mort d'un concurrent et une absence totale de contrôle d'une foule parmi laquelle des vandales avaient jeté des clous et du verre pilé sur la piste. Le circuit fut modifié et la surveillance renforcée à mesure des années, sans résoudre pourtant ni le problème du public ni celui des accidents, et la scène de New York fut abandonnée lorsque d'autres morts survinrent lors des courses organisées ensuite (sauf en 1907, sans compétition).

Stripped for action

Before the advantages of streamlining were fully understood, maximum power with minimum weight was the key to speed, and many early racing cars dispensed with anything that was not considered absolutely necessary, bodywork included. (From top to bottom) J.E. Hutton's four-cylinder Hutton, 'Little Dorrit', entirely devoid of bodywork, at Brooklands around 1907; a Fiat at Brooklands in 1908, with no protection, even against a snow shower; and Captain C.A. Glentworth's Napier at Bexhill in 1907, with the distinctive tube radiator providing some streamlining around the engine, but little else.

Je weniger, desto schneller

Bevor die Vorteile der Stromlinienform erkannt wurden, war ein Maximum an Motorkraft bei einem Minimum an Gewicht der Schlüssel zur Geschwindigkeit. Frühen Rennwagen fehlte alles, was nicht unbedingt notwendig war, bis hin zur Karosserie. (Von oben nach unten) J. E. Huttons Vierzylinder-Hutton »Little Dorrit« als reines Chassis in Brooklands, etwa 1907; ein Fiat in Brooklands, 1908, ohne jeden Schutz, nicht einmal gegen Schneeschauer; und Captain C. A. Glentworths Napier in Bexhill, 1907, mit dem charakteristischen Röhrenkühler und einer leicht aerodynamischen Haube, doch sonst fast nackt.

Dépouillement et vitesse

Avant que l'on ne comprenne vraiment tout l'intérêt de l'aérodynamique, la clé de la vitesse était de disposer du maximum de puissance pour un poids de voiture minimum. Nombre des premières voitures de course se passaient donc de tout ce qui n'était pas considéré comme absolument nécessaire, carrosserie comprise. (De haut en bas) La Hutton quatre cylindres de J. E. Hutton, « Little Dorrit », entièrement dépourvue de sa carrosserie, à Brooklands vers 1907 ; une Fiat à Brooklands en 1908, sans protection, même par temps de neige ; et la Napier du capitaine C. A. Glentworth à Bexhill en 1907, dont les tubes de radiateur apparents donnent l'illusion d'un certain aérodynamisme.

The days of 'anything goes'

The sheer variety of racing machinery which took to the track at Brooklands in its early days is shown in this starting line-up for one of the track's popular relay races. What made it possible for the minnows to take on the giants in many races at Brooklands was a superb system of handicapping, which often brought very close finishes between unlikely rivals.

Erlaubt ist, was gefällt

Diese Aufnahme vom Start eines der populären Stafettenrennen zeigt die bunte Vielfalt der Wagen in den Anfangstagen von Brooklands. Dass in vielen dieser Rennen die Zwerge die Giganten herausforderten, wurde durch ein ausgeklügeltes System von Handicaps ermöglicht, das oft zu einem sehr knappen Ausgang zwischen den ungleichen Konkurrenten führte.

Les jours où « tout va »

Une grande diversité de voitures pouvaient courir ensemble aux premiers jours de Brooklands, comme on peut le constater en voyant la ligne de départ de l'une des populaires épreuves de relais organisées sur le circuit. Un système de handicap élaboré permettait ainsi au menu fretin de se frotter à armes égales (ou presque) aux gros poissons, offrant parfois la surprise d'arrivées disputées entre véhicules très différents.

A recipe for disaster

At its worst, the crowd control problem in the early American 'road' races, and especially the Vanderbilt Cup races around New York which could attract more than a quarter of a million spectators, was frightening – and completely unacceptable. From the earliest races, lap speeds were more than 70mph, and this is how close to disaster a car like this Bianchi often came.

Flirten mit dem Risiko

Die Zuschauer waren bei den ersten amerikanischen Straßenrennen eine ständige Gefahr, gerade bei den Fahrten um den Vanderbilt Cup im New Yorker Umland, die gut eine Viertelmillion Schaulustige anlockten. Schon bei den frühesten Rennen lagen die Rundenzeiten bei gut 110 Stundenkilometern, und Wagen wie dieser Bianchi bewegten sich oft am Rande einer Katastrophe.

La recette d'un désastre

Le contrôle de la foule dans les premières courses sur route américaines, notamment pour les épreuves de la Coupe Vanderbilt autour de New York, capables d'attirer plus de 250 000 spectateurs, posait un vrai problème. Dès les premières courses, les vitesses au tour de voitures comme cette Bianchi dépassaient 112 km/h sur une route encombrée par un public en totale liberté.

Natural hazards

Even when they were not hemmed in by living walls of unruly spectators, competitors in the New York races faced the dangers of the everyday roadside. There were no crash barriers to protect them from the trees, banks and ditches, and even the road surface itself was often totally unpredictable and barely suitable for a horse-drawn cart, let alone a 100mph racing car.

Feindliche Natur

Selbst wenn sie nicht zwischen lebendigen Mauern aus unberechenbaren Zuschauern hindurchrasten, blieben den Teilnehmern der New Yorker Rennen die Gefahren der Landstraße. Es gab keine Leitplanken, die sie vor den Bäumen, Abhängen und Gräben geschützt hätten, und auch die Straßenoberfläche war oft kaum für Pferd und Wagen geeignet, geschweige denn für Rennwagen mit Geschwindigkeiten bis zu 160 km/h.

Des dangers naturels

Même s'ils ne devaient pas courir entre deux murs de spectateurs incontrôlables, les concurrents des épreuves de New York devaient affronter les dangers du bord de la route, sans barrières pour les protéger des arbres, des fossés ou des bas-côtés. Le revêtement de la chaussée était incertain et à peine adapté à la circulation d'un char à bœufs, sans parler d'une voiture roulant à 160 km/h !

A day at the races

Long before it became an institution in Europe with classic events like Le Mans, the 24-hour race was a popular format in America, with spectators and promoters alike. America's first 24-hour race was held in Columbus, Ohio, in 1905, and here the cars line up at one of two 24-hour races held on the one-mile dirt track at Point Breeze, Philadelphia, in the summer of 1907.

Ein Tag beim Rennen

Lange bevor sie sich mit klassischen Veranstaltungen wie Le Mans in Europa durchsetzten, erfreuten sich 24-Stunden-Rennen in den USA bei Zuschauern und Veranstaltern großer Beliebtheit. Das erste fand 1905 in Columbus, Ohio statt, und auf unserem Bild nehmen die Wagen zu einem der beiden Rennen Aufstellung, die im Sommer 1907 auf der unbefestigten Einmeilenpiste von Point Breeze, Philadelphia, liefen.

Un jour aux courses

Bien avant qu'elles ne deviennent une institution en Europe, grâce à des classiques comme Le Mans, les épreuves d'endurance sur 24 heures étaient populaires aux États-Unis auprès des spectateurs comme de leurs promoteurs. La première course américaine de 24 heures fut organisée à Columbus (Ohio) en 1905. On voit ici les voitures s'aligner pour l'une de ces épreuves sur la piste en terre de Point Breeze, 1907.

— 2 —
The Pioneering Years

Previous pages: The opening of Brooklands had linked the sport with the needs of the industry. The track gave car makers a controlled environment in which to test their products and a means of promoting them – through records of every kind. This is L.G. Hornsted's 200hp Benz during an attempt on the hour record in May 1914. In June he set a new land speed record, at 124.1mph.

Vorherige Seiten: Die Rennstrecke von Brooklands diente nicht nur dem Sport, sondern auch der Industrie. Hersteller konnten dort ungestört ihre Produkte testen und zugleich Werbung für sie machen – durch Rekorde aller Arten. Hier sehen wir L. G. Hornsteds 200-PS-Benz im Mai 1914 bei einer Fahrt um den Stundenrekord. Im Juni stellte er mit 199,7 km/h einen neuen Geschwindigkeitsweltrekord auf.

Pages précédentes : L'ouverture de Brooklands a permis d'associer le sport aux besoins de l'industrie automobile. Ce circuit offre en effet aux constructeurs non seulement un cadre pour tester leurs produits mais aussi le moyen de les promouvoir grâce aux records de tous genres qui y sont établis. On voit ici la Benz 200 ch de L. G. Hornsted lors d'une tentative de record de l'heure en mai 1914 ; le mois suivant, il établissait le nouveau record du monde de vitesse sur terre à 199,7 km/h.

By 1910, both the motor car and motor sport were well established in the popular consciousness, if not yet very accessible to the ordinary man or always welcomed by the authorities. By now, the automobile had proved both its speed and its improving reliability. The French Grands Prix (and the Grands Prix of the Automobile Club of France, which were not the same thing), the Gordon Bennett, Vanderbilt, Kaiserpreis and Targa Florio or Florio Cup races had taken over from the city-to-city races as the sport's pinnacle, and the fastest lap speeds on the closed-road courses had risen to around 80mph. The world's land speed record had been pushed to 115.9mph in 1909 by Victor Hémery in what was in effect a modified racing Benz, while the American Barney Oldfield hit 131.7mph, also in a Benz, in America in 1910, but before American speed records were universally recognised.

Anything less than 1,000 miles was no longer seen as a particularly serious trial. The car's ability to cover huge distances even with appalling road and weather conditions (sometimes with no roads at all) had been proved by events like the Peking–Paris race of 1907, won by Prince Scipio Borghese's Itala, and the controversial New York–Paris race in 1908, won by Montague Roberts and George Shuster on the American Thomas Flyer (various rivals had caught trains and missed out entire countries). But those long distance events had already become an anachronism, and by the 1910s the more conventional races were becoming true tests of speed rather than simply the ability to complete the distance in one piece. Motor racing was indeed growing up.

By the 1910s the exaggerated demands of motoring competition were already beginning to teach lessons to the broader motoring movement. Those lessons were not only in increased power and performance but in better brakes and suspensions, and in practical improvements such as, first, detachable wheel rims, and then quickly removable wheels – the answer to the problem of early tyres being very vulnerable to punctures on the frequently awful road surfaces of those pioneering years. The roads themselves were improving to keep pace with the faster car, which was here to stay.

Europe was still the focus of the most important races, and the source of most of the leading cars and drivers, although America had also discovered motor sport before the 20th century was much older. By 1910, France had established the Grand Prix, organised by the Automobile Club de France, as the world's most important single race, supported by a number of important races for cars of lesser formulae, such as the Coupe de l'Auto and the Grand Prix des Voiturettes – prompting improvements in light cars and touring cars in just the same way that the Grand Prix pushed the development of the ultimate motoring technology of the early years. Italy, meanwhile, had the Giro di Sicilia (otherwise known as the Targa Florio), and Britain had Brooklands, which was proving to be a hugely successful venture, for both racers and spectators, with lap speeds already climbing far beyond what was possible on even the fastest of the road-based courses. In February 1913 Percy Lambert became the first man to cover 100 miles in an hour on the track, with his streamlined, single-seater 4.5-litre Talbot. That was a feat that only Brooklands could have accommodated at the time. Brooklands was fast enough for outright speed records, and in June 1914 L.G. Hornsted, driving a Benz, raised the world's land speed record to 124.1mph, an average speed set, under new land speed record rules, in two directions on the long finishing straight.

Britain was fortunate to have Brooklands because the attitude of the authorities to racing on the public highway had not changed during the 1910s, and it never would. Road racing in the British Isles had so far been represented by events in Ireland and the Isle of Man, ironically creating some of the most famous races in British motor sporting history. The Tourist Trophy (TT) series was first run on the Isle of Man in 1905, a year before either the Targa Florio or the Grand Prix, but it had disappeared from the calendar after the 'Four-Inch' race of 1908 (which limited cylinder bores to four inches and no more than four cylinders). It was revived in 1914, and the entry for that year's race provided a fine illustration of how far automobile technology had advanced since the end of the previous decade. In the 1914 TT, sporting cars like the twin-overhead-camshaft Sunbeams and Vauxhalls brought a new generation of highly efficient, high-revving engines that pointed the way to the next generation of racing car design. Unfortunately, in Europe at least, such designs would be put on hold for most of the rest of the decade; only weeks after Kenelm Lee Guinness took one of those Sunbeams to victory in that 1914 Tourist Trophy war was declared.

Like Europe, America had embraced road racing, with events like the Vanderbilt Cup and the Savannah races run on road courses around Long Island, New York, and Savannah, Georgia, respectively, and American drivers such as George

Heath, Lewis Strang, George Robertson and Ralph de Palma showing that they could more than hold their own against Europe's finest. But America also had a tradition of track racing events, which took a great leap in the middle of this decade. In the early days, America had raced on the same 1-mile dirt tracks used for horse racing and the shorter tracks used for running, on frozen lakes, on beaches and mountain climbs. In August 1909 America had opened its answer to Brooklands, and another of the world's most famous racing venues, in the shape of a track which is just as famous today – Indianapolis. It started an American tradition by offering the largest cash prizes available in the sport, but, much more, it started the legend of ultra-fast American track racing, even though Indianapolis was a long way behind Brooklands itself in terms of outright speed.

Like Brooklands, Indianapolis was promoted as a proving ground for the motor industry, but it was quite different from the high-banked, egg-shaped English track, comprising two long and two short straights linked by shallow banking at the four quarter-mile-long corners of the 2.5-mile lap. Where Brooklands had pioneered the use of reinforced concrete, Indianapolis's original surface comprised crushed stone and asphalt over a base of packed clay, but it did not work very well. The two inaugural meetings (the first for motor cycles, the second for cars) were abandoned, but not before Barney Oldfield in the Benz had covered one mile at more than 85mph and a riding mechanic had been killed in the 250-mile feature race, which was won by Bob Burman's Buick. After more track deterioration and another fatality over the same weekend, the track was resurfaced with more than three million bricks; it has been known as the 'Brickyard' since.

In 1910 Indianapolis started the tradition of running its major meeting during the Memorial Day holiday at the end of May, and in 1911, after a lean time of falling crowd attendances, it inaugurated a new 500-mile race, advertised as the greatest race the world had yet seen and with the massive purse of $25,000. Many drivers chose to run imported European racing cars, but the first Indianapolis 500 was won by an American driver in an American car – Ray Harroun in the Marmon Wasp – which famously claimed the first use of a rear-view mirror on a racing automobile instead of a riding mechanic.

While Europe was at war, however, American racing flourished, and alongside Indianapolis came a brief fashion for one of the most spectacular but dangerous forms of motor racing

ever devised, the high-banked board speedways. These remarkable speed bowls were built from tens of thousands of wooden planks, normally laid on edge to produce a smooth, hard surface which allowed incredible speeds – far faster, in fact, than Indianapolis's famous bricks. They spread from the West Coast, where the first board tracks were built in 1910, throughout the USA. By 1915 their brand of racing circus was booming, with lap speeds nudging 120mph, but great speeds also meant great dangers, and it was remarkable that they survived into the 1920s, when the fastest tracks of all saw 145mph-plus laps.

Then in November 1919, with the war over, racing returned to Europe with the Targa Florio. The winner of the race, André Boillot, initially crossed the line backwards in his Peugeot, having spun to avoid some errant spectators, but he turned around and finished a second time pointing in the right direction. It signalled a strange end to a difficult decade.

Um das Jahr 1910 waren Automobile und Motorsport nichts Ungewöhnliches mehr, wenn auch noch längst nicht für jeden erreichbar und bei den Behörden nicht immer gern gesehen. Inzwischen hatten die Fahrzeuge bewiesen, wie schnell sie sein konnten, und auch die Zuverlässigkeit besserte sich. Rennen um den Großen Preis von Frankreich (und den Großen Preis des Automobilclubs von Frankreich, was nicht dasselbe war), die Gordon-Bennett-Trophäe, um Kaiserpreis, Vanderbilt-, Targa-Florio- und Florio-Pokal hatten als Großereignisse die Stadt-zu-Stadt-Rennen abgelöst, und die schnellsten Runden auf den abgesperrten Rundstrecken lagen nun bei 130 Stundenkilometern. Den Geschwindigkeitsweltrekord hatte Victor Hémery in einem modifizierten Benz-Rennwagen im Jahr 1909 auf 186,5 km/h gebracht; der Amerikaner Barney Oldfield, ebenfalls auf Benz, erreichte 1910 sogar 211,9 Stundenkilometer, doch wurden damals die amerikanischen Rekorde noch nicht international anerkannt.

Alles, was kürzer als tausend Meilen war, galt nicht mehr als ernsthafte Belastungsprobe. Dass der Motorwagen gewaltige Entfernungen selbst unter schlechtesten Straßenbedingungen (oder sogar ganz ohne Straßen) bewältigen konnte, hatten Rennen wie die Fahrt Peking–Paris im Jahr 1907 bewiesen, aus der Fürst Scipio Borghese auf einem Itala als Sieger hervorgegangen war, und 1908 das umstrittene Rennen New York–Paris, das schließlich Montague Roberts und George Shuster im amerikanischen Thomas Flyer für sich entschieden (manche Konkurrenten durchquerten ganze Länder mit dem Zug). Doch solche Langstreckenfahrten hatten sich bereits überlebt, und die konventionelleren Rennen wurden immer mehr zu Geschwindigkeitswettbewerben und nicht mehr zu bloßen Belastungsproben. Der Sport wurde allmählich erwachsen.

Um 1910 fanden die hohen Anforderungen, die an Rennwagen gestellt wurden, bereits ihren Niederschlag in der Technik der zivileren Fahrzeuge. Dazu zählten nicht nur mehr Motorkraft und Leistung, sondern auch bessere Bremsen und Radaufhängungen und praktische Erleichterungen wie die abnehmbare Felge und bald darauf das abnehmbare Rad mit Schnellverschluss – eine große Hilfe, denn auf den oft äußerst schlechten Straßen der Zeit waren Reifenpannen an der Tagesordnung. Doch auch die Straßen besserten sich mit den schnelleren Wagen, und dass das Automobil eine Zukunft hatte, daran zweifelte nun niemand mehr.

Die meisten wichtigen Rennen fanden nach wie vor in Europa statt, und die führenden Wagen und Fahrer kamen größtenteils von dort – obwohl in den ersten Jahren des neuen Jahrhunderts auch die Amerikaner den Sport für sich entdeckten. In Frankreich hatte sich 1910 der Grand Prix, organisiert vom französischen Automobilclub, bereits als wichtigste Rennform herauskristallisiert, und in seinem Schatten fand eine Reihe weiterer Rennen in kleineren Formeln statt, etwa der Coupe de l'Auto und der Grand Prix des Voiturettes; diese Rennen trieben die Entwicklung von leichten Wagen und Tourenwagen genauso voran wie die Grand-Prix-Rennen stets den neuesten technischen Fortschritt auf die Straße brachten. Die Italiener hatten ihre Giro di Sicilia (besser bekannt als Targa Florio), und die Briten hatten Brooklands, das von Fahrern wie Zuschauern begeistert aufgenommen wurde und wo bereits Rundenzeiten gefahren wurden, die weit über allem lagen, was selbst auf den besten Straßenkursen möglich war. Percy Lambert legte im Februar 1913 auf dieser Strecke mit einem stromlinienverkleideten 4,5-Liter-Talbot-Einsitzer erstmals 100 Meilen (160 km) binnen einer Stunde zurück. Solche Fahrleistungen waren damals auf keiner anderen Strecke als in Brooklands möglich, und selbst Weltrekorde wurden dort noch aufgestellt; im Juni 1914 erreichte L. G. Hornsted mit einem Benz auf der langen Zielgeraden die Bestzeit von 199,7 Stundenkilometern gemäß den neu festgelegten Regeln, die Fahrten in beide Richtungen vorschrieben.

Großbritannien konnte von Glück sagen, dass es Brooklands hatte, denn die Behörden änderten ihre Einstellung zu Rennen auf öffentlichen Straßen nicht – weder in jenem Jahrzehnt noch überhaupt jemals. Diese Regelung führte dazu, dass einige der berühmtesten britischen Rennen in Irland oder auf der Isle of Man stattfanden. Das erste Tourist-Trophy-Rennen wurde schon 1905 auf der Isle of Man gefahren, ein Jahr vor der Targa Florio und dem Grand Prix, doch 1908 traten zunächst die »Four Inch«-Rennen an ihre Stelle (bei denen vier Zoll Bohrung und vier Zylinder vorgeschrieben waren). 1914 kehrte die TT zurück, und die Wagen, die in jenem Jahr antraten, waren schöne Beispiele für die großen Fortschritte, die die Technik seit dem Ende des vorangegangenen Jahrzehnts gemacht hatte. Mit den Sunbeams und Vauxhalls der TT von 1914 kam eine neue Generation von drehfreudigen Hochleistungsmotoren mit zwei oben liegende Nockenwellen auf die Straßen, die schon den Weg zu den

Rennwagen der nächsten Epoche wiesen. Doch für den Rest des Jahrzehnts sollte die Entwicklung stillstehen: Nur wenige Wochen nachdem Kenelm Lee Guinness in jener Tourist Trophy von 1914 mit seinem Sunbeam als Sieger ins Ziel gegangen war, begann der Erste Weltkrieg.

Wie auf dem europäischen Kontinent hatten sich auch in den Vereinigten Staaten Straßenrennen etabliert. Auf Long Island, New York, fand das Rennen um den Vanderbilt Cup statt, und zu einem zweiten großen Rennen traf man sich in Savannah in Georgia, und amerikanische Fahrer wie George Heath, Lewis Strang, George Robertson und Ralph de Palma bewiesen, dass sie sich durchaus mit den Besten Europas messen konnten. Doch die Amerikaner fuhren auch auf Rundkursen, und Mitte des Jahrzehnts schneller als irgendwo sonst. Die ersten amerikanischen Rennen fanden auf den eine Meile langen Sandpisten statt, auf denen sonst Pferderennen veranstaltet wurden, manche auch auf Sportplätzen, gefrorenen Seen, auf Stränden oder an Berghängen. Im August 1909 hatte Amerika seine Antwort auf Brooklands eröffnet – Indianapolis, bis heute eine der großen Rennstrecken der Welt. Nirgends winkten größere Geldpreise – der Beginn einer amerikanischen Tradition –, und vor allem standen von nun an Rundstrecken mit möglichst hohen Geschwindigkeiten im Mittelpunkt der amerikanischen Aufmerksamkeit, auch wenn das Tempo, das in Indianapolis möglich war, weit unter jenem von Brooklands lag.

Wie Brooklands galt auch Indianapolis als Testgelände für die Industrie, aber es war gänzlich anders aufgebaut als der eiförmige englische Kurs mit seiner stark abgeschrägten Piste; die zweieinhalb Meilen von Indianapolis bestanden aus zwei langen und zwei kurzen Geraden, und die vier jeweils eine Viertelmeile langen Kurven waren nur leicht geneigt. Brooklands war im damals neuartigen Stahlbeton erbaut, Indianapolis bestand zunächst nur aus Splitt und Asphalt auf einem Fundament aus gestampftem Lehm, doch dieser Belag erwies sich als nicht haltbar genug. Beide Einweihungsrennen (eines für Motorräder, eines für Automobile) wurden abgebrochen; zum Sieger des 250-Meilen-Hauptrennens, in dem ein Beifahrer den Tod fand und Barney Oldfield mit seinem Benz die schnellste Runde mit 133,5 Stundenkilometern fuhr, wurde Bob Burman auf Buick erklärt. Nach weiteren Fahrbahnschäden und einem zweiten tödlichen Unfall am selben Wochenende wurde die Strecke mit über drei Millionen Backsteinen ausgekleidet und trägt ihren Spitznamen »Brickyard« bis heute.

Ende Mai 1910 fand erstmals ein Indianapolis-Rennen am Memorial-Day-Wochenende statt, der Anfang einer langen Reihe, und 1911 wurde als Mittel gegen schwindende Zuschauerzahlen das 500-Meilen-Rennen lanciert, das als größtes der Welt beworben wurde und bei dem Preise im Wert von $ 25 000 winkten. Viele Fahrer traten mit europäischen Wagen an, doch der Sieger der ersten 500 Meilen von Indianapolis war ein Amerikaner auf einem amerikanischen Modell – Ray Harroun auf einem Marmon Wasp, der als Erster den Beifahrer durch einen Rückspiegel ersetzte.

Während Europa im Krieg lag, blühte der Rennbetrieb in Amerika, und neben Indianapolis kam, wenn es auch eine vorübergehende Erscheinung blieb, die spektakulärste Form des Motorsports überhaupt auf, allerdings auch die gefährlichste – das Motodrom mit einem stark geneigten Rundkurs aus Holzbohlen. Diese Arenen waren aus Zehntausenden von Planken zusammengesetzt, meist bündig verlegt, sodass eine glatte, harte Oberfläche entstand, die unglaubliche Geschwindigkeiten erlaubte – weitaus höhere als auf den berühmten Ziegeln von Indianapolis. Von der Westküste aus, wo die ersten Motodrome 1910 entstanden, verbreiteten sie sich über die gesamte USA. 1915 blühte dieser Rennzirkus, und die Rundengeschwindigkeiten näherten sich der 120-Meilen-Marke (193 km/h); doch hohe Geschwindigkeiten bedeuteten hier große Gefahren, und es war erstaunlich, dass sich die Motodrome bis in die zwanziger Jahre hielten, als in den schnellsten unter ihnen Rundengeschwindigkeiten von über 230 Stundenkilometern erreicht wurden.

Im November 1919 nahm mit der Targa Florio auch Europa nach überstandenem Krieg den Rennbetrieb wieder auf. Der Sieger in diesem Rennen, André Boillot, ging mit seinem Peugeot zunächst rückwärts über die Ziellinie, denn der Wagen hatte sich gedreht, als er unvorsichtigen Zuschauern auswich; Boillot wendete dann und überfuhr die Linie noch einmal, damit er auch in der richtigen Richtung ankam. Es war ein passendes Ende für ein wirres und schwieriges Jahrzehnt.

One of the greatest designers with one of his earliest sporting creations – Ferdinand Porsche driving the winning Austro-Daimler during the 1910 Prince Henry Trial.

Ein Konstrukteur, der zu den größten zählte, mit einem seiner frühen Sportwagen: Ferdinand Porsche am Steuer des Austro-Daimler, des Siegers der Prinz-Heinrich-Fahrt von 1910.

L'un des plus grands concepteurs d'automobiles avec l'une de ses premières créations sportives : Ferdinand Porsche au volant de l'Austro-Daimler victorieuse lors du Concours du Prince Henri de 1910.

Paddock fashions at Brooklands at a spring meeting in 1914: tweeds and checks for the driver and admirer, wire wheels and open cockpit for the TT Sunbeam.

Mode in Brooklands bei einem Sportwagenrennen 1914: Tweed für den Fahrer, Karo für die Dame und Speichenräder und offenes Cockpit für den TT Sunbeam.

Présentation de mode au paddock de Brooklands lors d'une réunion de printemps en 1914 : tweed à carreaux pour le pilote et son admiratrice, roues à rayons et habitacle découvert pour la Sunbeam TT.

En 1910, la voiture et le sport automobile sont déjà bien acceptés dans la conscience populaire, à défaut d'être toujours accessibles à l'homme ordinaire ou bien accueillis par les autorités. L'automobile a déjà prouvé qu'elle était rapide et sa fiabilité s'est améliorée au fil des ans. Si les automobiles atteignent désormais 130 km/h sur circuit, en 1909 le record de vitesse sur terre est établi à 186,5 km/h par le Français Victor Hémery dans une Benz de course modifiée, tandis que l'Américain Barney Oldfield, également sur Benz, atteint l'année suivante 211 km/h aux États-Unis (mais à une date où les records de vitesse américains ne sont pas encore reconnus). Les Grand Prix de France (et les Grand Prix de l'Automobile Club de France, ce qui est différent), les épreuves des coupes Gordon Bennett, Vanderbilt, du Kaiserpreis et de la Targa Florio (ou coupe Florio) ont progressivement remplacé les courses de ville à ville au panthéon du sport.

Désormais, les épreuves se disputant sur un parcours d'une longueur inférieure à 1600 km ne sont plus considérées comme suffisamment intéressantes puisque l'automobile a déjà prouvé qu'elle pouvait parcourir de grandes distances dans des conditions météorologiques et sur des routes effroyables (parfois sans route du tout) grâce notamment aux courses Paris–Pékin de 1907, remportée par l'Itala du prince Scipio Borghese, et New York–Paris de 1908, remportée par Montague Roberts et George Shuster sur une Thomas Flyer américaine (le classement final de la course fut cependant controversé car de nombreux concurrents avaient pris le train en évitant des pays entiers). Mais ces grandes « croisières » sont déjà un anachronisme dans ces années 1910 et les courses automobiles les plus « ordinaires » sont de véritables épreuves de vitesse et non plus de simples rallyes d'endurance où il s'agit de couvrir la plus longue distance.

En cette décennie 1910, les exigences exagérées de la compétition portent déjà leurs fruits dans le monde automobile, qui profite de cette expérience non seulement pour augmenter la puissance et les performances mais perfectionner aussi les freins et les suspensions des voitures, ou inventer des solutions pratiques comme les jantes amovibles – puis les roues à démontage rapide – pour pallier l'extrême vulnérabilité à la crevaison des premiers pneumatiques sur les revêtements abrasifs des voies de circulation. Les routes elles-mêmes sont aménagées pour s'adapter aux conditions de roulage des véhicules les plus rapides.

L'Europe demeure le lieu d'accueil des plus grandes compétitions et le berceau de la plupart des pilotes et des principales marques, même si l'Amérique découvre le sport automobile depuis quelques années. En 1910, la France a fait du Grand Prix organisé par l'Automobile Club de France l'épreuve la plus importante du monde, en parallèle avec un certain nombre d'autres courses intéressantes mais qui suivent des formules moins rigoureuses, telles que la Coupe de l'Auto ou le Grand Prix des Voiturettes. Ce sont d'ailleurs ces compétitions qui font progresser les voitures légères et de tourisme, de la même manière que les Grand Prix ont accéléré le développement technique des moteurs. Entre-temps, l'Italie a créé le Giro di Sicilia (un avatar de la Targa Florio) et la Grande-Bretagne a construit Brooklands, qui remporte un énorme succès tant auprès des spectateurs que des concurrents, qui peuvent y enregistrer des vitesses au tour déjà bien supérieures à ce qu'il est possible d'atteindre lors des courses sur route les plus rapides. En février 1913, Percy Lambert devient ainsi, sur une Talbot monoplace profilée de 4,5 litres de cylindrée, le premier homme à couvrir 160 km en une heure, un exploit alors uniquement réalisable sur l'autodrome de Brooklands. Le circuit se révélant suffisamment rapide pour y établir des records de vitesse, L. G. Hornsted, au volant d'une Benz, s'arroge en juin 1914 le record du monde de vitesse à 199,7 km/h, calculé, suivant les nouvelles règles, sur la moyenne réalisée en parcourant la ligne droite des stands dans les deux sens.

Il est heureux que la Grande-Bretagne dispose du circuit de Brooklands car l'attitude des autorités vis-à-vis des courses sur la voie publique n'a toujours pas évolué. Les compétitions sur route organisées au Royaume-Uni, sans doute les plus célèbres courses de l'histoire du sport automobile britannique, se sont jusque là déroulées en Irlande et sur l'île de Man. D'abord disputées sur l'île de Man en 1905, un an avant la Targa Florio et le Grand Prix, les épreuves du Tourist Trophy (TT) disparaissent ensuite du calendrier après la course dite « Four Inch » (parce que limitant les moteurs à quatre cylindres d'un alésage de quatre pouces) de 1908. Les machines des concurrents qui s'inscrivent en 1914 au Tourist Trophy, relancé cette année-là, illustrent parfaitement l'évolution de la technique automobile depuis la fin de la dernière décennie. Les Sunbeam et les Vauxhall, notamment, disposent de moteurs modernes à double arbre à came en tête très efficaces et tournant à un régime élevé qui annoncent la prochaine génération de voitures de course. Malheureusement, ces idées vont devoir rester quelque temps dans les cartons, en Europe tout au moins, car la guerre est déclarée quelques semaines après la victoire de la Sunbeam de Kenelm Lee Guinness dans ce dernier Tourist Trophy.

Suivant l'exemple de l'Europe, les États-Unis ont adopté la compétition automobile sur route en organisant des épreuves comme la Coupe Vanderbilt, disputée autour de Long Island (New York), et les courses de Savannah (Georgie), au cours desquelles les pilotes américains George Heath, Lewis Strang, George Robertson et Ralph de Palma se montrent à la hauteur des meilleurs Européens. Mais les États-Unis, qui conservent le goût des épreuves sur circuit, font formidablement évoluer le sport automobile au milieu de la décennie. Jusqu'à présent, les Américains couraient sur les pistes en terre des hippodromes, d'une longueur de 1 mile (1,6 km), celles plus courtes encore des stades, sur des lacs gelés, des plages et des pistes de montagne. C'est en août 1909 que les États-Unis créent l'un des plus célèbres circuits du monde, équivalent américain de Brooklands : Indianapolis. Cet ovale inaugure la tradition américaine des compétitions les plus richement dotées et, plus encore, lance la légende des courses sur piste ultra-rapides – quand bien même les vitesses qui y sont atteintes restent de loin inférieures à celles réalisables à Brooklands.

Indianapolis présente toutefois d'assez grandes différences avec le circuit ovoïde anglais et ses hauts virages relevés, puisqu'il offre quatre lignes droites, deux longues et deux courtes, reliées entre elles par quatre virages très relevés de 400 m de longueur sur un tracé total de 4 km. De plus, alors que la piste de Brooklands est en béton armé, celle d'Indianapolis est en pierres concassées et asphalte sur lit de terre battue. Mais la mauvaise qualité de ce type de revêtement contraint finalement les organisateurs à annuler les deux compétitions d'inauguration (la première pour motocyclettes, la seconde pour voitures) – toutefois après que Barney Oldfield sur Benz a couvert 1,6 km à plus de 133,5 km/h et qu'un mécanicien « embarqué » se soit tué lors de la course des 250 miles (400 km), remportée par la Buick de Bob Burman. La dégradation de la piste, et un nouvel accident survenu le même week-end, imposent sa réfection ; elle sera refaite en utilisant plus de trois millions de briques, ce qui vaut au circuit son surnom de « brickyard » (champ de briques).

La direction d'Indianapolis ayant décidé en 1910 d'organiser régulièrement son principal meeting fin mai, lors du Memorial Day, c'est en 1911, après une brève époque de désaffection du public, qu'elle inaugure une nouvelle course de 500 miles (805 km), annoncée comme étant la plus grande compétition du monde et dotée d'un prix du montant considérable de 25 000 dollars. Si la plupart des pilotes choisissent de courir sur des voitures importées d'Europe, ces premiers 500 Miles d'Indianapolis sont remportés par un pilote américain dans une voiture américaine – une Marmon Wasp pilotée par Ray Harroun, qui se rend célèbre pour avoir utilisé pour la première fois un rétroviseur sur une voiture de course plutôt que d'embarquer un mécanicien.

Les compétitions se multiplient aux États-Unis pendant que l'Europe est en guerre. Les Américains, sans pour autant délaisser Indianapolis, prennent brièvement goût aux courses sur speedways, sans doute l'une des courses automobiles les plus spectaculaires mais aussi les plus dangereuses jamais inventées. Les pistes de ces extraordinaires ovales, un tracé très rapide aux virages fortement relevés, sont construites avec des dizaines de milliers de planches de bois assemblées sur chant pour offrir une surface à la fois souple et résistante, qui autorise des vitesses incroyables, bien supérieures en fait aux célèbres briques d'Indianapolis. Ce genre de circuit s'étend progressivement de la côte Ouest, où il apparaît dès 1910, à l'ensemble des États-Unis et rencontre un succès formidable. En 1915, les concurrents des courses sur speedway atteignent des vitesses au tour approchant les 193 km/h. Le danger augmentant en proportion, il est remarquable que ces courses aient perduré jusque dans les années 1920, à une époque où l'on dépassait déjà les 233 km/h sur les circuits les plus rapides.

La guerre terminée, la compétition reprend sur le sol européen dès novembre 1919 avec la Targa Florio, dont le vainqueur de l'épreuve, André Boillot, sur Peugeot, va d'abord franchir la ligne dans le mauvais sens après avoir fait un tête-à-queue pour éviter des spectateurs, puis faire demi-tour et terminer enfin le capot orienté dans la bonne direction. Cet épisode marque ainsi étrangement la fin d'une décennie difficile pour l'automobile.

On road and track

Closed circuit road racing in France, for the pinnacle of motor racing, the Grand Prix, and racing in Britain on the world's first purpose-built track, at Brooklands. The French style is epitomised by Louis Wagner's Fiat, rounding the fork in Dieppe during the 1912 French Grand Prix (left), en route to second place behind Georges Boillot's Peugeot. The scale of Brooklands (above) is revealed by three cars line-abreast on the huge banking with masses of room to spare in a race for standard production cars just a few weeks later.

Auf Straßen und Pisten

Ein Straßenrennen auf einem abgeschlossenen Rundkurs in Frankreich für die Perle des Motorsports, den Grand Prix, und eine Veranstaltung in Großbritannien auf der ersten speziell dafür gebauten Rennstrecke in Brooklands. Wie Louis Wagner im Fiat (links) beim Großen Preis von Frankreich, 1912 in Dieppe, aus der Kurve kommt, ist französischer Rennstil par excellence; Wagner belegte den zweiten Platz hinter Georges Boillots Peugeot. Die Aufnahme aus Brooklands (oben), nur ein paar Wochen später bei einem Rennen für Serienwagen entstanden, zeigt die Größenverhältnisse: Drei Wagen haben in der mächtigen Steilkurve bequem nebeneinander Platz.

Sur route et sur circuit

Si, en France, on court sur route en Grand Prix, le nec plus ultra de la course automobile, en Grande-Bretagne la compétition a pour cadre Brooklands, le premier autodrome du monde. La compétition de style français est illustré par la Fiat de Louis Wagnere, passant à Dieppe lors du Grand Prix de France de 1912 (à gauche), où elle finira à la seconde place derrière la Peugeot de Georges Boillot. On se rend compte des dimensions du circuit de Brooklands (ci-dessus) en découvrant la place dont disposent ces trois automobiles, de front dans le grand virage relevé lors d'une course de voitures de production quelques semaines plus tard.

Over and under

Boillot's Peugeot (above) passes under a viaduct on the Dieppe circuit on its way to winning the 1912 French Grand Prix, while Kenelm Lee Guinness's winning Sunbeam (opposite, above) races over Quarter Bridge on the Isle of Man course during the 1914 Tourist Trophy. A competitor (opposite, below) makes more leisurely progress through the tunnel under the Brooklands banking.

Drunter und drüber

Boillots Peugeot (oben), auf dem Weg zum Sieg beim Großen Preis von Frankreich 1912, unterquert eine Brücke bei Dieppe, und Kenelm Lee Guinness' siegreicher Sunbeam nimmt in voller Fahrt (gegenüber, oben) die Quarter Bridge, 1914 bei der Tourist Trophy auf der Isle of Man. Gemächlicher (gegenüber, unten) durchquert ein Besucher den Tunnel unter der Steilkurve von Brooklands.

Dessus et dessous

La Peugeot de Boillot (ci-dessus) passe sous un viaduc du circuit de Dieppe lors du Grand Prix de France de 1912 qu'elle va remporter, tandis que la Sunbeam de Kenelm Lee Guinness (ci-contre, en haut) franchit le Quarter Bridge lors du Tourist Trophy de 1914, organisé sur l'île de Man. Un des concurrents a adopté, quant à lui, une vitesse de croisière pour passer le tunnel ménagé sous l'un des virages relevés de Brooklands (ci-contre, en bas).

A sport and an entertainment

As motor racing grew in stature, its appeal as a spectator sport grew with it. Crowds gather around the cars in the paddock (above) before the 75mph short handicap race at the Brooklands 1914 Easter meeting; watch one of the New York races from an adapted railway wagon (opposite, above); and greet 1914 Tourist Trophy winner Kenelm Lee Guinness (opposite, below) after his victory.

Sport und Unterhaltung

Je mehr das Ansehen des Motorsports wuchs, desto mehr Zuschauer zog er an. Schaulustige (oben) haben sich Ostern 1914 in der Arena von Brooklands vor dem 75-Meilen-Handikap-rennen um die Wagen versammelt, verfolgen (gegenüber, oben) eines der New Yorker Rennen von einem Eisenbahnwaggon aus und applaudieren (gegenüber, unten) dem Sieger der Tourist Trophy von 1914, Kenelm Lee Guinness.

Sport et spectacle

L'attrait du public augmente à mesure que le sport automobile prend de l'importance. La foule se rassemble dans le paddock autour des voitures (ci-dessus) avant l'épreuve à handicap de Pâques à Brooklands. Le public assiste aux épreuves de New York depuis une voiture de chemin de fer aménagée (ci-contre, en haut), ou salue le vainqueur du Tourist Trophy de 1914, Kenelm Lee Guinness, après la course (ci-contre en bas).

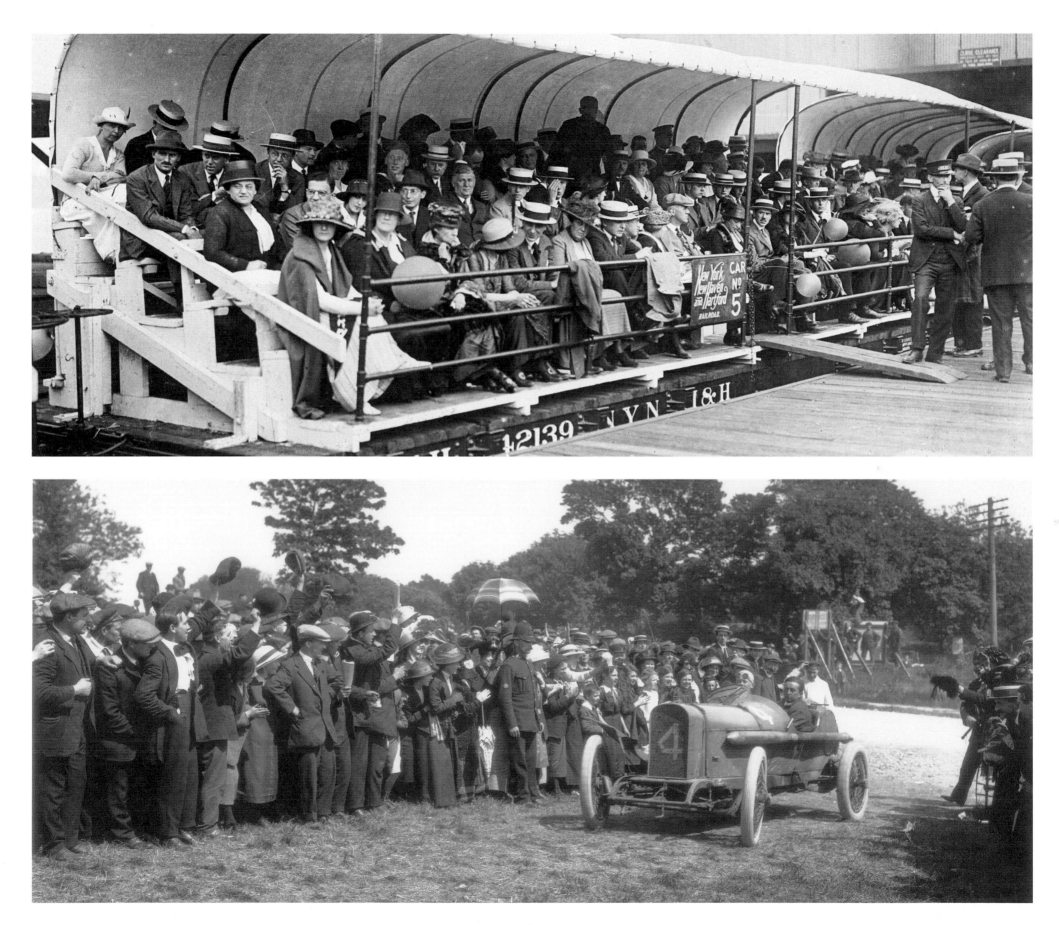

Aiming for the top

Speed hillclimbing had a following all of its own. (Opposite, clockwise from top left) C.A. Bird's Sunbeam leaves the line at Shelsley Walsh in June 1913; J.A. Barber Lomax's Vauxhall nears the top at Shelsley on the same day; C. Inglefield's 8hp Enfield cyclecar on a Lancashire hill in 1913; and Mr Bayliss's Sunbeam in Yorkshire in 1912. (Above) H.G. Day's Talbot slides through a corner on the Caerphilly climb, also in 1913.

Auf zum Gipfel

Bergrennen waren eine Welt für sich. (Gegenüber, im Uhrzeigersinn von oben links) C. A. Bird startet mit seinem Sunbeam in Shelsley Walsh, Juni 1913; J. A. Barber Lomax' Vauxhall nähert sich der Bergkuppe von Shelsley; C. Inglefield mit einem 8-PS-Kleinwagen von Enfield an einem Hügel in Lancashire, 1913; Mr. Bayliss' Sunbeam in Yorkshire, 1912. (Oben) H. G. Day mit seinem Talbot bei der Caerphilly-Bergprüfung, ebenfalls 1913.

Viser les sommets

La course de côte a ses passionnés. (Ci-contre, dans le sens des aiguilles d'une montre, à partir du haut à gauche) La Sunbeam de C. A. Bird s'élance à Shelsley Walsh, en juin 1913. La Vauxhall de J. A. Barber Lomax approche de l'arrivée au sommet ; le cyclecar Enfield 8 ch de C. Inglefield, Lancashire, 1913. La Sunbeam de M. Bayliss, Yorkshire, 1912. (Ci-dessus) La Talbot de H. G. Day part en dérapage lors de la course de Caerphilly, 1913.

Occupational hazards

Pushing the limits of roadholding and driver skill always had its dangers. Johnny Marquis in a Sunbeam, the only British car ever to contest this race, discovered the point of no return at Death Curve during the 1914 Grand Prize. Marquis and his mechanic survived; the race, on the shores of the Pacific at Santa Monica, California, was won by Joe Pullen's Mercer, a popular all-American victory.

Berufsrisiko

Bis an die Grenzen von Straßenlage und fahrerischem Können zu gehen, war gefährlich. Beim Großen Preis von Kalifornien, 1914 in Santa Monica überschritt Johnny Marquis mit seinem Sunbeam (dem einzigen britischen Wagen, der je in diesem Rennen antrat) in der »Todeskurve« die kritische Marke. Marquis und sein Mechaniker überlebten; Joe Pullen auf Mercer errang einen populären rein amerikanischen Sieg.

Les risques du métier

Il est dangereux de chercher à repousser les limites de tenue de route de la voiture ou d'habileté du pilote. J. Marquis et sa Sunbeam, la seule voiture britannique à avoir jamais participé à cette course, découvre le point de non-retour dans la *Death Curve*, lors du Grand Prix de 1914; Marquis et son mécanicien survécurent à l'accident. Cette course fut remportée par la Mercer de J. Pullen, une victoire américaine.

On both sides of the ocean

Gil Anderson's Stutz on the grid for the 1913 Indianapolis 500 (above right). He finished third, after five pit stops for tyres cost him the lead. Ralph de Palma (below right) winning the 1914 Vanderbilt Cup at Santa Monica for Mercedes. (Overleaf) Practice for the 1914 Tourist Trophy. Arthur Rawlinson's Sunbeam (number 10) failed to make the start on the following day; Lisle's Star (number 5) lasted only six laps.

Dies- und jenseits des Großen Teichs

Gil Anderson mit seinem Stutz bei den 500 Meilen von Indiana-polis, 1913 (oben). Er kam auf Rang drei – fünf Boxenstopps für Reifenwechsel kosteten ihn den Sieg. Ralph de Palma (unten) erringt 1914 in Santa Monica mit seinem Mercedes den Vanderbilt Cup. (Folgende Seiten) Training zur Tourist Trophy, 1914. Arthur Rawlinsons Sunbeam (Nummer 10) trat am folgenden Tag nicht an, Lisles Star (Nummer 5) schied nach sechs Runden aus.

Des deux côtés de l'océan

La Stutz de Gil Anderson sur la grille des 500 Miles d'Indiana-polis de 1913 (en haut à droite). Il termina troisième, ses cinq arrêts au stand lui ayant coûté la victoire. Ralph de Palma (en bas à droite), vainqueur pour Mercedes de la Coupe Vanderbilt, Santa Monica, 1914. (Pages suivantes) Les essais du Tourist Trophy de 1914. La Sunbeam d'Arthur Rawlinson (n° 10) ne prendra pas le départ et la Star de Lisle (n° 5) ne tiendra que six tours.

A severe test in the forests

In 1913, decades before Spa Francorchamps in the forests of the Ardennes became a venue for the modern Belgian Grand Prix, the area hosted a speed and reliability trial which bore the name Belgian Grand Prix. The scene before the start (left) shows some of the cars assembled in front of the waiting scoreboard. The event was marred by the death of the driver Baron de Woelmont (above), who was fatally injured when he crashed his Belgian-made SAVA racer.

Das Röhren im Walde

Jahrzehnte bevor die Strecke von Spa-Francorchamps mitten in den Ardennen zum Schauplatz für den heutigen Großen Preis von Belgien wurde, gab es im Jahr 1913 einen Geschwindigkeits- und Zuverlässigkeits-Wettbewerb, der als belgischer Grand Prix ausgeschrieben war. Die Szene vor dem Start (links) zeigt einige Teilnehmer vor der noch leeren Anzeigetafel versammelt. Das Rennen wurde vom tödlichen Unfall des Barons de Woelmont (oben) überschattet, der mit seinem belgischen SAVA angetreten war.

Essais difficiles en forêt

En 1913, c'est-à-dire plusieurs décennies avant que le circuit de Spa Francorchamps ne soit aussi tracé dans la forêt des Ardennes, la région accueillait déjà un concours de vitesse et d'endurance portant le nom de Grand Prix de Belgique. Quelques voitures sont rassemblées avant le départ devant le panneau d'affichage (à gauche). L'épreuve fut attristée par la mort du baron de Woelmont (ci-dessus) dans un grave accident survenu alors qu'il se trouvait au volant de sa SAVA, une voiture construite en Belgique.

Grand Prix masters

By the time war threatened, Grand Prix racing was the undisputed pinnacle of motor sport, Grand Prix cars were its cutting-edge technology and Grand Prix drivers its greatest heroes. Christian Lautenschlager and Mercedes (top) took an all-German win in the 1914 French Grand Prix; Georges Boillot and Peugeot (above) were all-French victors at Dieppe in 1912.

Grand-Prix-Meister

Vor dem Ersten Weltkrieg waren Grand-Prix-Rennen unbestritten die Krone des Motorsports, in Grand-Prix-Wagen fand sich das Fortschrittlichste an Autotechnik, und die Grand-Prix-Fahrer waren Helden. Christian Lautenschlager und Mercedes (oben) fuhren 1914 einen rein deutschen Sieg im Großen Preis von Frankreich ein; Georges Boillot und sein Peugeot sorgten dafür, dass der Preis 1912 in Dieppe im Lande blieb.

Les maîtres des Grand Prix

À l'époque où la guerre menace, la course de Grand Prix représente le nec plus ultra du sport automobile, avec des voitures à la pointe de la technologie et des pilotes considérés comme des héros. Après que Georges Boillot et sa Peugeot (ci-dessus) ont remporté une victoire française à Dieppe en 1912, Christian Lautenschlager et Mercedes (en haut) marquent une victoire allemande au Grand Prix de France de 1914.

Motor racing as theatre

Track racing in America started with head-to-head challenge races on small dirt tracks and horse racing tracks. Following the example of Indianapolis, they spread to purpose-built speedways with every kind of surface, from Indy's bricks to the high-speed wooden boards of some of the fastest tracks in the sport's early history. Everywhere the crowds were huge.

Motorsport als Showgeschäft

Die ersten amerikanischen Rennen waren reine Wettfahrten auf kurzen Sandpisten oder Pferderennbahnen. Nach dem Erfolg von Indianapolis kamen neu erbaute Rennstrecken mit unterschiedlichen Belägen hinzu, von den Backsteinen bis zu den Holzbohlen der Hochgeschwindigkeits-Motodrome, mit denen einige der schnellsten Strecken der Frühzeit des Sports entstanden. Alle zogen gewaltige Zuschauermengen an.

La course automobile comme spectacle

La course sur circuit a commencé aux États-Unis par l'organisation de duels sur des pistes en terre et des hippodromes. À l'instar d'Indianapolis, ces épreuves se disputent ensuite sur des speedways construits spécialement et aux revêtements très divers, depuis les briques d'Indianapolis jusqu'aux planches en bois de certaines des pistes les plus rapides de l'histoire du sport. Partout, l'assistance est considérable.

Motor sport for every man

Below the expensive and esoteric levels of Grand Prix racing, there have always been more accessible levels of motor sport, with room for far less exotic cars alongside the pure bred racers. Production cars and single-seaters (above) sit side by side at a sand race meeting, and (opposite) even a standard Model T (24M) could find a place in a Brooklands relay in 1912.

Motorsport für Jedermann

Grand-Prix-Wagen waren teuer und technisch aufwändig, doch von Anfang an gab es erschwinglichere Formen des Motorsports, und alltägliche Modelle fuhren neben reinrassigen Rennwagen. Bei einem Strandrennen (oben) stehen Serienwagen und Monoposti friedlich nebeneinander, und selbst ein gewöhnliches T-Modell (Startnummer 24M) fand seinen Platz bei einem Brooklands-Stafettenrennen von 1912 (gegenüber).

Le sport automobile à portée de tous

En dehors des courses de Grand Prix, onéreuses et souvent ésotériques au profane, il a toujours existé des niveaux plus accessibles du sport automobile, où s'affrontent des voitures moins exotiques et de purs bolides. Voitures de production et monoplaces voisinent lors d'une course sur plage (ci-dessus), et même une Ford Model T standard (24M) a sa place dans une course de relais à Brooklands en 1912 (ci-contre).

A poor weekend for Vauxhall

A.J. Hancock, Vauxhall's prolific record-breaker, was also a fine road racer. He is seen (opposite, below right) during scrutineering, (above) at Sulby Glen, and (opposite above) at Kirkmichael during the 1914 Tourist Trophy. It was not a good event for the Vauxhall team (opposite, below left): two of their cars retired on the first day of the two-day contest, and Hancock himself crashed heavily on the second day.

Vauxhall im Pech

A. J. Hancock, der für Vauxhall viele Rekorde brach, war auch in Straßenrennen erfolgreich. Hier sehen wir ihn bei der Tourist Trophy von 1914 bei der technischen Abnahme (gegenüber, unten rechts), in Sulby Glen (oben) und Kirkmichael (gegenüber, oben). Für Vauxhall (gegenüber, unten links) war es kein gutes Rennen: Zwei Wagen schieden nach dem ersten der beiden Renntage aus, und Hancock verunglückte am zweiten Tag.

Un mauvais week-end pour Vauxhall

A. J. Hancock, le prolifique briseur de records de Vauxhall, était aussi un excellent pilote sur route. On le voit ici lors du Tourist Trophy de 1914 au cours du contrôle (ci-contre, en bas à droite), à Sulby Glen (ci-dessus) et à Kirkmichael (ci-contre, en haut). L'épreuve ne fut pas favorable à l'écurie Vauxhall (ci-contre, en bas à gauche) : deux de leurs voitures abandonnèrent le premier jour, et Hancock eut un grave accident le second jour.

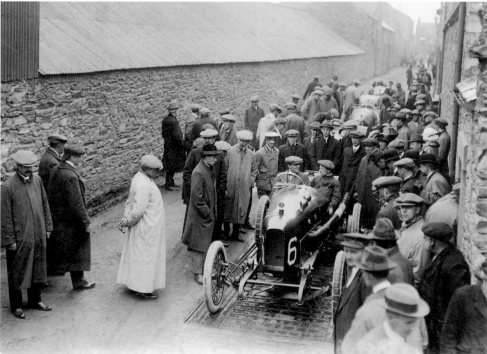

Serving the needs of the driver

Pit and paddock work has always played a vital role in the successful racing programme. Work goes on during Humber, Star and Sunbeam record attempts (above and below left, and opposite, below right) at Brooklands in 1913, 1912 and 1914. The Pope-Hartford crew gets ready to resume the race (opposite, above); and a punctured front tyre is replaced on Bianchi's Crossley (opposite, below left) during practice for the 1914 Tourist Trophy.

Alles, was der Fahrer braucht

Die Arbeit an den Boxen spielte für einen erfolgreichen Rennbetrieb von Anfang an eine entscheidende Rolle. Die Mechaniker von Humber, Star und Sunbeam (links oben, links unten und gegenüber unten rechts) in Aktion bei Rekordfahrten in Brooklands 1913, 1912 und 1914. Die Pope-Hartford-Mannschaft schickt den Wagen wieder ins Rennen (gegenüber, oben), und bei Bianchis Crossley (gegenüber, unten links) wird beim Training für die Tourist Trophy von 1914 ein Vorderreifen gewechselt.

Servir les besoins du pilote

La préparation des voitures au paddock comme aux stands a toujours été essentielle pour gagner une course. Les mécaniciens continuent de travailler pendant les tentatives de record d'une Humber, d'une Star et d'une Sunbeam à Brooklands en 1912, 1913 et 1914 (à gauche en bas et en haut, et ci-contre en bas à droite). L'équipe Pope-Hartford se tient prête à reprendre la course (ci-contre en haut). Changement du pneumatique avant de la Crossley de Bianchi après une crevaison lors des essais du Tourist Trophy de 1914 (ci-contre, en bas à gauche).

Containing the dangers...

Today, generous run-off areas and walls of tyre barriers are taken for granted. In the 1910s, effective means to keep cars and crowds apart were a rare but already desirable thing. Eddie Pullen's Mercer (centre) heads for the barriers after losing a wheel in the 1914 Vanderbilt Cup at Santa Monica, but two days later he won the Grand Prize at the same race track.

Die Gefahren klein halten ...

Heute sind breite Randstreifen und dicke Reifenbarrieren selbstverständlich, doch in den 1910er Jahren war es die Ausnahme, Wagen und Zuschauer voreinander zu schützen, auch wenn die Notwendigkeit längst erkannt war. Eddie Pullens Mercer (Mitte) hat beim Vanderbilt Cup von 1914 in Santa Monica ein Rad verloren und nimmt Kurs auf die Absperrung, zwei Tage später trat er auf derselben Strecke wieder an und errang den Großen Preis.

Réduire les risques ...

Si nous sommes désormais habitués à voir de vastes dégagements et des barrières de pneus en bord de piste, les moyens efficaces pour séparer les voitures et le public étaient rares mais souhaitables dans les années 1910. La Mercer de Eddie Pullen (au centre) fonce droit vers les barrières de sécurité lors de la Coupe Vanderbilt de 1914 à Santa Monica ; deux jours plus tard, elle remportera le Grand Prix sur le même circuit.

...and controlling the crowds

When the world's fastest racing cars competed on what were little more than ordinary roads, with all the problems of controlling public access, it was vital to warn of the imminent arrival of speeding cars. Waving flags (opposite, far left) was one option, and at the Coupe des Voiturettes in Boulogne the approach of the cars was signalled in some places by men with trumpets (right).

... und die Massen in Schach

Wenn die schnellsten Rennwagen der Welt über die nur notdürftig dafür hergerichteten Landstraßen rasten, war es lebenswichtig, die Zuschauer vor den herannahenden Wagen zu warnen. Eine Möglichkeit waren Flaggen (gegenüber, links), eine andere Trompetensignale wie beim Coupe des Voiturettes in Boulogne (rechts).

... et canaliser la foule

Lorsque les voitures les plus rapides du monde courent sur des routes rien de plus qu'ordinaires, avec tous les problèmes que pose le contrôle de l'accès du public, il est vital de prévenir les spectateurs de l'arrivée imminente des bolides. Il suffisait parfois d'agiter un drapeau (ci-contre, à l'extrême gauche) ou, comme lors de la Coupe des Voiturettes à Boulogne, de signaler l'arrivée des voitures d'un coup de trompette (à droite).

High and mighty...

When the rule makers limited the size of cylinder bores, the car makers found capacity, and power, from exaggeratedly long strokes, leading to tall engines and distinctively high-bonneted cars. This is Ralph de Palma's Fiat, still using chain drive, at the Dieppe fork during the 1912 French Grand Prix before he was disqualified for taking on fuel away from the pits.

Je höher die Haube ...

Als das Reglement bestimmte Zylinderbohrungen vorschrieb, suchten die Hersteller Heil und Motorkraft in unverhältnismäßig langem Hub, was zu sehr hohen Motoren mit entsprechend charakteristischen Hauben führte. Hier sehen wir Ralph de Palmas Fiat, noch mit Kettenantrieb, am Abzweig nach Dieppe beim Großen Preis von Frankreich 1912, bevor er disqualifiziert wurde, weil er außerhalb der Boxen nachgetankt hatte.

Haute et puissante ...

Lorsque les instances de régulation limitèrent l'alésage des cylindres, les constructeurs augmentèrent la puissance des moteurs en allongeant la course. Cela explique la grosseur des moteurs et la hauteur de capot, comme c'est le cas de la Fiat de Ralph de Palma, négociant l'épingle à cheveux de Dieppe lors du Grand Prix de France de 1912 avant sa disqualification pour avoir ravitaillé en carburant en dehors des stands.

...the shape of power

The long-stroke, tall bonnet configuration arose from Grand Prix rules, but its influence spread to all kinds of motor sport. Georges Boillot drove the Lion-Peugeot (top) in the 1910 Coupe des Voiturettes in Boulogne; Arthur Duray in a 200hp Benz (above left) at the 1914 Ostend Trials; and Boissy in the single-cylinder Lion-Peugeot (above right) at Brooklands in 1911.

... desto mächtiger der Motor

Die langhubigen Motoren mit den hohen Hauben waren eine Folge der Grand-Prix-Regeln, doch von da griff diese Mode auf alle Bereiche des Motorsports über. Georges Boillot fuhr den Lion-Peugeot (ganz oben) 1910 beim Coupe des Voiturettes in Boulogne, Arthur Duray den 200-PS-Benz (oben links) 1914 bei Versuchsfahrten in Ostende und Boissy den Einzylinder-Lion-Peugeot (oben rechts) 1911 in Brooklands.

... la silhouette de la puissance

Si la configuration à course longue découle des règles de Grand Prix, son influence s'étend bientôt à tous les genres du sport automobile, qu'il s'agisse de la Lion-Peugeot de Georges Boillot dans la Coupe des Voiturettes de 1910 à Boulogne (en haut), de la Benz 200 ch d'Arthur Duray lors du Concours d'Ostende de 1914 (ci-dessus à gauche), ou de la monocylindre Lion-Peugeot de Boissy à Brooklands en 1911 (en haut à droite).

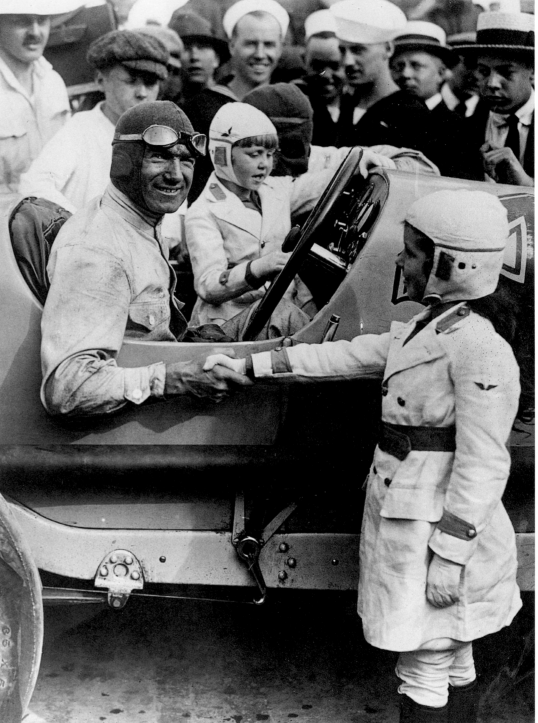

Famous men and pioneers

Before he became a car maker, W.O. Bentley raced both motorcycles and cars and pioneered aluminium pistons in the French DFP, as at Brooklands in 1914 (top). American George Robertson, Vanderbilt Cup winner, in his Simplex (above) for the opening of the Los Angeles board speedway in 1917; and fellow American Ralph de Palma (right), with young fans.

Pioniere und berühmte Männer

Bevor er seine eigenen Wagen baute, trat W. O. Bentley als Motorrad- und als Automobilrennfahrer an, unter anderem 1914 in Brooklands (ganz oben) mit dem französischen DFP, der erstmals Kolben aus Aluminium aufwies. Der Amerikaner George Robertson, Gewinner des Vanderbilt Cups, kam 1917 in seinem Simplex (oben) zur Eröffnung des Motodroms in Los Angeles. Ralph de Palma (rechts) begrüßt junge Verehrer.

Des hommes et des pionniers célèbres

Avant de devenir constructeur, W. O. Bentley a participé à des courses de motocyclettes et d'automobiles mais a aussi mis au point les pistons en aluminium de la DFP française, comme à Brooklands en 1914 (en haut). L'Américain George Robertson, le vainqueur de la Coupe Vanderbilt, dans sa Simplex à l'ouverture du speedway en bois de Los Angeles en 1917 (ci-dessus), et Ralph de Palma avec de jeunes admirateurs (à droite).

A talent for great design

Ernest Henry has been described as the father of Grand Prix design, and his ideas had great influence on both sides of the Atlantic, in his own work and in that of various admirers and imitators. His early Grand Prix Peugeots had an amazingly long life, as driven by Jules Goux at Brooklands in 1913 (below), and the 1912 7.6-litre Grand Prix model – still competitive for Captain Malcolm Campbell (above) at Brooklands ten years later.

Ein Meisterkonstrukteur

Ernest Henry gilt als Vater des Grand-Prix-Rennwagens und hatte mit seinen Ideen beiderseits des Atlantiks großen Einfluss, mit eigenen Konstruktionen wie auch mit denen seiner zahlreichen Bewunderer und Nachahmer. Seine frühen Peugeot-Grand-Prix-Wagen, wie Jules Goux einen (unten) 1913 in Brooklands fuhr, waren bemerkenswert langlebig – mit der 7,6-Liter-Version von 1912 startete Captain Malcolm Campbell (oben) dort noch zehn Jahre später.

Un talent pour les grands projets

Les idées d'Ernest Henry, décrit comme le père des voitures de Grand Prix, eurent une grande influence des deux côtés de l'Atlantique, dans son propre travail comme dans celui de nombreux admirateurs et imitateurs. Ses premières Peugeot de Grand Prix eurent une durée de vie extraordinairement longue, comme par exemple celle que pilote Jules Goux à Brooklands en 1913 (en bas) ou le modèle Grand Prix 7,6 litres de 1912, suffisamment compétitif dix ans plus tard pour le capitaine Malcolm Campbell à Brooklands (en haut).

Under starter's orders

In 1909 Harry Grant was virtually unknown until he won the Vanderbilt Cup at his first attempt, driving the American Alco car for which he was a dealer in Boston. He won again in 1910, but by 1914 Alco was out of business, while Grant (above, at the wheel) was driving for Isotta-Fraschini. He was first man away in that year's Vanderbilt (right), a race won by Ralph de Palma in a dramatic showdown with his arch-rival Barney Oldfield.

Das Wort des Starters gilt

Harry Grant war im Jahre 1909 so gut wie unbekannt, als er auf Anhieb den Vanderbilt Cup mit einem Alco gewann, einem amerikanischen Fabrikat, für das er in Boston die Vertretung hatte. 1910 wiederholte er seinen Erfolg, doch 1914 gab es Alco nicht mehr, und Grant (oben, am Steuer) war auf Isotta-Fraschini umgestiegen. Im Rennen jenes Jahres startete er als erster (rechts), doch als Sieger ins Ziel kam Ralph de Palma nach einem dramatischen Zweikampf mit seinem Erzrivalen Barney Oldfield.

Aux ordres du starter

En 1909, Harry Grant était pratiquement inconnu jusqu'à ce qu'il gagne la Coupe Vanderbilt dès sa première tentative au volant d'une Alco, une marque américaine dont il était un revendeur à Boston, avant de remporter de nouveau la coupe en 1910. En 1914, Alco n'existant plus, Grant (ci-dessus, au volant) pilote pour Isotta-Fraschini. Il est le premier à s'élancer lors de l'épreuve de cette année-là (à droite) mais c'est Ralph de Palma qui, après un duel fantastique contre son grand rival Barney Oldfield, gagne la course.

Innovation and tradition at Indy

The first Indianapolis 500 was won by Ray Harroun's Marmon Wasp, the only car in the 1911 race to run without a riding mechanic but with a rear-view mirror. The Wasp (number 32) and Joe Dawson's National, which won in 1912, were on show at the 1913 race, near the 'pagoda' which housed race officials and the press, but which burnt down in the 1920s.

Tradition und Erneuerung in Indianapolis

Die ersten »Indy 500« gewann Ray Harroun auf einem Marmon Wasp, dem einzigen Wagen im Rennen von 1911, der keinen Beifahrer, dafür jedoch einen Rückspiegel hatte. Der Wasp (Nummer 32) und Joe Dawsons National, der Sieger von 1912, waren beim Rennen von 1913 vor der »Pagode« zu sehen, wo Rennleitung und Presse residierten, bis sie in den zwanziger Jahren abbrannte.

Innovation et tradition à Indianapolis

La première course des 500 Miles d'Indianapolis, en 1911, est remportée par Ray Harroun sur une Marmon Wasp, la seule voiture à disposer d'un rétroviseur à la place du mécanicien navigant. La Wasp (numéro 32) et la National de Joe Dawson, vainqueur en 1912, sont exposées pour l'édition 1913 près de la « pagode » qui abritait les officiels et la presse et fut détruite dans un incendie dans les années 1920.

Preliminaries and outcomes

In the early days of Indianapolis, cars had to pass a 'brake test' (top) before they were allowed to race. There was no Vanderbilt Cup in 1913, but there was plenty of other racing in America. In that year's Santa Monica races in August, Barney Oldfield in his Mercer (centre) scored a second place while Earl Cooper, the 1913 national champion, was a winner in his Stutz (bottom).

Vorleistungen und Resultate

In den ersten Tagen von Indianapolis mussten die Wagen einen Bremstest absolvieren (oben), bevor sie ins Rennen durften. 1913 gab es keinen Vanderbilt Cup, doch Amerika kannte genügend andere Rennen. Im Santa-Monica-Rennen im August jenes Jahres kam Barney Oldfield in seinem Mercer (Mitte) auf den zweiten Platz, Earl Cooper, Landesmeister von 1913, kam mit dem Stutz (unten) als Sieger ins Ziel.

Préliminaires et résultats

Lors des premières éditions d'Indianapolis, les voitures devaient subir un « test de freinage » avant d'être admises à concourir (en haut). Beaucoup d'épreuves se sont déroulées aux États-Unis en 1913, à l'exception notable de la Coupe Vanderbilt. Lors des courses de Santa Monica, au mois d'août, Barney Oldfield et sa Mercer (au centre) s'arrogent la seconde place tandis que Earl Cooper, le champion national en 1913, remporte la victoire dans sa Stutz (en bas).

Fighting on the beaches
Cars line up on the sand for the Irish Automobile Club's speed trials at Rosslare, and for the South Wales and Cardiff Motor Club's trials at Porthcawl (with H.F.S. Morgan's Morgan on the left), both in 1913 (previous spread, above and below). L.G. 'Cupid' Hornsted's Benz (above) approaching 100mph on Saltburn Sands, Yorkshire, July 1912; sometimes the tide came in or the rain came down (left).

Rangelei am Strand
Zum Sandrennen nehmen die Teilnehmer der Geschwindigkeitsprüfung des Irish Automobile Club in Rosslare und der Wettfahrt des Cardiff Motor Club in Porthcawl Aufstellung (links H. F. S. Morgan mit einer sciner Konstruktionen), beides 1913 (vorherige Doppelseite, oben und unten). Der Benz von L. G. (»Cupid«) Hornsted nähert sich im Juli 1912 in Saltburn Sands, Yorkshire, der 160-Stundenkilometer-Grenze. Manchmal kam die Flut zu früh (links) – oder ist es Regen?

Affrontements sur le sable
Les plages sont le théâtre de nombreuses épreuves, parfois sous la pluie ou à marée montante (à gauche) : la Benz de L. G. « Cupid » Hornsted approche les 160 km/h à Saltburn Sands (Yorkshire) en juillet 1912 (ci-dessus) ; la grille de départ du concours de vitesse organisé à Rosslare par l'Irish Automobile Club et lors d'une compétition du South Wales and Cardiff Motor Club à Porthcawl (on reconnaît la Morgan de H. F. S. Morgan sur la gauche), en 1913 (pages précédentes, en haut et en bas).

An opportunity for everyone

Sand racing created a competitive arena for almost every kind of amateur driver in the early years, including the ladies lining up in their virtually standard sporting tourers at Porthcawl at the turn of the 1920s (above), and every kind of machinery, including Mr George's stripped Ford Model T (left), winning on Saltburn Sands in July 1912 at the other end of the entry list from Hornsted's Benz (opposite).

Eine Gelegenheit für jeden

In den ersten Jahren waren die Sandrennen eine Rennform, an der fast jeder Amateur teilnehmen konnte, so etwa die Damen, die in Porthcawl um 1920 in ihren fast serienmäßigen Tourensportwagen antreten (oben), und mit jedem anderen erdenklichen Gefährt – wie Mr. George (links) beweist, der im Juli 1912 in Saltburn Sands auf seinem Ford-T-Chassis erfolgreich war; am anderen Ende der Startliste stand Hornsteds Benz (gegenüber).

La compétition pour tous

Les courses sur plage ont permis d'ouvrir la compétition automobile à presque tous les pilotes amateurs, notamment à ces femmes au volant de voitures de tourisme presque standard à Porthcawl au début des années 1920 (ci-dessus), et à tous types de machines, dont cette Ford Model T dépouillée de Mr George (à gauche), victorieuse à Saltburn Sands en juillet 1912 et très éloignée de la Benz de Hornsted (page précédente).

The charge of the light brigade
The cyclecar was popular in Europe before the First World War
– a very lightweight vehicle filling the gap between motorcycle
and sidecar and conventional light car, usually helped by tax
advantages. Cyclecar racing was popular, too; this is Frenchman
Ronteix in a car of his own make at the French Cyclecar Grand
Prix at Amiens in 1913, a race won by W. Gordon McMinnies in
the three-wheeler Morgan.

Der Angriff der leichten Brigade
Cyclecars waren vor dem Ersten Weltkrieg in Europa beliebt –
Modelle, die auf halbem Wege zwischen Motorrad mit Beiwagen
und einem konventionellen Kleinwagen standen und steuerlich
begünstigt waren. Solche Wagen hatten ihre eigenen Rennen –
der Franzose Ronteix in einer Eigenkonstruktion bei den
französischen Meisterschaften in Amiens, 1913; Sieger wurde
W. Gordon McMinnies auf einem Morgan-Dreirad.

La charge de la brigade légère
Le cyclecar – une voiture très légère, souvent vendue avec une
taxe réduite, comblant le vide entre motocyclette, sidecar et
voiture – et les courses qui leur étaient réservées furent très
populaires en Europe avant la Première Guerre mondiale. On
voit ici le Français Ronteix dans une voiture de sa marque lors
du Grand Prix des Cyclecars d'Amiens de 1913, remporté par
W. Gordon McMinnies sur un tricycle Morgan.

The fine line

Motor racing revolves around treading the fine line between triumph and disaster, calculating risks without overstepping the mark. In practice for the 1914 Tourist Trophy (above), Algernon Lee Guinness's Sunbeam speeds between solid walls and even more solid trees, while the competitor in the French race (below) did not judge the margins quite so well.

Der schmale Grat

Motorsportler bewegen sich stets auf dem schmalen Grat zwischen Triumph und Katastrophe, sie müssen Risiken eingehen, ohne dass sie den Schritt zu viel tun. Beim Training für die Tourist Trophy von 1914 donnert Algernon Lee Guinness' Sunbeam zwischen massiven Steinmauern und nicht minder massiven Bäumen entlang (oben), während der Konkurrent im französischen Rennen (unten) die Streckenbegrenzung nicht richtig einschätzte.

Sur le fil

La course automobile implique de piloter en permanence sur le fil du rasoir en frôlant souvent la catastrophe, comme la Sunbeam d'Algernon Lee Guinness lors du Tourist Trophy de 1914 (ci-dessus), qui fonce entre murs et arbres. Les conséquences d'une erreur sont bien démontrées par l'accident de ce concurrent d'une épreuve française (en bas), qui a mal jugé de sa marge de manœuvre.

European winners at an American institution

The Indianapolis Motor Speedway (above), with its gently banked turns and the famous brick paving of its early years, found everlasting fame when it introduced its annual 500-mile Memorial Day Sweepstakes. The great race quickly attracted European interest, and in 1913 Jules Goux, in his Peugeot (opposite, above and below), became the first European victor.

Europäische Sieger, amerikanische Institution

Der Indianapolis Motor Speedway (oben) mit den leicht angeschrägten Kurven und dem berühmten Backstein-Straßenbelag der frühen Jahre wurde durch seine 500-Meilen-Rennen am Memorial Day weltberühmt. Bald lockte das Rennen auch Europäer an. Der erste europäische Sieger war im Jahre 1913 Jules Goux mit seinem Peugeot (gegenüber, oben und unten).

Victoire européenne dans une institution américaine

L'Indianapolis Motor Speedway (ci-dessus), avec ses virages légèrement relevés et le célèbre pavement de briques de ses débuts, acquiert une célébrité durable en créant le célèbre 500-Mile Memorial Day Sweepstakes annuel. Cette grande course attire rapidement l'attention des pilotes européens et c'est Jules Goux sur une Peugeot qui, en 1913, devient le premier vainqueur européen de l'épreuve (ci-contre, en haut et en bas).

The all-round racing driver
Georges Boillot was already a very successful driver in Europe before he made various forays to America, with mixed results. In 1910 he had won the Targa Florio, then in 1912 (above) he won the two-day French Grand Prix on the Dieppe circuit, again for Peugeot. Sadly, Boillot's talent would be cut short: he enlisted as a pilot in the forthcoming war and was shot down and killed in 1916.

Siegreich auf allen Pisten
Georges Boillot war bereits ein erfolgreicher Fahrer in Europa, als er die ersten Rennen in Amerika, mit unterschiedlichen Ergebnissen, bestritt. 1910 hatte er die Targa Florio gewonnen, 1912 den zweitägigen Großen Preis von Frankreich in Dieppe, wiederum für Peugeot. Leider sollte Boillot die Früchte seines Ruhms nicht lange genießen können: Im Weltkrieg meldete er sich als Pilot und wurde 1916 abgeschossen.

Le pilote polyvalent
Georges Boillot était déjà un pilote très connu en Europe avant qu'il ne vienne se faire aussi un nom aux États-Unis, où il obtient des résultats mitigés. En 1910, il avait déjà gagné la Targa Florio et, en 1912, le Grand Prix de France, disputé sur deux jours sur le circuit de Dieppe (ci-dessus), pour Peugeot. Sa brillante carrière fut hélas écourtée par la guerre : engagé dans l'aviation, il fut abattu au cours d'une mission en 1916.

The circus comes to town

In the days of the great road races the cars' passages through towns were usually subject to strict speed limits, but, with the coming of road 'circuits' and better spectator control, the towns became unrestricted parts of the race track. These are two views of one corner, through Moreuil, during the 1913 French Grand Prix – with Champoiseau's Th Schneider (above) and winner Boillot's Peugeot (below) coping with the slippery surface.

Der Zirkus kommt

Zur Zeit der großen Straßenrennen gab es für Stadtdurchfahrten in der Regel strikte Geschwindigkeitsbeschränkungen, doch mit den Rundkursen und besser abgeschirmten Zuschauern wurden auch die Ortschaften zum vollwertigen Teil der Strecke. Hier sehen wir dieselbe Kurve in Moreuil, aufgenommen beim Großen Preis von Frankreich 1913, aus zwei Perspektiven – mit Champoiseaus Th Schneider (oben) und dem Peugeot des Siegers Boillot (unten); beide haben mit dem rutschigen Straßenbelag zu kämpfen.

Le cirque vient en ville

À l'époque des grandes courses sur route, les voitures devaient généralement limiter leur vitesse dans la traversée des villes et des villages jusqu'à ce que cette mesure ne soit plus utile avec la création de « circuits » routiers et un meilleur contrôle de la foule des spectateurs.
Voici deux vues du même virage de Moreuil lors du Grand Prix de France 1913 : la Th Schneider de Champoiseau (en haut) et la Peugeot victorieuse de Boillot (en bas), en plein dérapage.

California dreaming

The 8.4-mile Santa Monica circuit in California provided a
fine new home for the Vanderbilt Cup and Grand Prize races
in 1914, without the crowd control problems of the old
New York courses. Ed Pullen's Mercer (above) won the
1914 Grand Prize for the first American car and driver victory in
an era when pollution control (opposite) was not such a
sensitive issue in America.

California dreaming

Der 13,5 Kilometer lange Rundkurs im kalifornischen Santa
Monica bot den Rennen um den Vanderbilt Cup und den
Großen Preis von Amerika 1914 ein schönes neues Zuhause,
ohne die New Yorker Schwierigkeiten, die Zuschauer im Zaum
zu halten. Ed Pullen errang auf seinem Mercer (oben) 1914 den
ersten rein amerikanischen Grand-Prix-Sieg – in einer Zeit, als
dort Umweltverschmutzung noch kein Thema war (links).

Rêve californien

En 1914, le circuit de 13,5 km de Santa Monica offre un beau
décor à la Coupe Vanderbilt et aux épreuves du Grand Prix,
sans pâtir du problème de contrôle de la foule qu'ont connu les
épreuves à New York. En remportant l'édition 1914 du Grand
Prix, Ed Pullen et sa Mercer (ci-dessus) signent la 1re victoire
d'une voiture et d'un pilote américains, à une époque où la
pollution ne pose pas encore problème (ci-contre).

3
Entering a Golden Era

After the interruption of some five years of war, motor racing entered a golden era in the 1920s. The machinery made great advances thanks to the lessons learned in the world's first highly mechanised war and the public were increasingly hungry for entertainment and excitement to help them forget the horrors of the past few years.

Motor sport was pushing its limits. Throughout the 1920s a fierce battle raged on both sides of the Atlantic for the world's land speed record, with America trying desperately to challenge Europe's superiority in this increasingly specialised branch of the sport. By the end of the 1920s, land speed record cars would be a breed of their own, but at the beginning of the decade the fastest cars in the world were essentially highly developed racing cars; the fastest came from America, although before the 1920s records set in the USA had not been recognised by the sporting authorities in Europe. The last official world record before 1920 was that 124.1mph run by Hornsted's Benz at Brooklands in 1914, after which Europe's interest in such matters had been diverted by the war. In America, meanwhile, Ralph de Palma had reached 149.9mph with his Packard in 1919 and Tommy Milton had been the first man to exceed 150mph, with an unofficial mark of 156.0mph in his Duesenberg in 1920. He gave the new decade the flying start it needed.

Ignoring those outstanding achievements, the official record books credit Kenelm Lee Guinness in his 350hp Sunbeam with being the first man to beat Hornsted's pre-war mark, in May 1922 at Brooklands with a speed of 'only' 129.2mph. It was the last time the record was set on a closed circuit, and now the land speed record scene moved to the sands, and into a period through the 1920s and the 1930s where the ultimate mark changed hands sometimes several times a year. The gentlemanly rivalry between the British racing driver record breakers Malcolm Campbell and Henry Segrave saw the record pass new landmarks. In July 1925 on Pendine Sands in South Wales, Campbell, with the 350hp Sunbeam, became the first man to hold the official record at more than 150mph, with a speed of 150.9mph. In February 1927, again at Pendine, he almost posted 175mph, but was about one tenth of a mile-per-hour short, and he was beaten to 200mph by arch-rival Segrave, who took his enormous chain-driven 1,000hp Sunbeam streamliner to a speed of 203.8mph at Daytona Beach, Florida, in March 1927.

Oddly, chain drive was still common in record-breaking circles in the mid-1920s, although it was now considered archaic in racing cars, but it was a chain drive that brought one of record breaking's great tragedies in March 1927 when Parry Thomas was killed by the broken, flailing chain of his car, Babs, while chasing Campbell's 175mph mark at Pendine. Thomas was not the only victim of the period. In America, Ray Keech with the monstrous White-Triplex Special with its three Liberty V12 aero engines and spectacularly crude chassis had officially held the record with 207.5mph at Daytona Beach in April 1928. Also in 1928, Frank Lockhart in his tiny Stutz Black Hawk had proved that two compact racing engines and around 400hp in a light and highly streamlined car could threaten the 200mph mark, but both Lee Bible, the man who later took over the Triplex Special from Keech, and Lockhart died in pursuit of their goals. By March 1929, Segrave had raised the record to 231.4mph with the 1,400hp Napier-engined Sunbeam Golden Arrow at Daytona, and that mark survived into the 1930s.

On the racing front, there were other great rivalries in several different branches of the sport. In 1923 a new race was inaugurated in France, one which would become one of the world's most famous. It brought international motor racing back to Le Mans, scene of one of the earliest closed courses in France around the turn of the century, and the course for the Grand Prix de France from 1911 to 1913. The new course was again based on public roads, and the race was dubbed the Grand Prix d'Endurance des 24 Heures du Mans – the Le Mans 24-Hour race. It was intended to demonstrate the speed and reliability of the fast touring cars of the day, and not least their lighting equipment during the night-time hours. It was also intended to be more of a trial than a race, but that was not how its future turned out, and André Lagache and René Leonard in a Chenard & Walcker went down in history as the first winners, having covered the greatest distance.

Soon, the Le Mans event was unequivocally a race, and through the 1920s it saw some famous battles, and the emergence of the British Bentleys, with wins in 1924, 1927, 1928 and 1929 (as well as in 1930), as the dominant marque in what was widely hailed as the greatest race in the world. Ettore Bugatti, whose light and elegantly designed racing cars dominated Grand Prix and shorter distance sports car racing during the 1920s, was not as impressed by the massively engineered

Bentleys as some. Disparagingly, he called them *'les plus vites* (sic) *camions du monde'* – 'the fastest lorries in the world', but the races between the green Bentleys and the blue Bugattis became a symbol of the decade. Brooklands was back in action by the 1920s, too, with lap speeds rising inexorably and the great track's reputation as a social as well as a racing venue growing with them. By the end of the decade the outer-circuit lap record had been taken to 134.2mph by Kaye Don's 4-litre V12 Sunbeam, and the circuit's eclectic mixture was as popular as ever. It was getting towards the end, though, for the massive racers of the older school, and even at Brooklands it became abundantly clear that brute force was no longer the only way to go.

Grand Prix racing not only revived in the 1920s but it spread its wings beyond France, to include before the end of the decade Grand Prix races in Italy, Belgium, Spain, Germany, Great Britain and Monaco – all the major motor racing nations plus the tiny principality that would immediately become motor sport's most glamorous venue. Grand Prix formulae increasingly emphasised science over brute force, with smaller but more efficient engines in lighter, more technically sophisticated chassis. The decade saw much new technology, including hydraulic brakes, roller-bearing crankshafts, multi-valve cylinder heads and, perhaps most far-reaching of all, Europe's first supercharged racing cars, from Mercedes, building on the lessons learned with aero-engines during the recent war to produce prodigious amounts of power from relatively light engines and exotic alcohol fuels. With more power and more speed, aerodynamics began to be ever more important, too, and again the racing car built on the lessons learned by the aero industry – while experimenting with new and often bizarre shapes all of its own.

When the decade started, the American Duesenberg, bene-fiting from continuous development while European manu-facturers had been held back by the war, was a force in European Grand Prix racing, but as the decade progressed Europe regained its dominance, with marques like Fiat, Sun-beam, Alfa Romeo, Maserati, Delage, and most of all Bugatti, especially with the ultra successful Type 35 Grand Prix cars.

Another major change in the shape of the cars came during the 1920s, and it has continued to define the Grand Prix car to this day. In the early days of the sport, in many racing disciplines it was obligatory (and in other areas permissible) to carry a 'riding mechanic', who, with the driver, was the

only person permitted to work on the car during the race. In accidents, the riding mechanic was every bit as vulnerable as the driver, and many mechanics were killed in the sport's pioneering days, but in 1924 the riding mechanic was finally banned, for the first time in the sport's history. Originally, the car's bodywork still had to allow space for a second seat (and only one mechanic at the roadside was allowed to work on the car), but by 1927 the notional mechanic's seat was no longer obligatory, and the single-seater Grand Prix car was born.

Oddly though, towards the end of the decade, Grand Prix racing in particular lost its momentum, and for the last two years of the 1920s the official formulae were largely dispensed with and cars ran to a virtually free formula. That did not appeal to the major manufacturers as much as the technical challenges, and commercial benefits, of development under the stricter formulae had; for a while they stayed away from the sport, taking more interest in sports car racing while the Grand Prix scene was confined mainly to wealthy amateurs driving privately owned cars. But the low-key approach at the sport's highest levels would only be temporary.

At the 1928 Tourist Trophy on the Dundonald circuit, near Belfast, Viscount Curzon's Bugatti was put out by a leaking fuel tank. Malcolm Campbell (in cap), whose own Bugatti had burnt out after a fuel fire in the pits, went to sympathise.

Bei der Tourist Trophy von 1928 auf dem Dundonald-Kurs bei Belfast schied der Bugatti von Viscount Curzon mit leckem Benzintank aus. Malcolm Campbell (mit Schlägermütze), dessen eigener Bugatti in den Boxen aus-gebrannt war, tröstet ihn.

Le vicomte Curzon dut abandonner à cause d'une fuite du réservoir d'essence de sa Bugatti lors de l'édition 1928 du Tourist Trophy, disputé sur le circuit de Dundonald, près de Belfast. Malcolm Campbell (avec la casquette), dont la Bugatti a été détruite par un feu de carburant aux stands, vient le réconforter.

Nach der fast fünfjährigen Unterbrechung durch den Krieg begannen für den Motorsport die Goldenen Zwanziger. Viele Erfahrungen des weltweit ersten hoch technisierten Krieges kamen nun der Automobiltechnik zugute. Die Öffentlichkeit hungerte nach Spannung und Unterhaltung, um die Schrecken der vergangenen Jahre zu vergessen.

Der Motorsport stieß über seine alten Grenzen hinaus. Das ganze Jahrzehnt hindurch tobte beiderseits des Atlantiks ein erbitterter Wettbewerb um den Geschwindigkeitsweltrekord, und die Amerikaner taten alles, um sich in dieser Sparte, die immer mehr ihre eigenen Wege ging, eine Überlegenheit gegenüber Europa zu sichern. Ende der zwanziger Jahre waren Rekordwagen eine Welt für sich, doch zu Anfang des Jahrzehnts traten zu den Rekordfahrten noch besonders hoch entwickelte Rennwagen an; die schnellsten kamen aus Amerika, auch wenn die europäischen Motorsportverbände damals die amerikanischen Rekorde noch nicht anerkannten. Den letzten offiziellen Rekord vor dem Jahr 1920 hatte Hornsted auf seinem Benz schon 1914 in Brooklands gefahren, und danach hatte der Krieg verhindert, dass jemand seine 199,7 km/h überbot. In Amerika hatte jedoch Ralph de Palma mit seinem Packard im Jahr 1919 bereits 241,2 Stundenkilometer erreicht. Bei einer inoffiziellen Fahrt mit einem Duesenberg überschritt Tommy Milton 1920 mit 156 mph (251 km/h) erstmals die 150-Meilen-Grenze. Das war der fliegende Start, den die neue Dekade brauchte.

Doch die offiziellen Rekordlisten nahmen diese bemerkenswerten Leistungen nicht wahr, für sie war Kenelm Lee Guinness der Erste, der Hornsteds Vorkriegswert überbot, obwohl er im Mai 1922 in Brooklands mit seinem 350-PS-Sunbeam »nur« 207,9 Stundenkilometer erreichte. Es war das letzte Mal, dass der Rekord auf einem Rundkurs aufgestellt wurde, von nun an fanden die Rekordfahrten auf Stränden statt. In den zwanziger und dreißiger Jahren wurde die neueste Höchstmarke oft mehrmals im Jahr überboten. Zwischen den beiden britischen Rekordfahrern Malcolm Campbell und Henry Segrave entwickelte sich eine gepflegte Rivalität, mit der sie das Tempo vorantrieben. Im Juli 1925 überschritt Campbell auf dem Sand von Pendine in Südwales mit dem 350-PS-Sunbeam erstmals offiziell die 150-Meilen-Marke; er erreichte 150,9 mph (242,8 km/h). Im Februar 1927, ebenfalls in Pendine, fehlte ihm nur eine Zehntelmeile zum 175-Meilen-Rekord, und beim Kampf um die 200-Meilen-Grenze schlug ihn Erzrivale Segrave, der mit dem gewaltigen kettengetriebenen, stromlinienverkleideten 1000-PS-Sunbeam im März 1927 in Daytona Beach, Florida, 203,8 mph (327,9 km/h) erreichte.

Seltsamerweise wurden auch Mitte der zwanziger Jahre Rekordwagen noch mit Kettenantrieb gebaut, der bei Rennwagen längst als veraltet galt, und dieser Antrieb führte im März 1927 zu einer der großen Rennsporttragödien, als Parry Thomas, der mit seinem Babs in Pendine angetreten war, um Campbells 175-Meilen-Rekord zu brechen, von einer gerissenen Kette erschlagen wurde. Thomas war nicht das einzige Opfer dieser Zeit. Den amerikanischen Rekord von 333,9 km/h hatte Ray Keech im April 1928 in Daytona Beach mit dem monströsen White-Triplex Special aufgestellt, dessen drei Liberty V12-Flugzeugmotoren in einem geradezu spektakulär primitiven Chassis saßen. Ebenfalls 1928 hatte Frank Lockhart mit einem winzigen Stutz Black Hawk bewiesen, dass zwei kompakte 400-PS-Rennmotoren in einem leichten und sorgfältig stromlinienverkleideten Wagen ausreichten, um an die 200-Meilen-Marke heranzukommen, doch Lockhart ließ genauso wie Lee Bible (der als Fahrer des Triplex Special Keechs Nachfolge angetreten hatte) bei der Rekordjagd sein Leben. Im März 1929 erreichte Segrave in Daytona mit dem von einem 1400 PS starken Napier-Flugzeugmotor angetriebenen Sunbeam Golden Arrow 372,3 Stundenkilometer. Dieser Rekord blieb bis in die Dreißiger bestehen.

Auch beim eigentlichen Rennsport gab es große Rivalitäten in einer Reihe von Disziplinen. 1923 wurde in Frankreich ein neues Rennen veranstaltet, das sich zu einem der berühmtesten überhaupt entwickeln sollte. Es holte den internationalen Rennbetrieb zurück nach Le Mans, wo zur Jahrhundertwende eines der ersten französischen Rundstreckenrennen und von 1911 bis 1913 die Großen Preise von Frankreich stattgefunden hatten. Auch das neue Rennen wurde auf öffentlichen Straßen gefahren. Mit vollem Namen hieß es Grand Prix d'Endurance des 24 Heures du Mans – das erste 24-Stunden-Rennen von Le Mans. Es sollte zeigen, wie schnell und verlässlich die Tourenwagen jener Zeit waren, und auch die Qualität ihrer Beleuchtung demonstrieren. Ursprünglich war es eher als Testfahrt und nicht als Rennen gedacht, doch das änderte sich bald; als erste Sieger gingen André Lagache und René Leonard, die auf ihrem Chenard & Walcker die größte Distanz zurückgelegt hatten, in die Geschichte ein.

Es dauerte nicht lange, bis Le Mans unverkennbar den Charakter eines Rennens hatte, und die zwanziger Jahre sahen einige berühmte Schlachten; das Rennen galt bald als das größte der Welt, und als Champions erwiesen sich die britischen Bentleys, die 1924, 1927, 1928 und 1929 (und auch 1930) siegreich waren. Ettore Bugatti, dessen leichte und raffiniert konstruierte Wagen in den zwanziger Jahren die Grand Prix und die Rennen über kürzere Distanzen beherrschten, ließ sich von den wuchtigen Bentleys nicht beeindrucken – »les plus vites (sic) camions du monde« nannte er sie, »die schnellsten Lastwagen der Welt« –, doch der Wettstreit zwischen den grünen Bentleys und den blauen Bugattis wurde zum Inbegriff des Jahrzehnts. Inzwischen war auch Brooklands wiederhergestellt, und mit immer schnelleren Rundenzeiten war es nicht nur beim Publikum, sondern auch bei den Fahrern beliebter denn je. Am Ende der Dekade lag der Rundenrekord bei 215,9 Stundenkilometern, aufgestellt von Kaye Don mit einem 4-Liter-Sunbeam-V12, und die Vielfalt der Strecke faszinierte wie eh und je. Doch für die schweren Rennwagen der alten Schule waren die Tage gezählt, und selbst in Brooklands war allen klar, dass Kraft allein nicht mehr genügte.

Die Grand-Prix-Rennen lebten in den zwanziger Jahren nicht nur in Frankreich wieder auf, sondern breiteten sich auch in Nachbarländer aus. Am Ende des Jahrzehnts gab es bereits Große Preise von Italien, Belgien, Spanien, Deutschland, Großbritannien und Monaco – alle großen Motorsportnationen und dazu das winzige Fürstentum, das auf Anhieb zum spektakulärsten Austragungsort wurde. Die Grand-Prix-Formeln legten immer mehr Gewicht auf die Konstruktion statt auf die Motorleistung und bevorzugten kleinere, doch leistungsstärkere Maschinen in technisch aufwändigeren Chassis. Das Jahrzehnt sah eine Reihe von Neuerungen, darunter hydraulische Bremsen, kugelgelagerte Kurbelwellen, Mehrventiler und – vielleicht die einflussreichste Entwicklung – bei Mercedes die ersten europäischen Wagen mit Kompressormotor, ein Konzept, das im Weltkrieg für Flugmotoren entstanden war, die bei geringem Gewicht und mit exotischen Alkoholtreibstoffen hohe Leistung brachten. Je stärker Motorleistung und Geschwindigkeit stiegen, desto größer war der Stellenwert der Aerodynamik, und auch hier profitierten die Konstrukteure von Lösungen aus dem Flugzeugbau, auch wenn sie die oft bizarren Formen, mit denen sie experimentierten, selbst ersannen.

Zu Anfang des Jahrzehnts war der amerikanische Duesenberg, der im Krieg kontinuierlich weiterentwickelt wurde,

während die europäischen Wagen in den Garagen standen, ein ernsthafter Konkurrent auf den Grand-Prix-Strecken Europas, doch im Lauf der Dekade errangen die einheimischen Marken wieder die Oberhand – Marken wie Fiat, Sunbeam, Alfa Romeo, Maserati, Delage und vor allem Bugatti mit seinem höchst erfolgreichen Typ 35.

Eine weitere wichtige Veränderung, die bis heute das Erscheinungsbild von Grand-Prix-Wagen prägt, gab es in den zwanziger Jahren. In den Anfangstagen des Sports war für viele Rennklassen obligatorisch (bei anderen erlaubt), dass ein Mechaniker mitfuhr, der neben dem Fahrer der Einzige war, der während des Rennens Reparaturen vornehmen durfte. Dieser Beifahrer riskierte genau wie der Fahrer sein Leben, und in der Pionierzeit kamen viele Mechaniker um; 1924 wurde deshalb schließlich die Mitnahme eines Beifahrers untersagt. Zunächst war für die Wagen trotzdem noch ein zweiter Sitz vorgeschrieben (und nur ein einzelner Mechaniker am Straßenrand durfte Wartungsarbeiten vornehmen), doch 1927 wurde der nominelle Mechanikersitz abgeschafft, und der einsitzige Grand-Prix-Rennwagen war geboren.

Doch gerade in der Grand-Prix-Sparte kam es gegen Ende der Dekade zu einer unerklärlichen Flaute. In den letzten beiden Jahren der 1920er fuhren die Wagen weitgehend ohne Formelvorschriften. Den großen Herstellern behagte das weniger als die technischen Herausforderungen und der kommerzielle Nutzen der strengeren Formeln. Sie konzentrierten sich auf Sportwagen und überließen die Grand-Prix-Rennen den wohlhabenden Amateuren, die mit Privatwagen antraten. Doch dieser Rückzug aus den höheren Sphären des Motorsports sollte nur vorübergehend sein.

One of Germany's greatest ever drivers, Rudolf Caracciola, with his wife Charly in the Mercedes pits during the Irish Grand Prix meeting in Dublin in July 1930, where he won the Grand Prix title by winning the Eireann Cup, one of the two qualifying events. He raced, in spite of many bad accidents, until 1954, and died in 1959, aged only fifty-eight.

Einer der größten deutschen Fahrer aller Zeiten, Rudolf Caracciola, im Juli 1930 beim Großen Preis von Irland in Dublin mit seiner Frau Charly an den Mercedes-Boxen. Caracciola siegte im Eireann Cup, einem der beiden Läufe, und errang damit den Grand-Prix-Titel. Trotz vieler schwerer Unfälle fuhr er bis 1954 Rennen und starb 1959, nur 58 Jahre alt.

L'un des plus grands pilotes d'Allemagne, Rudolf Caracciola, ici avec son épouse Charly dans le stand Mercedes lors du Grand Prix d'Irlande à Dublin en juillet, remporte le titre après avoir gagné la Eireann Cup, l'une des deux épreuves qualificatives de la réunion. Malgré plusieurs accidents graves, il pilota jusqu'en 1954 et mourut en 1959 à l'âge de cinquante-huit ans seulement.

La course automobile entre dans son âge d'or en 1920, après cinq années d'interruption dues à la guerre. En effet, non seulement les machines ont fait de grands progrès grâce aux leçons apprises pendant la précédente guerre mondiale – le premier conflit mécanisé – mais le public se montre également de plus en plus avide de spectacle, sans doute pour mieux oublier les horreurs du passé récent.

Le sport automobile s'emploie toujours à repousser les limites des hommes et des mécaniques. Ces années 1920 sont marquées par l'ardente bataille qu'on se livre des deux côtés de l'Atlantique pour s'arroger le record du monde de vitesse sur terre, les États-Unis contestant avec acharnement la supériorité de l'Europe dans ce domaine particulier et spécialisé du sport automobile. Mais, alors que les engins des courses au record ne forment une classe à part qu'au début de la décennie suivante, les automobiles les plus rapides sont encore essentiellement de « simples » voitures de course adaptées spécifiquement pour la vitesse, conçues d'ailleurs pour la plupart aux États-Unis. Comme les performances qui y sont enregistrées ne sont pas reconnues en Europe avant 1920, le dernier record du monde officiel, qui date de 1914, a été établi par Hornsted, dont la Benz a atteint 199,7 km/h sur le circuit de Brooklands. En 1919, aux États-Unis, Ralph de Palma parvient à 241,2 km/h avec sa Packard, mais est dépassé un an plus tard par Tommy Hilton, chronométré (mais pour un résultat officieux) à 251 km/h dans sa Duesenberg. Il donne ainsi l'élan nécessaire à la nouvelle décennie.

Ignorant ces extraordinaires résultats d'outre-Atlantique, le livre officiel des records attribue à Kenelm Lee Guinness l'honneur d'être le premier homme à battre le record établi avant-guerre par Hornsted, lorsqu'il atteint la vitesse de 207,9 km/h « seulement » avec sa Sunbeam de 350 ch, en mai 1922 à Brooklands. C'est en fait la dernière fois qu'un record de vitesse est établi sur circuit, puisque les tentatives auront désormais pour cadre des plages de sable. Les décennies 1920–1930 vont voir ce record changer plusieurs fois de mains, souvent la même année. Leur rivalité amicale aiguillonne les pilotes recordmen de vitesse britanniques Malcolm Campbell et Henry Segrave, qui vont franchir de nouvelles limites au record. En juillet 1925, à Pendine Sands (Galles du Sud), Campbell devient, avec sa Sunbeam 350 ch, le premier homme à dépasser officiellement les 150 mph (241,4 km/h) à la vitesse de 242,8 km/h. En février 1927, toujours à Pendine, il atteint 281,6 km/h mais se fait battre en mars par son rival Segrave, qui pousse à 327,9 km/h son énorme Sunbeam profilée à moteur de 1000 ch sur la plage de Daytona Beach en Floride.

Curieusement, la plupart des pilotes de vitesse du milieu des années 1920 conservent la transmission par chaîne bien qu'elle soit désormais considérée comme dépassée pour les voitures de course. Une rupture de chaîne de sa Babs provoquera d'ailleurs la mort de Parry Thomas en mars 1927, lors de sa tentative de battre le record de Campbell à Pendine. Il ne sera pas la seule victime ni de cette période ni de cette course aux records aux États-Unis. En avril 1928, Ray Keech et sa monstrueuse White-Triplex Special, équipée de 3 aéromoteurs Liberty V12 montés sur un châssis extrêmement dépouillé, s'arroge officiellement le record à 333,9 km/h à Daytona Beach ; la même année Frank Lockhart, avec une minuscule Stutz Black Hawk, prouve qu'une voiture légère à carrosserie aérodynamique, propulsée par 2 moteurs de course compacts de 400 ch environ, peut atteindre 321,8 km/h. Lockhart et Lee Bible, qui a repris la White-Triplex Special de Keech, mourront tous deux dans leur quête insatiable. En mars 1929, à Daytona toujours, Segrave améliore le record à 372,3 km/h sur sa Sunbeam Golden Arrow à moteur Napier de 1400 ch, une performance qui restera inégalée jusque dans les années 1930.

Le monde de la course proprement dit, quelles que soient les branches du sport automobile, est animé par les rivalités entre pilotes, marques et circuits. Une nouvelle épreuve, qui va bientôt devenir l'une des plus célèbres au monde, naît en France en 1923 et ramène la compétition automobile internationale au Mans, sur un tracé en grande partie routier semblable à celui où avait déjà été organisée, vers le tournant du siècle, une des plus anciennes courses sur circuit et où s'étaient déroulés les Grand Prix de France de 1911 à 1913. Appelée le Grand Prix d'Endurance des 24 Heures du Mans, cette épreuve – qui se veut d'ailleurs plus un concours qu'une course (mais l'avenir en décidera autrement) – vise à démontrer la fiabilité (accessoirement la vitesse) des voitures de tourisme de l'époque et, notamment, leur dispositif d'éclairage nocturne. Après André Lagache et René Léonard, qui vont entrer dans l'histoire de la course automobile au volant d'une Chenard et Walcker comme les premiers vainqueurs des 24 Heures du Mans, le circuit français devient sans équivoque possible une véritable course, où s'illustrent les Bentley britanniques, victorieuses en 1924, 1927, 1928, 1929 et 1930. Si ces automobiles équipées d'énormes moteurs dominent ce que tous saluent comme la plus grande course du monde, elles n'impressionnent guère Ettore Bugatti, dont les voitures de course élégantes et légères se distinguent en Grand Prix et sur des distances plus courtes, puisqu'il les appelle de manière assez désobligeante « les plus vites (sic) camions du monde ». La lutte que se livrent alors les vertes Bentley et les Bugatti bleues symbolise bien l'esprit des courses de cette décennie. C'est à cette époque que Brooklands retrouve son rôle de piste de vitesse – le record du tour est établi à 215,9 km/h par la Sunbeam à moteur V12 de 4 litres de Kaye Don peu avant les années 1930 –, de circuit éclectique ouvert à tous les types de voitures et de lieu social. Mais les grosses voitures de course ont fait leur temps et il est clair que, même à Brooklands, la puissance brute n'a plus d'avenir.

Les courses de Grand Prix non seulement renaissent en France dans les années 1920 mais s'organisent aussi, avant la fin de la décennie, dans toutes les grandes nations du sport automobile – Italie, Belgique, Espagne, Allemagne, Grande-Bretagne – sans oublier la minuscule principauté de Monaco, qui va immédiatement devenir le cadre le plus élégant des manifestations du sport automobile. La formule Grand Prix conduit les ingénieurs à mettre l'accent sur la technologie plutôt que sur la puissance brute d'une machine de grosse capacité, et donc à concevoir des moteurs plus petits mais plus efficaces à l'intérieur de châssis plus légers et plus sophistiqués. Les ingénieurs de cette décennie apportent nombre de perfectionnements techniques aux voitures, notamment les freins hydrauliques, les vilebrequins à roulement à bille, les têtes de cylindre multisoupapes et, ce qui aura une portée bien plus considérable, la suralimentation. Les premières voitures de course à moteur suralimenté furent construites en Europe par Mercedes, qui tire parti des leçons apprises avec les aéromoteurs de la précédente guerre mondiale pour fournir une puissance prodigieuse à des moteurs relativement légers et fonctionnant avec un carburant exotique composé de plus d'alcool que d'essence. Puissance et vitesse ayant augmenté, on accorde une importance accrue à la forme aérodynamique des voitures, là encore en s'inspirant de l'expérience acquise par l'industrie aéronautique sinon en essayant empiriquement de nouvelles et souvent étranges carrosseries.

Ayant bénéficié d'améliorations constantes aux États-Unis pendant la dernière guerre alors que les constructeurs automobiles européens devaient travailler pour l'armement, la Duesenberg américaine domine les Grand Prix d'Europe

The epitome of British motor racing in the 1920s – the paddock, crowded with race-goers, before the first race of the bank holiday meeting at Brooklands in August 1922.

Typisch britischer Rennbetrieb der zwanziger Jahre – Zuschauer in der Arena von Brooklands vor dem ersten Lauf zum Bank-Holiday-Rennen vom August 1922.

Le sport automobile britannique des années 1920 est illustré par cette photo du paddock de Brooklands où se pressent la foule des amateurs avant la première course de la réunion de Bank Holiday, en août 1922.

au début des années 1920 mais se fait ensuite rattraper progressivement par des marques comme Fiat, Sunbeam, Alfa Romeo, Mascrati, Delage et, surtout, Bugatti, dont la Type 35 Grand Prix remporte d'innombrables succès.

Mais les Années folles sont surtout marquées par une transformation majeure des voitures de Grand Prix. Dans les débuts du sport automobile, le châssis des voitures de course devait offrir l'emplacement pour un second siège car la plupart des épreuves rendaient obligatoire (parfois facultatif) d'embarquer un « mécanicien navigant », seule personne autorisée, avec le pilote, à travailler sur la voiture pendant la course. Ce mécanicien est aussi vulnérable que le pilote et beaucoup trouveront la mort dans des accidents en course. Ce n'est qu'en 1924 que sa présence physique est interdite à bord de la voiture et en 1927 que le siège qu'il occupait n'est plus obligatoire. La monoplace de Grand Prix est née.

Et pourtant, malgré cette évolution du sport automobile de la fin des années 1920, les courses – et plus particulièrement les épreuves de Grand Prix – manquent de dynamisme. Peu avant 1930, on commence à courir sans plus tenir compte des formules officielles ou, à la limite, en suivant un règlement assez libre. Du coup, les épreuves attirent moins les grands constructeurs, qui n'ont plus alors ni de défis techniques à affronter ni de bénéfices commerciaux à retirer du développement des automobiles. Abandonnant les Grand Prix à de riches amateurs pilotant des voitures privées, ils se tournent alors pendant quelque temps vers les courses de voitures de sport. Mais leur éloignement des niveaux les plus élevés de la compétition ne sera heureusement que temporaire.

The last throes of the opening era

The 1914 Tourist Trophy had taken place only weeks before the outbreak of war brought the first great age of motor sport to a close. R.S. Witchell's 3.3-litre Straker Squire, having been held up by a broken petrol pipe, failed by only thirty seconds to take third place, after 600 miles of racing. The race was won by Kenelm Lee Guinness's Sunbeam, and the 1920s began where the 1910s left off.

Die Pionierzeit ist vorbei

Mit der Tourist Trophy von 1914, nur wenige Wochen vor Kriegsausbruch, war die erste Epoche des Motorsports zu Ende gegangen. R. S. Witchells 3,3-Liter-Straker Squire, den ein Schaden an der Benzinleitung aufgehalten hatte, verpasste mit nur dreißig Sekunden Abstand den dritten Platz – bei einem Rennen von fast tausend Kilometern. Sieger war Sunbeam-Fahrer Kenelm Lee Guinness, der nach dem Krieg an diesen Erfolg anknüpfen sollte.

Les derniers soubresauts de la genèse automobile

L'édition 1914 du Tourist Trophy se déroule quelques semaines seulement avant que le déclenchement de la Première Guerre mondiale ne mette un coup de frein brutal au sport automobile. La Straker Squire 3,3 litres de R. S. Witchell, ralentie par une rupture du tuyau d'arrivée d'essence, manque la troisième place à trente secondes seulement après 965 km de course, dans une épreuve remportée par la Sunbeam de Kenelm Lee Guinness. Les années 1920 commencent où s'arrêtent les années 1910.

The fastest men in the world

In the 1920s, the race for the land speed record became an obsession to several famous drivers, but perhaps most of all to Captain Malcolm Campbell, whose series of Bluebird cars held the record many times. Campbell's early cars were aero-engined Sunbeams, including the car he drove at Saltburn in 1922 (above) and the 350hp car he ran at Pendine, South Wales, in 1924 (below).

Die schnellsten Männer der Welt

In den zwanziger Jahren wurde die Jagd nach dem Geschwindigkeitsweltrekord für eine Reihe von berühmten Fahrern geradezu zur Obsession, am stärksten vielleicht für Captain Malcolm Campbell, der mit seiner Serie von Bluebird-Wagen den Rekord immer wieder neu errang. Zunächst trat er in Sunbeams mit Flugzeugmotoren an, wie hier 1922 (oben) in Saltburn und 1924 (unten) mit einem 350 PS starken Exemplar in Pendine, Südwales.

Les hommes les plus rapides du monde

Dans les années 1920, la course au record de vitesse sur terre devient l'obsession de plusieurs célèbres pilotes mais surtout du capitaine Malcolm Campbell, dont les différentes Bluebird ont détenu plusieurs fois le record. Les premières voitures de Campbell étaient des Sunbeam propulsées par un aéromoteur, comme celle qu'il pilotait à Saltburn en 1922 (en haut) et la 350 ch avec laquelle il courut à Pendine (Galles du Sud) en 1924 (en bas).

Preparing for the attack

Campbell, in helmet and goggles and wrapped up against the miserable weather, watches as his mechanics prepare the Sunbeam for a run at Pendine Sands in 1924. His runs with this car at Pendine in September eventually raised the record to 146.2mph, and in July 1925 he took the record beyond 150mph with a development of the same car, again at Pendine.

Bereit zum Angriff

Campbell, mit Helm und Schutzbrille, dick eingepackt gegen das kalte Wetter, verfolgt, wie seine Mechaniker den Sunbeam für eine Fahrt am Strand von Pendine vorbereiten, 1924. Im September desselben Jahres stellte er mit diesem Wagen einen neuen Rekord von 146,2 mph (235,2 km/h) auf, und mit einer verbesserten Version überschritt er im Juli 1925, wiederum in Pendine, die 150-Meilen-Marke.

Prêt à attaquer

Campbell, portant casque et lunettes et emmitouflé dans sa combinaison contre le mauvais temps, regarde ses mécaniciens préparer la Sunbeam avant une tentative à Pendine Sands en 1924. En septembre, elle lui permit d'établir le record à 235,2 km/h avant de le porter un an plus tard, en juillet 1925 et toujours à Pendine, au-delà de 241,4 km/h (150 miles) dans une version améliorée de cette même voiture.

Informing the enthusiast

With its system of handicapping and its stops for fuel, tyres and other repairs, motor racing was not always easy to follow for the ordinary spectator in the public enclosures. By August 1922, Brooklands could offer a public address system broadcasting race information; and if it looked primitive, it was better than nothing.

Immer gut informiert

Aufgrund der Handikap-Regeln und der Boxenstopps zum Tanken, für Reifenwechsel und Reparatur war der Stand eines Rennens für die begeisterten Zuschauer auf den Rängen nicht leicht zu verfolgen. Im August 1922 wurden deshalb in Brooklands erstmals Informationen per Lautsprecher gegeben; die Anlage macht einen sehr improvisierten Eindruck, aber sie war doch immerhin besser als nichts.

Informer les passionnés

Avec son système de handicap et les arrêts au stand pour le ravitaillement en essence, le changement de pneumatiques et autres réparations, une course automobile n'était pas toujours facile à suivre pour le spectateur ordinaire. En août 1922, Brooklands proposa un système sonore diffusant des informations sur la course qui, bien qu'assez rudimentaire, valait finalement mieux que rien.

A race to start the race

What became widely known as the Le Mans start, with drivers sprinting across the track to leap into their cars, was not confined only to Le Mans. Here drivers from five nations sprint towards their mounts for the start of the six-hour race at Brooklands in June 1929, on a circuit which combined the banked track with an artificial 'road' circuit.

Das Rennen zum Rennen

Der Le-Mans-Start, bei dem die Fahrer zu den Wagen sprinteten und sie dann anließen, wurde auch anderswo praktiziert. Hier sehen wir Fahrer aus fünf Nationen beim Spurt zum Cockpit, aufgenommen im Juni 1929 in Brooklands; es war der Auftakt zum Sechs-Stunden-Rennen auf einem Kurs, der die Steil-kurven-Rundstrecke mit einer künstlichen »Straßenstrecke« verband.

Une course au départ

Ce que l'on va appeler un « départ Le Mans », où les pilotes doivent traverser la piste en courant avant de bondir dans leur voiture, n'avait pas lieu qu'au Mans. Les pilotes de cinq nations se précipitent ici au départ de la course des 6 heures de Brook-lands en juin 1929, sur un circuit artificiellement « routier » disposant de virages relevés.

On the beach...

On a weekend in June 1922, when Campbell's Sunbeam broke the British speed record with a run of more than 133mph, missing the world record by less than one mile per hour, there were also races for many less extreme sporting cars. This group is led away from the line by the diminutive but very rapid Brescia Bugatti, driven by Raymond Mays.

Am Strand ...

An einem Renntag im Juni 1922, als Campbells Sunbeam mit 214 km/h zwar einen neuen britischen Rekord aufstellte, den internationalen jedoch knapp verfehlte, traten auch etliche nicht ganz so spektakuläre Sportwagen an. Bei dieser Gruppe ist auf Anhieb der winzige, doch äußerst schnelle Brescia-Bugatti in Führung gegangen; am Steuer sitzt Raymond Mays.

Sur la plage ...

Ce week-end de juin 1922 où la Sunbeam de Campbell s'attribue le record de vitesse britannique à 214 km/h, manquant de moins de 1,6 km/h le record du monde, d'autres courses étaient disputées par des voitures de sport bien moins extrêmes. Ce petit groupe est emmené dès le départ par la petite mais très rapide Bugatti Brescia de Raymond Mays.

...and on the promenade

Racing on long, straight, well-paved promenades had been a sporting tradition on both sides of the Channel since early speed record runs had been held in France. This is the start of one such race in the light car class during the trials at Westcliff-on-Sea, Essex, in July 1922, with the famous GN cyclecar Kim (number 106) prominent in the line-up.

... und auf der Promenade

Rennen auf den langen, geraden, gut ausgebauten Strandpromenaden waren beiderseits des Ärmelkanals eine Tradition, seit dort in der Frühzeit in Frankreich Wettfahrten stattgefunden hatten. Hier sehen wir den Start eines solchen Rennens in der Leichtbau-Kategorie, aufgenommen im Juli 1922 in Westcliff-on-Sea, Essex. Der berühmte »Kim«-Cyclecar von GN (Nummer 106) steht ganz vorn.

... et sur la promenade

Les courses de voitures sur les longues lignes droites de promenades bien pavées étaient devenues une tradition des deux côtés de la Manche depuis que le premier record de vitesse avait été établi en France. On assiste ici au départ d'une de ces courses de voitures légères lors des concours de Westcliff-on-Sea (Essex) en juillet 1922, avec le célèbre cyclecar GN Kim (numéro 106) en bonne position sur la grille.

Ready for the off

Cars waiting their turn at the Westcliff Trials of July 1922, with the promenade stretching into the distance and the early summer holiday crowds getting close to the action. This type of trial generally tested straight-line acceleration, manœuvrability and braking ability against the clock, and attracted a huge variety of machinery, ranging here from the tiny GN to the sportiest 30/98 Vauxhall.

Bereit zum Start

Wagen warten auf ihren Start bei den Wettfahrten von Westcliff, Juli 1922. Die Promenade erstreckt sich bis zum Horizont. Die frühsommerlichen Feriengäste mustern neugierig das Aufgebot. Die Wagen maßen sich in Beschleunigung, Wendigkeit und Bremsleistung. Die Wettbewerbe zogen ein breites Feld von Teilnehmern an, hier vom winzigen GN bis zum sportlichen Vauxhall 30/98.

Prêts à s'élancer

La foule des estivants circule au milieu des voitures des concurrents qui attendent leur tour pour participer au Concours de Westcliff de juillet 1922, dont on aperçoit la promenade au loin. Ce genre de concours, qui offrait des épreuves contre la montre d'accélération, de manœuvrabilité et de freinage, attirait des machines très diverses, allant de la minuscule GN à la sportive Vauxhall 30/98.

Following a family tradition

When Raymond Mays was a boy he used to watch his father competing in trials and hillclimbs, and when he was old enough his father gave him a car of his own, a much modified Hillman. In the early 1920s, selling the Hillman provided part of the finance for Mays' famous Brescia Bugatti, seen here at speed in the Westcliff Trials in July 1922.

Eine Familientradition

Als Junge war Raymond Mays dabei, wenn sein Vater an Trials und Bergrennen teilnahm, und als er alt genug war, bekam er einen eigenen Wagen, einen frisierten Hillman. Anfang der Zwanziger verkaufte er den Hillman und zahlte mit dem Geld seinen berühmten Brescia-Bugatti an, hier beim Geschwindig-keitswettbewerb von Westcliff im Juli 1922.

Une tradition familiale

Enfant, Raymond Mays avait l'habitude d'aller voir courir son père dans divers concours et courses de côte. Lorsqu'il fut un peu plus âgé, son père lui offrit une Hillman très modifiée. Au début des années 1920, la vente de cette voiture lui permit d'acquérir cette célèbre Bugatti Brescia, ici à pleine vitesse lors du Concours de Westcliff en juillet 1922.

Every schoolboy's dream

Malcolm Campbell's newest Bluebird (above left and right) rolled out in January 1929 and reached 218mph at Verneuk Pan, South Africa – not quite fast enough to take the record. Sunbeam's 1,000hp car for Segrave evolved during 1927 from its original form (opposite, above) to the twin-engined, chain-driven monster (opposite, below) which first broke the 200mph barrier, reaching 203.8mph at Daytona Beach in March 1927.

Der Traum jedes Schuljungen

Malcolm Campbells Bluebird (oben links und rechts) erreichte 1929 auf dem Salzsee von Verneuk 351 km/h – kein neuer Rekord. Der 1000-PS-Wagen, den Sunbeam für Segrave baute, entwickelte sich 1927 von der ursprünglichen Form (gegenüber, oben) zum kettengetriebenen zweimotorigen Monstrum (gegenüber, unten), mit dem er im März 1927 in Daytona Beach mit 327,9 km/h die 200-Meilen-Grenze durchbrach.

Le rêve de tous les écoliers

La nouvelle Bluebird de Malcolm Campbell (ci-dessus à gauche et à droite) s'élança en janvier 1929 à Verneuk Pan pour atteindre 351 km/h – une vitesse toutefois insuffisante pour s'attribuer le record de vitesse. En 1927, la Sunbeam de 1000 ch de Segrave (ci-contre, en haut) devint ce monstre bimoteur à transmission par chaîne (ci-contre, en bas) qui franchit le premier la barrière des 321 km/h, atteignant 327,9 km/h à Daytona Beach en mars.

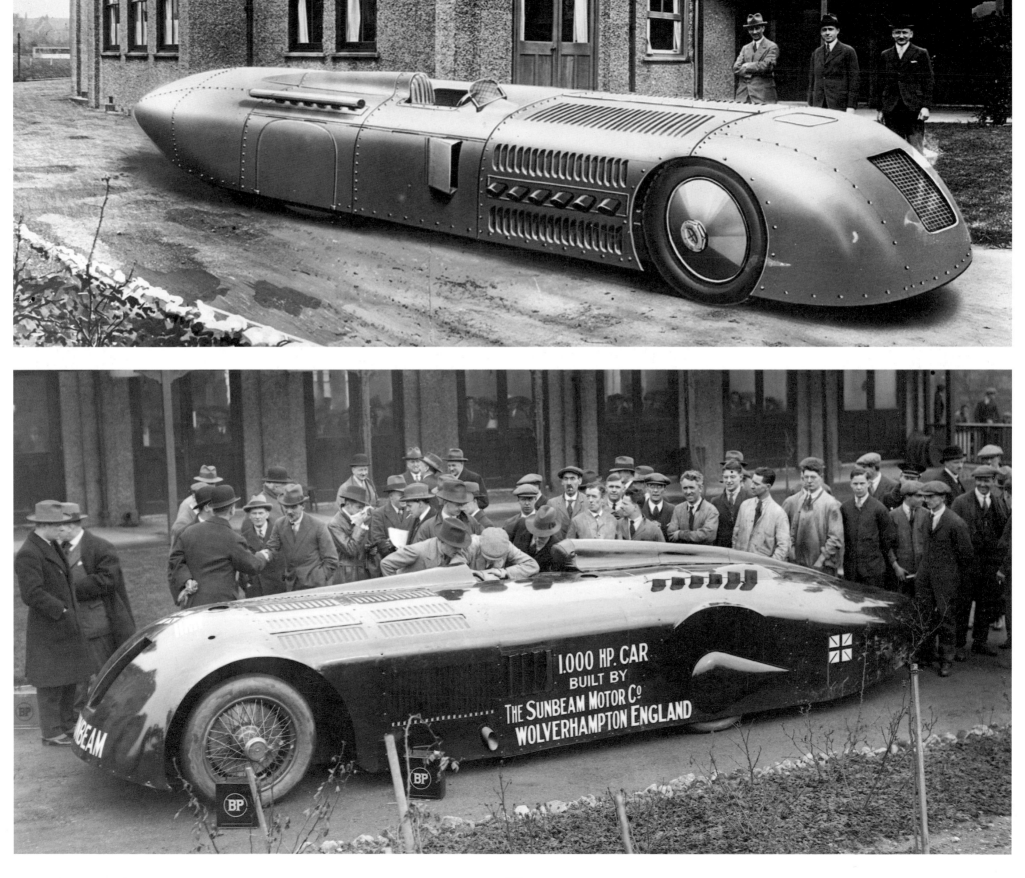

Rain and dust

Umbrellas for the spectators, a slippery track for the drivers (left) at the North Curve of Berlin's Avus circuit in July 1926, where Rudi Caracciola, in a 2-litre Mercedes, scored the first of his six German Grands Prix wins – and showed his genius in wet conditions. In a sunnier climate, Jules Goux's Ballot (above) kicks up the dust in the mountains of Sicily on its way to second place in the 1922 Targa Florio, behind Masetti's Mercedes.

Regen und Staub

Schirme für die Zuschauer, eine glitschige Piste für die Fahrer (links) in der Nordkurve der Berliner Avus, Juli 1926; Rudi Caracciola errang hier auf dem 2-Liter-Mercedes den ersten seiner sechs Siege beim Großen Preis von Deutschland und stellte wieder einmal sein Können im Regen unter Beweis. Jules Goux' Ballot (oben) wirbelt in sonnigerem Klima Staub auf, unterwegs in den sizilianischen Bergen zum zweiten Platz bei der Targa Florio von 1922; Sieger wurde Masetti auf Mercedes.

Pluie et poussière

Une foule de parapluies et une piste glissante accueillent les pilotes au virage Nord du circuit Avus de Berlin en juillet 1926 (à gauche), dans une épreuve où Rudi Caracciola, montrant son génie du pilotage sur piste mouillée avec sa Mercedes 2 litres, remporte la première de ses six victoires dans le Grand Prix d'Allemagne. Dans une région au climat plus ensoleillé, la Ballot de Jules Goux (ci-dessus) fait voler la poussière dans les montagnes de Sicile avant de finir second derrière la Mercedes de Masetti dans la Targa Florio de 1922.

Against the clock

Brooklands' famous timekeeper and handicapper A.V. 'Ebby' Ebblewhite, with stopwatch and flag (left), preparing to release the next car on handicap from a mixed grid at the track in August 1923. According to Ebby's calculations, the faster cars started later and later, and in theory all should finish close together. The 1928 Tourist Trophy also ran to handicap, and Kaye Don's Lea Francis (above), with two laps start over the largest cars, won the 410-mile race by just thirteen seconds.

Die Uhr läuft

A. V. »Ebby« Ebblewhite, der berühmte Zeitnehmer und Handicapper von Brooklands, steht im August 1923 mit Stoppuhr und Flagge bereit (links), um den nächsten Wagen aus der bunten Versammlung auf die Strecke zu schicken. Ebby kalkulierte die Stärke der Wagen und ließ die Kräftigsten zuletzt starten, sodass sich, zumindest in der Theorie, ein gegen Ende immer spannenderes Rennen ergab. Die Tourist Trophy von 1928 wurde ebenfalls nach diesem Handicap-System veranstaltet; Kaye Dons Lea Francis (oben) startete zwei Runden vor den stärksten Wagen und gewann das 660 Kilometer lange Rennen mit gerade einmal dreizehn Sekunden Vorsprung.

Contre la montre

Le célèbre chronométreur et handicapeur de Brooklands, A.V. « Ebby » Ebblewhite, armé d'un drapeau et d'un chronomètre (à gauche), se prépare à libérer le prochain concurrent d'une grille assez mélangée en août 1923. D'après les calculs d'Ebby, les voitures les plus rapides partaient de plus en plus tard et, en théorie, finissaient proches les unes des autres. Le Tourist Trophy de 1928 était également couru suivant un handicap ; la Lea Francis de Kaye Don (ci-dessus), avec deux tours d'avance sur des voitures plus grosses, remporta l'épreuve de 660 km avec trente secondes d'avance seulement.

A German triumph in Ireland

Many people believe that the 1929 Tourist Trophy on the Ards circuit was the greatest TT of them all. Rudi Caracciola won in one of the magnificent supercharged 7.1-litre Mercedes SS sports cars, sister car to the one shown here, driven by Otto Merz. Again, Caracciola demonstrated his mastery of wet conditions, lapping faster in the rain than any other car had in the dry.

Deutscher Triumph in Irland

Vielen gilt die Tourist Trophy von 1929 auf dem Rundkurs von Ards als größte ihrer Art. Rudi Caracciola siegte in einem prachtvollen Mercedes SS 7,1-Liter-Kompressorwagen, hier ein zweites Exemplar mit Otto Merz am Steuer. Wieder bewies Caracciola seine Fähigkeiten im Regen und erreichte auf der nassen Strecke schnellere Rundenzeiten als die Konkurrenten zuvor auf trockener.

Un triomphe allemand en Irlande

Beaucoup de gens pensent que le Tourist Trophy de 1929, couru sur le circuit de Ards, fut le plus grand de tous. Rudi Caracciola gagna dans l'une des magnifiques Mercedes SS à moteur surali-menté de 7,1 litres, identique à celle-ci pilotée par Otto Merz. Caracciola démontra sa maîtrise par temps humide, tournant plus vite sous la pluie qu'aucune autre voiture sur le sec.

Speed – the common link

On the concrete bankings of Brooklands, on the beaches, or on the hills, speed was king. On the track in 1923 (top) the riding mechanic in Captain J.E.P. Howey's Leyland-Thomas hides from the slipstream. On Southport sands in March 1926 (centre) Major H.O.D. Segrave's Sunbeam failed in its record attempts after mechanical problems. Slightly lower down the speed scale, T.R. Tunnard-Moore (bottom), representing Oxford, attacks Aston Clinton hill in his Amilcar during the Inter-Varsity Hillclimb in 1925.

Allen gemeinsam: das Tempo

Ob auf der Betonpiste von Brooklands, am Meeresstrand oder in den Bergen: Immer drehte sich alles um die Geschwindigkeit. Auf der Rennstrecke (oben) duckt sich 1923 der Beifahrer in Captain J. E. P. Howeys Leyland-Thomas, um dem Fahrtwind zu entgehen. Im März 1926 jagt Major H. O. D. Segrave im Sunbeam (mittig) am Strand von Southport Rekorde, kommt jedoch wegen technischer Schwierigkeiten nicht recht in Fahrt. Ein wenig weiter unten auf der Temposkala rangiert T. R. Tunnard-Moore (unten), der beim Universitäts-Bergrennen von 1925 für Oxford startete und hier mit seinem Amilcar Anlauf zum Hügel von Aston Clinton nimmt.

Vitesse – un trait d'union

Dans les virages relevés de Brooklands, sur les plages ou dans les collines, la vitesse est reine. En 1923, le mécanicien navigant de la Leyland-Thomas du capitaine J. E. P. Howey rentre à l'intérieur du baquet pour éviter de perturber l'aérodynamique (en haut). Sur la plage de Southport, en mars 1926, la Sunbeam du major H. O. D. Segrave échoue dans sa tentative de record à la suite de problèmes mécaniques (au centre). À un niveau de vitesse légèrement inférieur, T. R. Tunnard-Moore, représentant Oxford, attaque la colline d'Aston Clinton dans son Amilcar lors de la course de côte Inter-Varsity en 1925 (en bas).

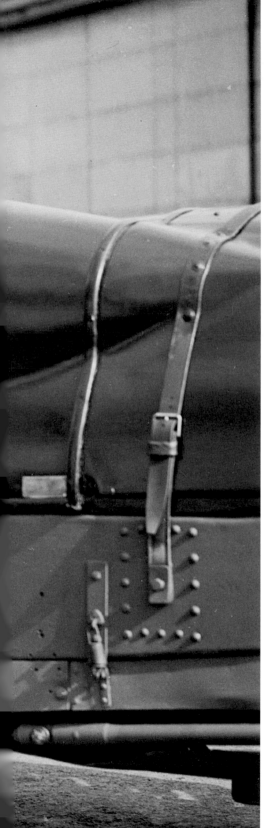

Fast ladies at Brooklands

Racing at Brooklands, perhaps more than any other form of motor sport, attracted a substantial number of lady drivers, some of whom were more than capable of beating the men. Mrs W.B. Scott (left) and her husband acquired Parry Thomas's Leyland-Thomas after Thomas's death in 1927 and raced it with considerable success until 1930. Mrs V. Dykes and Miss D. Burnett (above) were Brooklands ladies' race winners in May 1929.

Damen mit Tempo

Vielleicht mehr als jede andere Motorsportform zogen die Rennen in Brooklands auch Frauen als Fahrerinnen an, und einige hatten durchaus das Zeug, den Männern davonzufahren. Mrs. W. B. Scott (links) erwarb zusammen mit ihrem Mann den Leyland-Thomas von Parry Thomas, nachdem dieser 1927 umgekommen war, und trat darin mit beträchtlichem Erfolg bis 1930 an. Mrs. V. Dykes und Miss D. Burnett (oben) siegten im Damenrennen, das im Mai 1929 in Brooklands stattfand.

Femmes de vitesse à Brooklands

Les courses de Brooklands attiraient, peut-être plus que toute autre forme de sport automobile, un nombre assez important de femmes pilotes, parmi lesquelles certaines étaient plus que capables de battre les hommes. Madame W.B. Scott (à gauche) et son mari achetèrent la Leyland-Thomas de Parry Thomas après sa mort en 1927 et obtinrent grâce à elle de nombreux succès jusqu'en 1930. Madame V. Dykes et mademoiselle D. Burnett (ci-dessus) après avoir gagné la course des dames de Brooklands en mai 1929.

A variety of challenges

Brooklands offered many variations over the years, including
artificial 'road' circuits within the oval. John Cobb leads George
Eyston on the banking in April 1923 (top), 'Cupid' Hornsted's
Mathis leads Vernon Balls's Amilcar during a 100-mile light car
trial in 1925 (above), and Eyston hauls his Bugatti through one
of the chicanes (above right) during a 1927 200-mile race.

Für jeden etwas

Im Laufe der Jahre bot Brooklands viele Rennvarianten an, teils
auf künstlichen »Straßenstrecken« im Oval. John Cobb führt im
April 1923 in der Steilkurve vor George Eyston (ganz oben),
»Cupid« Hornsted fährt 1925 auf einem Mathis (oben links)
beim 100-Meilen-Rennen für leichte Wagen dem Amilcar von
Vernon Balls voraus, und Eyston steuert seinen Bugatti beim
200-Meilen-Rennen von 1927 durch die Schikanen.

Des défis divers

Le circuit de Brooklands pouvait aménager différentes variantes,
notamment des circuits « routiers » artificiels tracés à l'intérieur
de l'ovale. J. Cobb mène devant G. Eyston en avril 1923 (en haut).
La Mathis de « Cupid » Hornsted devance l'Amilcar de Vernon
Balls lors de l'épreuve de 160 km (100 miles) d'un concours de
voitures légères en 1925 (ci-dessus). Eyston, sur Bugatti, lors
d'une course de 320 km (200 miles) en 1927 (ci-dessus à droite).

Just add corners

Henry Segrave's Talbot during practice for the first British Grand Prix, held at Brooklands in August 1926 on a course which included sandbank chicanes to give some semblance of a road race. In the race, all three of the Talbot team cars, driven by Segrave, Divo and Moriceau, retired, victory going to Robert Sénéchal and Louis Wagner, driving for Delage.

Ecken und Kanten

Henry Segrave im Talbot beim Training zum Großen Preis von England, der im August 1926 in Brooklands auf einem Kurs stattfand, auf dem Schikanen aus Sand aufgeschüttet waren, um die Kurven einer Straßenstrecke nachzuahmen. Alle drei Talbot-Werkswagen mit Segrave, Divo und Moriceau am Steuer fielen aus, und die beiden ersten Plätze gingen an Robert Sénéchal und Louis Wagner auf Delage.

Pour quelques virages de plus

La Talbot de Henry Segrave lors des essais du premier Grand Prix de Grande-Bretagne, organisé à Brooklands en août 1926 sur un tracé agrémenté de chicanes de sable pour rappeler une course sur route. Les trois voitures de l'écurie Talbot, pilotées par Segrave, Divo et Moriceau, abandonnèrent, la victoire revenant à Robert Sénéchal et Louis Wagner sur Delage.

MG, a sporting marque, from road races…

The supercharged 750cc C-Type MG Midget was a small car capable of humbling far larger opponents. In 1931, one of three C-Types run by the Earl of March won the Tourist Trophy, driven by Norman Black. A year later Major 'Goldie' Gardner (left, and above, in the middle) with Cyril Paul and Eddie Hall (above, in car and on the right) contested the TT. Gardner crashed, Paul retired, Hall finished third, an easy class winner behind two 1100cc Rileys.

MG-Sportwagen für jeden Anlass, vom Straßenrennen…

Der MG Midget Typ C mit 750-ccm-Kompressormotor war ein kleiner Wagen, der weit größere Konkurrenten das Fürchten lehrte. 1931 gewann einer von drei C-Typen, die der Earl of March ins Rennen schickte, mit Norman Black am Steuer die Tourist Trophy. Im Jahr darauf traten Major »Goldie« Gardner (links und oben, der Mittlere im Trio), Cyril Paul und Eddie Hall (oben, am Steuer und im weißen Kittel) zur TT an. Gardner, der verunglückte, und Paul schieden aus, Hall belegte den dritten Platz hinter zwei 1100-ccm-Rileys und gewann mühelos seine Klasse.

MG, la marque du sport, des courses sur route…

La MG Midget Type-C à moteur suralimenté de 750 cm³ était une petite voiture capable d'humilier des adversaires beaucoup plus importants. En 1931, l'une des trois Type-C engagées par le comte de March, remporte le Tourist Trophy, pilotée par Norman Black. Un an plus tard, le major « Goldie » Gardner (à gauche et ci-dessus, au centre) avec Cyril Paul et Eddie Hall (ci-dessus, dans la voiture et à droite) dispute le Tourist Trophy. Gardner accidenté, Paul ayant abandonné, Hall termine troisième de sa catégorie derrière deux Riley de 1100 cm³.

...to hillclimbs

The MG marque was conceived by William Kimber in 1924, initially to build more sporting cars based on Morris chassis, and soon to be a sporting make in its own right. MG's strengths were in highly successful competition cars and very affordable everyday sports cars – many of the latter having their own competition careers, like this Midget on the Land's End Trial.

... zur Bergprüfung

William Kimber hatte MG 1924 gegründet, zunächst mit sportlichen Modellen auf Morris-Chassis, doch schon bald als eigenständige Sportwagenmarke. Die beiden Stärken von MG waren die äußerst erfolgreichen Wettbewerbswagen und die preisgünstigen Sportwagen für den Alltagsgebrauch – von denen dann viele wiederum Sportkarriere machten, wie hier der Midget bei der Bergprüfung von Land's End.

... à la course de côte

La firme MG, créée par William Kimber en 1924 pour construire des voitures plus sportives sur la base du châssis Morris, devient bientôt une marque de voitures de course. La force de MG était de proposer d'excellentes automobiles pour la compétition et des voitures de sport très abordables pour le grand public, dont certaines – comme cette Midget dans le Land's End Trial – firent une carrière en compétition.

Homage to a record-breaker

When Major Henry Segrave went to Daytona to attack the land speed record with his 1,000hp Sunbeam, local professional racing drivers in slightly less powerful machinery put on a demonstration race in his honour. This took place on the same stretch of beach where Segrave would become the first man on earth to exceed 200mph, with his record of 203.8mph in March 1927.

Salut für den Weltrekordler

Als Major Henry Segrave mit dem 1000-PS-Sunbeam zu einer seiner Rekordfahrten nach Daytona kam, veranstalteten die dortigen Fahrer auf nicht ganz so kraftvollen Fahrzeugen ihm zu Ehren ein Rennen. Es fand auf demselben Sandstreifen statt, auf dem Segrave im März 1927 die Rekordgeschwindigkeit von 203,8 mph (327,9 km/h) erreichte und damit der erste war, der schneller als 200 Meilen die Stunde fuhr.

Hommage à un briseur de records

Lorsque le major Henry Segrave vint à Daytona s'attaquer au record de vitesse sur terre avec sa Sunbeam 1000 ch, les pilotes professionnels locaux organisèrent une course de démonstration en son honneur avec des machines légèrement moins puissantes sur la plage même où Segrave allait devenir le premier homme à dépasser les 322 km/h (200 miles/h) en atteignant 327,9 km/h en mars 1927.

Friendly rivalries

Drivers and riding mechanics in relaxed mood as they line
up for the start of a Brooklands race at the Whitsuntide meeting
in May 1923. The cars are a typically mixed Brooklands bunch,
including the Wolseley Moth (17), a Bugatti (16),
a Horstmann, a GN (12), a 15hp Wolseley (11), a Bentley (7)
and a Star, with the track's special emphasis on streamlining
clearly in evidence.

Freundschaftliche Rivalen

Fahrer und Mechaniker in entspannter Stimmung beim Start
zum Pfingstrennen in Brooklands, Mai 1923. Die Wagen boten
die übliche bunte Mischung, darunter ein Wolseley Moth (17),
ein Bugatti (16), ein Horstmann, ein GN (12), ein 15-PS-Wolseley
(11), ein Bentley (7) und ein Star; deutlich ist zu sehen, dass die
Aerodynamik an Bedeutung gewinnt.

Des compétitions amicales

Les pilotes et leurs mécaniciens paraissent plutôt détendus sur
la grille de départ de Brooklands lors de la réunion de Whitsuntide en mai 1923. Exemples parfaits du mélange des genres
que l'on pouvait rencontrer à Brooklands, on reconnaît : une
Wolseley Moth (17), une Bugatti (16), une Hortsmann, une
GN (12), une Wolseley 15 ch (11), une Bentley (7) et une Star,
toutes ayant mis l'accent sur l'aérodynamisme.

The gentleman racers...

Captain, later Sir, Malcolm Campbell was one of a special breed of British record-breakers of the 1920s and 1930s, men with ample funds and military backgrounds – which included the likes of Major Segrave and Major Gardner. This is Campbell with one of his Bugattis in his garage at home in Horley in 1928; all his racing cars were, however, looked after by professionals.

Die Gentlemen-Fahrer ...

Captain (später Sir) Malcolm Campbell gehörte zu jener typisch britischen Gruppe von Rekordfahrern, die aus wohlhabenden Familien mit militärischer Tradition kamen – andere Vertreter sind Major Segrave und Major Gardner. Hier sehen wir Campbell 1928 zu Hause in Horley in der Garage mit einem seiner Bugattis; die Rekordwagen wurden allerdings von professionellen Mechanikern betreut.

Les gentlemen pilotes ...

Le capitaine Malcolm Campbell, anobli par la suite, est, avec le major Segrave et le major Gardner, le digne représentant de ces briseurs de records britanniques des années 1920–1930, qui disposaient d'amples moyens financiers et d'un passé militaire. Sir Malcolm Campbell en 1928, dans le garage de sa maison de Horley près d'une de ses Bugatti ; toutes ses voitures étaient cependant révisées par des professionnels.

...and the Welsh Wizard

Welshman Parry Thomas (above) not only drove racing cars and record-breakers, he designed and built them, while living in a house at Brooklands. His Leyland-Thomas specials included the record-breaking Babs and low-slung 'flat-irons'. He took the land speed record to 171.0mph on Pendine Sands (below) in April 1926 but died there in 1927, chasing 180mph. (Overleaf) Campbell's Sunbeam reached 135mph at Saltburn Sands, Yorkshire, in June 1922, but failed to take the record.

... und der Teufelskerl aus Wales

Der Waliser Parry Thomas (oben) fuhr die Renn- und Rekordwagen nicht nur, er konstruierte und baute sie auch und wohnte in einem Haus in Brooklands. Zu seinen Leyland-Thomas gehörten der Rekordwagen Babs und die flachen »Bügeleisen«. Am Strand von Pendine (unten) stellte er im April 1926 mit 275,1 km/h einen neuen Weltrekord auf und verlor dort 1927 auf der Jagd nach dem 180-Meilen-Rekord (289 km/h) sein Leben. (Folgende Doppelseite) Campbells Sunbeam erreichte im Juni 1922 in Saltburn Sands, Yorkshire, 217 km/h, doch für einen neuen Rekord reichte das nicht.

... et le sorcier gallois

Le Gallois Parry Thomas (en haut), qui vivait à Brooklands, était non seulement un pilote de course et un briseur de records mais également le concepteur et le constructeur de ses voitures, des Leyland-Thomas spéciales, dont la Babs détentrice d'un record de vitesse et le « fer à repasser » à carrosserie surbaissée. Il s'octroie en avril 1926 le record de vitesse à 275,1 km/h à Pendine Sands (en bas), où il se tue en 1927 en cherchant à atteindre 289 km/h. Bien que la Sunbeam de Campbell ait atteint 217 km/h à Saltburn Sands (Yorkshire) en juin 1922, elle ne parvient pas toutefois à s'attribuer le record (pages suivantes).

An also-ran

The Italian Giulio Foresti was a racing driver, agent for Itala cars in England and another land speed record challenger. In 1927 he went to Pendine with the Djelmo (above and opposite), a 400hp car designed by an Italian engineer called Moglia, built in France and financed by an Egyptian prince named Djelaleddin. The car never approached the record and was ultimately wrecked in a high-speed crash.

Unter ferner liefen

Der Italiener Giulio Foresti war englischer Itala-Importeur und selbst Renn- und Rekordfahrer. 1927 trat er in Pendine mit dem Djelmo an (oben und gegenüber); konstruiert hatte den 400-PS-Boliden der Italiener Moglia, gebaut wurde er in Frankreich, und das Geld dazu hatte ein ägyptischer Prinz namens Djelaleddin gegeben. Der Wagen erreichte nicht annähernd die Rekordmarke und wurde bei einem Unfall zerstört.

Un autre concurrent

L'Italien Giulio Foresti, agent de la firme Itala en Grande-Bretagne, était aussi un pilote de course et un concurrent au record de vitesse. Il vient en 1927 à Pendine avec sa Djelmo (ci-dessus et ci-contre), une voiture de 400 ch dessinée par l'ingénieur italien Moglia, construite en France et financée par le prince égyptien Djelaleddin. La voiture ne parvint jamais à approcher le record et fut détruite lors d'un accident.

Almost the water speed record

Malcolm Campbell attempts to clear the windscreen of his Napier-Campbell Bluebird, powered by a 12-cylinder 'broad arrow' 450hp Napier Lion aero-engine, during his attack on the land speed record at Pendine, early in 1927. On 4 February, in spite of appalling conditions in his early runs, and after losing his goggles on one run, he managed to raise the record to 174.9mph.

Zu Land oder zu Wasser?

Malcolm Campbell versucht Anfang 1927 bei einer Rekordfahrt in Pendine die Windschutzscheibe seines Napier-Campbell-Bluebird, angetrieben von einem 450 PS starken zwölfzylindrigen Napier-Lion-Flugzeugmotor, freizuwischen. Trotz schlechter Witterung bei den ersten Läufen und nachdem er bei einem Rennen seine Schutzbrille verloren hatte, stellte er am 4. Februar mit 281,4 km/h einen neuen Rekord auf.

Presque un record sur l'eau

Malcolm Campbell essaie d'essuyer le pare-brise de sa Napier-Campbell Bluebird, propulsée par un aéromoteur Napier Lion 12 cylindres en « V large » de 450 ch, lors de sa tentative de record de vitesse à Pendine au début 1927. Le 4 février, malgré les conditions météo épouvantables pour ses premiers essais et la perte de ses lunettes, il parvint à améliorer le record à 281,4 km/h.

The pleasure and spoils of victory

Campbell was usually a serious man, and in later years often showed the strain of what had become an obsession with both land and water speed records, but the joy of success shows as he lifts the Daytona Beach Trophy. It was his reward for setting another new record on the Florida sands in March 1928, when he reached 206.9mph in a further developed Bluebird, now boasting some 900hp.

Zwei strahlen um die Wette

In der Regel war Campbell ein ernster Mann, und in späteren Jahren spürte man ihm die Anspannung der obsessiven Jagd nach dem Geschwindigkeitsweltrekord zu Lande und zu Wasser oft an, doch hier, wo er den Pokal von Daytona entgegennimmt, ist er ganz der strahlende Sieger. Es war sein Lohn für einen neuen Rekord von 332,9 Stundenkilometern, den er im März 1928 auf dem Strand von Florida mit einem weiterentwickelten, auf 900 PS Leistung erstarkten Bluebird aufstellte.

Plaisir et avantages de la victoire

Campbell était habituellement un homme sérieux qui montra souvent, les dernières années de sa vie, les stigmates de cette course au record de vitesse sur terre et sur eau qui était devenue pour lui une obsession. La joie se lit cependant sur son visage lorsqu'il reçoit le trophée de Daytona Beach (Floride), obtenu en mars 1928 après avoir amélioré le record en atteignant 332,9 km/h dans une Bluebird améliorée, développant près de 900 chevaux.

A dangerous game

In the era of the fast and dangerous board speedways in
America, California became the country's busiest racing venue,
the crowds drawn by drama such as this car losing a wheel
(top) at Culver City Speedway in Los Angeles in 1924. Malcolm
Campbell (above) tried in vain to save his Bugatti after it
erupted in flames in the pits during the 1928 Tourist Trophy.

Ein riskantes Spiel

In der Zeit der schnellen und gefährlichen Motodrome sah kein
amerikanischer Bundesstaat mehr Rennen als Kalifornien, wo
spektakuläre Unfälle wie dieser 1924, bei dem ein Wagen auf
dem Culver City Speedway in Los Angeles ein Rad verliert
(ganz oben), die Massen anzogen. Malcolm Campbell (oben)
versucht vergebens, seinen Bugatti zu retten, der bei der Tourist
Trophy von 1928 an den Boxen in Flammen aufgegangen ist.

Un jeu dangereux

À l'époque des speedways américains en bois, rapides et
dangereux, la Californie devient le plus actif théâtre de
compétitions du pays. La foule y est attirée par les nombreux
accidents, comme celui de cette voiture perdant une roue
(en haut) sur le Culver City Speedway de Los Angeles en 1924.
Malcolm Campbell (ci-dessus) tente vainement de sauver sa
Bugatti qui a pris feu au stand lors du Tourist Trophy de 1928.

Laying down the rules

Drivers at Brooklands (above) before the Junior Car Club's 200-mile race in August 1922, listening attentively to instructions from the officials of the meeting. The drivers' briefing, then as now, was primarily concerned with safety and fairness – and in 1922, as a notice in his office reminded all concerned, in all matters the decision of the Clerk of the Course was binding.

Fair Play

Fahrer in Brooklands (oben) hören aufmerksam zu, als vor dem Start zum 200-Meilen-Rennen des Junior Car Club im August 1922 die Regeln verlesen werden. Damals wie heute ging es in der Fahrerbesprechung vor allem um Sicherheit und Fairness – und 1922 hatte, damit keine Zweifel aufkamen, der Rennleiter in seinem Büro ein Schild aufgehängt, dass seine Entscheidungen in jedem Falle bindend sind.

La fixation des règles

Les pilotes se sont réunis à Brooklands (ci-dessus) avant la course de 200 miles du Junior Car Club d'août 1922, écoutant attentivement les instructions données par les officiels. Le briefing des pilotes, comme aujourd'hui, concernait essentielle-ment la sécurité et le fair play – et, en 1922, comme une note le rappelait à tous, la décision des Commissaires de course avait force de loi.

This island race

The start of the Mannin Moar race, for Grand Prix cars, on the Isle of Man in 1925. The venue was a legacy of the fact that mainland Britain still refused to countenance racing on public roads while the self-governed Isle of Man welcomed it with an enthusiasm which has never waned. The race was won by the Hon. Brian Lewis in Bugatti number 7, at an average speed of 75.6mph.

Rund um die Insel

Start zum Mannin-Moar-Rennen für Grand-Prix-Wagen, Isle of Man 1925. Nach wie vor waren auf der britischen Insel Rennen auf öffentlichen Straßen verboten, doch die unabhängige Verwaltung von Man hieß die Rennfahrer mit einer Herzlichkeit willkommen, die bis heute anhält. Als Sieger ging Brian Lewis auf dem Bugatti mit der Nummer 7 und einer Durchschnittsgeschwindigkeit von 121,6 km/h ins Ziel.

Une île de courses

Le départ de la course de Mannin Moar, réservée aux voitures de Grand Prix, est donné sur l'île de Man en 1925. Ce circuit était la conséquence du refus de la Grande-Bretagne d'accepter des compétitions sur la voie publique alors que le gouvernement autonome de l'île de Man les accueillait toujours avec enthousiasme. La course fut remportée par Brian Lewis sur la Bugatti numéro 7, à la moyenne de 121,6 km/h.

Road racing comes to the track

Cars leaving the starting line for a race on one of Brooklands'
early 'road' courses, in September 1925. Eventually the track
had a permanent infield road section in the form of the
Campbell Circuit, but the first events like this took cars off
the Outer Circuit via the paddock return and entrance roads,
by tunnel and bridge to descend the test hill and rejoin the
main track.

Straßenrennen auf der Piste

Start zu einem Rennen auf einem der frühen »Straßenkurse«
von Brooklands, September 1925. Später wurde der Campbell
Circuit angelegt, eine künstliche Straßen-Rundstrecke im
Inneren des Ovals, doch zuvor verließen die Wagen bei Rennen
wie diesem den Außenkurs über die Zugangsstraßen an Start
und Ziel, fuhren durch den Tunnel und über die Brücke und
kehrten über den Hügel zur Hauptstrecke zurück.

La course sur route vient à la piste

Le départ d'une des premières courses « sur route » organisées
à Brooklands, en septembre 1925, dans le périmètre duquel était
aménagé un tracé routier permanent, appelé le Campbell Circuit. Les épreuves comme celle-ci sortaient du circuit extérieur
par le paddock et les routes d'entrée en passant par un tunnel
et un pont avant de descendre la colline d'essais
et rejoindre la piste principale.

The featherweight brigade

Where engine size and power were limited, light weight and effective streamlining were keys to performance, and at Brooklands the pursuit of both led to some amazing machinery. The single-cylinder Jappic (above) was a record-breaker in which H.M. Walters set marks of up to 70.5mph with only 350cc in 1925. E.B. Ware's single-seat, twin-cylinder, three-wheel Morgan (left, in 1920 form) set a new 1100cc cyclecar record of 86.0mph in 1921.

Fliegengewicht

Wo Motorgröße und -leistung begrenzt waren, kam alles auf geringes Gewicht und gute Stromlinienform an, und diese Maxime brachte manch kurioses Gefährt nach Brooklands. Mit dem Jappic (oben), den ein nur 350 ccm großer Einzylinder trieb, stellte H. M. Walters im Jahr 1925 Rekorde von bis zu 113,4 Stundenkilometern auf. E. B. Wares einsitziges Morgan-Zweizylinder-Dreirad (links in der Version von 1920) erreichte 1921 mit 138,4 km/h eine neue Bestzeit für Cyclecars bis 1100 ccm.

La brigade légère

Avec la limitation du volume et de la puissance des moteurs, les clés de la performance sont la légèreté et l'aérodynamisme, dont la recherche entraîne la construction d'étranges machines. À Brooklands, on peut alors voir le tricycle monoplace bicylindre Morgan de E. B. Ware (à gauche, le modèle 1920), détenteur en 1921 du record de vitesse sur cyclecar de 1100 cm³ à 138,4 km/h, ou la Jappic monocylindre avec laquelle H. M. Walters s'octroie en 1925 le record de vitesse des 350 cm³ à 113,4 km/h (ci-dessus).

Blowers and rockets

Amherst Villiers (above, second left) was a brilliant British racing engineer with a reputation as one of the world's leading authorities on supercharging, as well as being a renowned chassis designer. His talents were combined in the fearsome supercharged Special he built for Raymond Mays (on right). Fritz von Opel's speciality, beyond the Opel production car, was a series of rocket-powered record cars (left).

Mit Dampf und Druck

Der brillante englische Rennwagenkonstrukteur Amherst Villiers (oben, Zweiter von links) galt nicht nur als weltweit führender Kompressorexperte, sondern auch als überlegener Fahrwerkstechniker. Beide Talente verband er in diesem eindrucksvollen Kompressorwagen, einem Einzelstück für Raymond Mays (rechts). Fritz von Opels Spezialität neben den zivileren Produkten der Opel-Werke war eine Serie von Raketenwagen (links).

Suralimentation et fusées

Amherst Villiers (ci-dessus, le deuxième à gauche) était un brillant ingénieur britannique qui avait la réputation d'être l'un des principaux experts mondiaux en suralimentation et un excellent concepteur de châssis. Il mit tous ces talents au service de Raymond Mays (à droite) en lui construisant cette Special suralimentée. Fritz von Opel, le fondateur de la marque qui porte son nom, s'était fait une spécialité de construire des voitures propulsées par des fusées (à gauche).

Tourist Trophy revived
Rudolf Caracciola in the Mercedes SS sports car during practice for the 1928 Tourist Trophy, revived after a six-year break on a new and challenging circuit at Ards, near Belfast. Mercedes withdrew at the last moment from the 1928 Tourist Trophy after a dispute over elements of the rules, but in 1929 Caracciola returned and scored one of the race's most famous wins.

Die Tourist Trophy ist wieder da
Rudolf Caracciola im Mercedes-SS-Sportwagen beim Training zur Tourist Trophy, die 1928 nach sechsjähriger Pause erstmals wieder stattfand, nun auf einem neuen und anspruchsvollen Kurs in Ards bei Belfast. In jenem Jahr zog sich Mercedes wegen eines Streits um die Regeln in letzter Minute zurück, doch 1929 war Caracciola wieder dabei und errang einen der spektakulärsten TT-Siege aller Zeiten.

La renaissance du Tourist Trophy
Rudolf Caracciola dans sa Mercedes SS de sport lors des essais de l'édition 1928 du Tourist Trophy, de nouveau organisé après une interruption de six ans sur le nouveau circuit de Ards, près de Belfast. Si Mercedes se retira au dernier moment de cette course après un différend sur des points de règlement, Caracciola revint en 1929 et remporta l'une des plus célèbres victoires de l'épreuve.

Leading the team effort

Giuseppe Campari's supercharged Alfa Romeo leading fellow 1500cc class entrant S.H. Newsome's very quick Lea Francis, in practice for the 1929 Tourist Trophy (above left). Campari finished the race second overall, won his class and led the three-car Alfa team to the team award. Felice Nazzaro in 1922 (right) when he rejoined Fiat shortly before he retired from the sport.

Bester im Team

Mit dem Kompressor getriebenen Alfa Romeo fährt Giuseppe Campari beim Training zur Tourist Trophy von 1929 dem Lea Francis von S. H. Newsome, seinem Konkurrenten in der 1500-ccm-Klasse, davon (oben links). Campari kam in der Gesamtwertung auf den zweiten Platz und sicherte dem Alfa-Team den Mannschaftspreis. Felice Nazzaro 1922 (rechts), als er noch einmal für Fiat fuhr, bevor er sich vom Rennsport zurückzog.

À la tête de l'équipe

Felice Nazzaro (à droite) entre chez Fiat en 1922 peu de temps avant d'abandonner la compétition automobile. L'Alfa Romeo suralimentée de Giuseppe Campari devance la Lea Francis, de 1500 cm⁵, de S. H. Newsome lors des essais du Tourist Trophy de 1929 (ci-dessus à gauche). Campari termina second au classement général, remportant sa catégorie et obtenant le titre des constructeurs à l'écurie Alfa, qui avait engagé trois voitures.

4
The Age of
Mercedes-Benz and
Auto Union

Grand Prix racing, the highest level of motor sport, entered the 1930s at a fairly low technical ebb, with formula racing largely replaced by free formulae, but it reached the end of the decade on a wave of politically-sponsored technological brilliance. That State-backed development moved the entire sport into new realms before wider political ambitions brought about another sporting suspension as a result of more serious conflicts.

As the 1930s dawned, the car manufacturers renewed their interest in the sport after a period dominated largely by private individuals. Once again, the main protagonists were those who had been dominant at the end of the 1920s, with the French Bugattis ranged against the well-established Alfa Romeos, and another Italian newcomer, Maserati, who were finding considerable success very early in what would become a long racing story. The cars of the late 1920s and early 1930s were still visibly descendants of the early 'upright' generations of sporting car, but, as Grand Prix racing reasserted itself as the pinnacle of the sport (with yet more countries joining the ranks of the Grand Prix hosts), the recent trend for multi-purpose Grand Prix-cum-sports models waned, and the narrow-bodied, single-seater became the pre-eminent shape.

For the first few years of the decade there was no official limit on engine capacity or weight for Grand Prix cars, but there were rules about the types of fuel which could be used, and on the minimum race distances or duration. In 1931, for instance, the duration of Grand Prix races had to be no less than ten hours. For 1932 they had to run for between five and ten hours, and by 1933 they were required to cover a distance of not less than 500km – which, given the physical and mental effort required to drive the cars of the period to their limits on the extremely demanding circuits of the day, was still a huge challenge.

What remained clear was that motor sport at the upper levels of Grand Prix cars, sports cars, even record breakers, now owed as much to science as to size. In sports car racing, events like the Targa Florio, the Mille Miglia, the Tourist Trophy and, most famously of all, Le Mans, were well-established as a parallel to Grand Prix racing, and the 1930s witnessed epic battles between Bentley, Alfa Romeo, Bugatti, Mercedes-Benz, Delahaye and MG among others across Europe, dominated by Alfa Romeo for the most part, and by drivers of the stature of Tazio Nuvolari, Achille Varzi and Rudi Caracciola.

The quest for outright speed was dominated through the early and mid-1930s by Malcolm Campbell and his series of Bluebird cars, now mostly built by Railton with power from either Napier or Rolls-Royce engines. They were no longer simply overgrown racing cars, although for the first half of the decade at least the ancestry was still apparent in the shape and mechanical layout; the difference was in the physical scale and the capacity of supercharged engines which by this stage were almost all derived from military aircraft rather than from automobiles. At the end of 1929 Henry Segrave held the record that he had broken in his Napier-engined Golden Arrow; the 1930s began with a famous land speed record failure for Kaye Don's highly-publicised 2,000hp Silver Bullet, which could not get beyond 180mph at Daytona Beach early in 1930 and was quietly retired, but others were more successful. By February 1932 Campbell had pushed the record beyond 250mph for the first time, to almost 254mph, and in September 1935 he became the first man in history to hold the record at more than 300mph, with a speed of 301.1mph. Such speeds were now beginning to outgrow even the vast Daytona Beach, and Campbell's 300-plus mark introduced a new and long-standing record venue in the dry beds of Bonneville Salt Flats, Utah. It was also to be Campbell's final record on land, as he switched his attention to the water where his record breaking exploits continued.

Campbell's final Bluebirds were glorious machines; majestic in scale, with increasingly sophisticated stream-lining, they were still, with their front engines and central single-seat cockpit, clearly related to the conventional racing car. The next generation of record breaker, as in George Eyston's eight-wheeled Thunderbolt, powered by two Rolls-Royce V12 aero engines producing a total of 4,800hp, and John Cobb's Railton-Mobil Special with its two supercharged 1,250hp Napier Lion V12s, finally broke the mould, with their drivers seated ahead of the engines, streamlining based on aircraft principles as the cars approached aircraft speeds, and hugely more complex and sophisticated chassis engineering under their sleek skins. With technology like this, the land speed record was pushed to 350.2mph by Cobb in September 1938, regained by Eyston within days at 357.5mph, and finally raised to its 1930s peak by Cobb again in August 1939, when he took the Railton-Mobil Special to 369.7mph at Bonneville. But record-breaking technology ultimately owed little to contemporary racing cars.

Many of the land speed record chasers were involved with records lower down the scale, in various capacity classes and in some cases in makes of car with which the public could readily identify. In October 1935 John Cobb set the ultimate Brooklands lap record at 143.4mph in his 24-litre Napier-Railton single seater, and at the same time recorded the highest speed ever attained at the famous track, at almost 152mph. Meanwhile, George Eyston, and later Goldie Gardner, continued to set remarkable straight-line records, over a large number of distances, in a long-running series of MG record breakers, the Magic Midgets – culminating in 1939, on the Frankfurt–Dessau autobahn, when Gardner took the 1100cc record (with supercharging) to an incredible 203mph.

The autobahn itself was a new concept, a high-speed road linking important cities, and it was one of the more positive achievements of the new National Socialist government in Germany in the early 1930s. Another was to be seen in Grand Prix racing, where in the second half of the 1930s the government-backed Mercedes-Benz and Auto Union teams simply rewrote the Grand Prix rule book, and ushered in an age of Grand Prix racing such as the world had never seen before, and arguably has not seen since.

At the outset of the decade, in the free formula era, the Grand Prix manufacturers themselves, having experimented with engines of 4 and even 5 litres, had generally settled on something rather smaller, lighter and relying on efficiency rather than simply big cubic capacity, typically around 3 litres and developing some 200hp, with light alloy construction becoming more common – to the great benefit of less exotic machinery as motor racing design lessons inevitably filtered down. In 1934 a new international formula was introduced, with no restriction on engine capacity but a minimum weight of 750kg, and now allowing up to four mechanics to work on each car during pit stops. It was a formula which encouraged technical innovation, but by its nature it favoured the marques with the greatest resources. And, as Adolf Hitler realised the publicity value of international motor sporting success, the teams with the best resources of all became Mercedes-Benz and Auto Union.

With huge budgets and access to extraordinary research and development facilities they were no longer so constrained by the conflict between big capacity and low weight. With exotic materials and inspired design, they could have the best of both worlds – hugely powerful large-capacity engines in

relatively light-weight cars with the most sophisticated chassis technology yet seen. Within a year, 400hp was possible, both Mercedes and Auto Union could boast all-independent suspensions, and the Auto Unions, designed by Ferdinand Porsche, had their engines behind the driver. From now until the next change of formula the German cars adopted 12 cylinders, even, in the case of Auto Union, 16 cylinders, their capacities grew to 6 litres and more, power to almost 650hp and maximum speeds nudged 200mph. They were ferocious cars to drive, but in the hands of geniuses like Caracciola, Nuvolari, Rosemeyer, Lang and Dick Seaman they swept almost all before them, with the occasional giant-killing efforts of Alfa Romeo serving only to make this latest golden era even more exceptional for European motor sport.

When the formula changed again in 1938, giving a sliding scale of weight depending on engine size, capacities typically dropped to 3 litres in a minimum weight of 850kg, but power outputs were soon back to around 500hp and further chassis, suspension, transmission, tyre and aerodynamic developments kept the whole process moving forwards, with the Mercedes and Auto Union Silver Arrows now virtually unbeatable. In the end, it was their own benefactors who provided the end of their spectacular reign, as the world was pushed into war.

Mechanics tending to Raymond Mays's ERA in April 1938. Mays was the driving force behind the birth of ERA, and its successor as the all-British racing marque, BRM.

Mechaniker versorgen Raymond Mays' ERA im April 1938. Mays war die treibende Kraft hinter dem ERA-Rennstall und später hinter dessen Nachfolger, der ebenfalls rein britischen Marke BRM.

Des mécaniciens au travail sur l'ERA de Raymond Mays, en avril 1938. Mays était l'instigateur de la création de ERA et de BRM, la marque britannique de voitures de course qui lui succéda.

Die Grand-Prix-Rennen galten als Krone des Motorsports, auch wenn sie Anfang der dreißiger Jahre mit einer weitgehend freien Formel nicht hoch im Kurs standen. Das Ende des Jahrzehnts sah sie, politisch unterstützt, auf einem Höhepunkt technischer Brillanz. Die staatliche Förderung veränderte den gesamten Sport, doch nationale Ambitionen sorgten auch dafür, dass die Fahrer von neuem eine Zwangspause einlegen mussten, als ernstere Konflikte entstanden.

Am Anfang der dreißiger Jahre wandten sich die großen Firmen wieder verstärkt dem Sport zu, nachdem ihn einige Jahre lang vor allem Privatleute am Leben gehalten hatten. Nun traten wieder die Kontrahenten an, die auch in den Zwanzigern das Renngeschehen bestimmt hatten, wobei sich die französischen Bugattis gegen die etablierten Alfa Romeos sowie den italienischen Neuling Maserati behaupten mussten, dessen zahlreiche Siege in diesem Jahrzehnt den Anfang einer langen, erfolgreichen Rennkarriere begründeten. Die Rennwagen der späten Zwanziger und frühen Dreißiger waren noch unverkennbar Weiterentwicklungen des schmalen und hohen Bautyps vom Anfang der Dekade. Nun, wo der Grand Prix wieder ins Rampenlicht rückte (auch neue Länder, die Rennen ausrichteten, kamen hinzu), verschwanden die multifunktionalen Sportwagen, die auch Grand-Prix-Rennen fuhren, und der schlanke Monoposto wurde zur vorherrschenden Form.

Anfangs waren Motorgröße und Gewicht nicht festgelegt; Vorschriften gab es für Treibstoff und für die minimale Streckenlänge und Renndauer. 1931 schrieben die Regeln für einen Großen Preis eine Mindestdauer von zehn Stunden vor. 1932 betrug die Renndauer zwischen fünf und zehn Stunden, 1933 die Entfernung mindestens 500 Kilometer – und wenn man bedenkt, welche körperliche Anstrengung und Konzentration notwendig waren, die damaligen Wagen auf den schwierigen Strecken der Zeit ständig mit Höchsttempo zu fahren, war das noch immer eine gewaltige Herausforderung.

Inzwischen war jedem klar, dass in den höheren Sphären des Motorsports – bei Grand-Prix-Wagen, Sportwagen, sogar bei Weltrekordfahrzeugen – nicht mehr die Größe zählte, sondern die Konstruktion. Parallel zu den Großen Preisen hatte sich eine Reihe von Sportwagenrennen etabliert, Veranstaltungen wie Targa Florio, Mille Miglia, Tourist Trophy und – die berühmteste von allen – Le Mans hatten ihren festen Platz im Renngeschehen, und die dreißiger Jahre sahen überall in Europa dramatische Wettkämpfe zwischen Bentley, Alfa Romeo, Bugatti, Mercedes-Benz, Delahaye, MG und anderen, wobei Alfa Romeo meist die Nase vorn hatte. Beherrscht wurden die Rennen nun auch von den großen Fahrern wie Tazio Nuvolari, Achille Varzi und Rudi Caracciola.

Den Wettlauf um den Weltrekord führte zu Beginn und in der Mitte der dreißiger Jahre Malcolm Campbell mit seinen diversen Bluebird-Wagen an, die nun meist bei Railton gebaut wurden, mit Motoren von Napier oder Rolls-Royce. An die Stelle der übergroßen Rennwagen waren eigene Konstruktionen getreten, auch wenn zumindest in der ersten Hälfte des Jahrzehnts die Herkunft und das traditionelle Grundprinzip noch deutlich zu erkennen waren; der Unterschied lag in der rein physischen Größe und der Leistung der Kompressormotoren, die inzwischen fast alle aus dem Militärflugzeugbau kamen. Zu Anfang des Jahrzehnts hielt Henry Segrave den Rekord, den er Ende 1929 mit seinem Golden Arrow mit Napier-Motor aufgestellt hatte. Die Dreißiger begannen mit einem spektakulären Misserfolg, als Kaye Dons mit großer Publicity vorgestellter 2.000 PS starker Silver Bullet im Januar 1930 in Daytona Beach noch nicht einmal 290 km/h erreichte; er wurde in aller Stille eingemottet, doch andere hatten mehr Erfolg. Im Februar 1932 erreichte Campbell mit fast 254 mph (408,7 km/h) erstmals die 250-Meilen-Grenze, und mit 301,1 mph (484,5 km/h) war er im September 1935 der Erste, der schneller als dreihundert Meilen pro Stunde fuhr. Für solche Geschwindigkeiten wurde allmählich selbst der weitläufige Strand von Daytona zu klein. Campbell fuhr den 300-Meilen-Rekord erstmals in der Salzwüste von Bonneville in Utah, der noch für viele Jahre ein Ort für Rekordfahrten bleiben sollte. Dies war auch Campbells letzter Rekord an Land, denn von nun an wandte er sich Rennbooten zu, in denen er seine wahre Berufung fand.

Campbells letzte Bluebirds waren prachtvolle Maschinen, gigantisch im Maßstab, mit immer ausgeklügelterer Stromlinienform, aber mit ihrem Frontmotor und dem einzelnen Fahrersitz in der Mitte doch eindeutig Verwandte der Rennwagen. Die nächste Generation von Weltrekordwagen wandte sich jedoch von diesem Vorbild ab, etwa mit George Eystons achträdrigem Thunderbolt, dessen zwei Rolls-Royce-V12-Flugzeugmotoren zusammen 4800 PS hatten, und John Cobbs Railton-Mobil Special mit zwei 1250 PS starken aufgeladenen Napier-Lion-V12-Aggregaten, denn bei beiden saßen die Fahrer nun vor den Motoren, die Karosserien waren nach Methoden des Flugzeugbaus konstruiert – die Wagen näherten sich ja auch Flugzeuggeschwindigkeiten –, und unter der schnittigen Karosse steckte eine wesentlich ausgefeiltere Fahrwerkstechnik. Mit solchen Fahrzeugen schraubte Cobb im September 1938 den Rekord auf 563,5 Stundenkilometer, den ihm Eyston wenige Tage darauf mit 575,2 km/h wieder abjagte. Den letzten Rekord des Jahrzehnts stellte wiederum Cobb im August 1939 mit dem Railton-Mobil in Bonneville auf, 594,8 Stundenkilometer – doch diese Rekordwagen hatten mit den Sportfahrzeugen kaum noch etwas gemein.

Viele Weltrekordfahrer wetteiferten auch in einer Reihe kleinerer Rekorddisziplinen miteinander, in Wettbewerben für bestimmte Größenklassen oder sogar Marken, mit denen das Publikum sich dann leicht identifizieren konnte. Im Oktober 1935 stellte John Cobb in seinem 24-Liter-Napier-Railton-Einsitzer mit 230,7 km/h den letzten Rundenrekord von Brooklands auf und erreichte auch mit fast 245 Stundenkilometern die höchste Geschwindigkeit, die je auf dem legendären Rundkurs gefahren wurde. Auf geraden Strecken fuhren George Eyston und später Goldie Gardner mit einer langen Reihe von MG-Rekordwagen, den Magic Midgets, neue Bestzeiten über die verschiedensten Entfernungen; Höhepunkt war 1939 eine Fahrt auf der Autobahn Frankfurt–Dessau, wo Gardner mit einem nur 1100 Kubikzentimeter großen Kompressormotor unglaubliche 326,6 Stundenkilometer erreichte.

Die deutschen Autobahnen setzten erstmals die Idee einer Schnellverbindung zwischen den großen Städten um, eine der positiveren Leistungen der nationalsozialistischen Regierung, die 1933 an die Macht kam. Ein weiterer Einfluss, den der neue deutsche Staat auf den Motorsport nahm, machte sich in der zweiten Hälfte der dreißiger Jahre bei den Grand-Prix-Rennen bemerkbar, als die staatlich unterstützten Rennställe von Mercedes-Benz und Auto Union bald überall den Ton angaben und der Sport einen Höhepunkt erreichte, wie die Welt ihn noch nicht gesehen hatte – und auch, würde manch einer sagen, nie wieder sah.

In der Zeit der freien Formel zu Anfang des Jahrzehnts pendelte sich die Motorgröße der Grand-Prix-Wagen, nachdem die Hersteller mit vier und sogar fünf Litern Hubraum experimentiert hatten, bei etwa 3 Litern und 200 PS ein, Aluminiumkonstruktionen setzten sich durch, und die Wagen wurden kleiner und leichter und verließen sich eher auf ihre Fahrtüchtigkeit als auf große Leistung – all das zum Nutzen der Konstrukteure von Alltagsfahrzeugen, bei denen sich die

Neuerungen nach und nach durchsetzten. 1934 wurde eine neue internationale Formel eingeführt, bei der zwar die Motorleistung beliebig war, das Minimalgewicht jedoch 750 Kilogramm betrug; von nun an durften bei den Boxenstopps auch bis zu vier Mechaniker gleichzeitig an den Wagen arbeiten. Die neue Formel diente dem technischen Fortschritt, doch sie bevorzugte die Firmen mit den größten Ressourcen. Und da Adolf Hitler wusste, wie werbewirksam internationale Rennerfolge waren, hatte niemand größere Ressourcen als die Mannschaften von Mercedes-Benz und Auto Union.

Mit großen Budgets und Zugang zu Forschungs- und Entwicklungsstätten war die Diskrepanz zwischen hoher Motorleistung und niedrigem Gewicht kein Hindernis mehr. Mit neuartigen Materialien und genialen Konstruktionen konnten sie beides zugleich haben – enorm kraftvolle Motoren in vergleichsweise leichten Wagen mit den raffiniertesten Chassis, die der Sport bis dahin kannte. Binnen eines Jahres waren 400 PS möglich, Mercedes und Auto Union konnten beide mit Einzelradaufhängung vorn und hinten aufwarten, und der von Ferdinand Porsche konstruierte Auto-Union-Wagen hatte als erster Grand-Prix-Wagen den Motor hinter dem Fahrer. Bis zur nächsten Reglementsänderung fuhren die Deutschen mit Zwölf- und bei Auto Union sogar Sechzehnzylindern, deren Hubraum auf 6 Liter und mehr und deren Leistung auf bis zu 650 PS anstieg, womit Spitzengeschwindigkeiten von 320 Stundenkilometern möglich wurden. Diese Monstren waren nur mit Mühe zu bändigen, doch mit Könnern wie Caracciola, Nuvolari, Rosemeyer, Lang und Dick Seaman am Steuer ließen sie alle Konkurrenten hinter sich, und nur dann und wann schwang sich ein Alfa Romeo zum Drachentöter auf, was dieser spektakulären Ära des europäischen Motorsports noch umso mehr Glanz verlieh.

Als 1938 von neuem die Formel geändert und das Gewicht nun relativ zur Motorgröße festgelegt wurde, ging der Hubraum im Schnitt auf etwa 3 Liter bei einem Gewicht von 850 Kilogramm zurück, doch bald waren auch hier die Leistungen wieder bei 500 PS angelangt, und weitere Fortschritte in Chassis-, Radaufhängungs- und Kraftübertragungstechnik und Verbesserungen bei Reifen und in der Aerodynamik sorgten dafür, dass diese Kraft auf die Straße kam. Die deutschen Silberpfeile waren so gut wie unschlagbar, und schließlich waren es ihre eigenen Gönner, die dieser Glanzzeit des Motorsports ein Ende bereiteten und die Welt in einen neuen Krieg stürzten.

Manfred von Brauchitsch in the Mercedes-Benz Grand Prix car at Donington Park in 1937 – when the State-sponsored German teams, Mercedes and Auto Union, showed a new level of racing car to Britain.

Manfred von Brauchitsch im Mercedes-Benz-Grand-Prix-Wagen 1937 in Donington Park, wo die staatlich unterstützten Mannschaften von Mercedes und Auto Union den Briten Rennwagen vorführten, wie sie sie noch nie gesehen hatten.

Manfred von Brauchitsch dans sa Mercedes-Benz Grand Prix à Donington Park en 1937, à une époque où les écuries allemandes – Mercedes et Auto Union – financées par l'État présentaient à la Grande-Bretagne une nouvelle philosophie de la voiture de course.

La course en Grand Prix, considérée comme le nec plus ultra du sport automobile, entre dans les années 1930 à un niveau technique assez bas en raison de l'introduction des formules libres, qui ont peu d'intérêt du point de vue du spectacle et n'incitent guère les constructeurs à faire évoluer leurs voitures. Mais elle va cependant brillamment achever cette décennie en s'ouvrant de nouvelles perspectives technologiques grâce au soutien politique et économique de certains des États européens qui vont faire du sport automobile le porte-drapeau de leur nationalisme avant que les ambitions démesurées et conflictuelles de leurs gouvernants ne provoquent, pour la seconde fois du siècle, l'interruption de la compétition.

Après une période où les engagements privés ont dominé la course, les constructeurs retrouvent quelque intérêt au sport automobile à l'aube des années 1930. Une fois encore, les principaux protagonistes sont les marques qui ont régné à la fin des années 1920, les Bugatti françaises affrontant les italiennes Alfa Romeo et Maserati, un nouveau constructeur qui rencontre un succès considérable dès les débuts de sa longue histoire en course automobile. Ces voitures de sport des années 1920–1930 ont conservé un lien de parenté évident avec celles «à caisse haute» de la première génération. Toutefois, la propension à adopter des modèles polyvalents décline rapidement au profit de voitures monoplaces étudiées plus spécialement pour disputer les Grand Prix, qui ont retrouvé leur auréole passée de compétition majeure du sport automobile et sont accueillies désormais par un nombre croissant de pays.

Les premières années de la décennie consacrent une formule de Grand Prix assez libre, qui ne limite ni la capacité du moteur ni le poids des voitures mais réglemente le type de carburant utilisable ainsi que la distance ou la durée minimum des épreuves. Alors qu'en 1931, un Grand Prix doit se courir au moins sur dix heures, en 1932 cette durée est réduite entre cinq et dix heures ; en 1933, le critère change et il s'agit de parcourir au moins 500 km, ce qui relève encore de l'exploit étant donné l'effort mental et physique nécessaire pour piloter les bolides de l'époque sur des circuits très éprouvants.

Il est toutefois évident que le sport automobile, pratiqué à son plus haut niveau, doit autant à la technologie qu'à la dimension des moteurs, qu'il s'agisse de monoplaces de Grand Prix, de voitures de sport voire d'engins de record de vitesse. Les épreuves «Grand Tourisme» organisées en parallèle aux courses de Grand Prix – la Targa Florio, les Mille Miglia, le Tourist Trophy et, la plus célèbre de toutes, les 24 Heures du Mans – sont alors le cadre de luttes épiques entre des pilotes de la stature de Tazio Nuvolari, Achille Varzi ou Rudi Caracciola au volant de Bentley, Bugatti, Mercedes-Benz, Delahaye et MG, toutes souvent surclassées par Alfa Romeo.

En cette première moitié des années 1930, la conquête de la vitesse pure est dominée par Malcolm Campbell et ses Bluebird, la plupart construites par Railton avec des moteurs fournis soit par Napier soit par Rolls-Royce. Même si ces bolides conservent encore quelque temps l'allure de leurs ancêtres dans la silhouette et la mécanique, ils sont désormais moins imposants et disposent de moteurs suralimentés, presque tous dérivés de ceux des avions militaires. Alors que Henry Segrave détient depuis la fin de l'année 1929 le record de vitesse sur terre avec sa Golden Arrow à moteur Napier, le début de la décennie suivante est marqué par l'échec – d'autant plus retentissant que la tentative a été annoncée à grand renfort de publicité – de Kaye Don qui, avec sa Silver Bullet de 2000 ch, ne parvient pas à franchir la barrière des 180 mph (289,6 km/h) à Daytona Beach et décide alors de prendre tranquillement sa retraite. D'autres coureurs ont plus de réussite que lui. En février 1932, Campbell établit le record à près de 408,7 km/h avant de devenir, en septembre 1935, le premier homme de l'histoire à atteindre 484,5 km/h (250 miles). La vaste plage de Daytona Beach étant désormais trop petite pour les vitesses visées, et atteintes, Campbell décide de faire sa prochaine tentative dans le lit à sec du lac de Bonneville Salt Flats (Utah), qui restera désormais le site privilégié des records de vitesse sur terre. Ce sera également la dernière tentative de record terrestre de Campbell, qui va désormais courir sur l'eau où il réalisera d'autres exploits.

Les dernières Bluebird de Campbell, de splendides machines aux dimensions majestueuses et à l'aérodynamisme particulièrement étudié, restent toutefois encore très proches des voitures de course conventionnelles, avec leur moteur à l'avant et leur cockpit central monoplace. Cette configuration démodée est bientôt abandonnée pour les engins de record de vitesse de la génération suivante, comme la Thunderbolt à huit roues de George Eyston, propulsée par 2 aéromoteurs Rolls-Royce V12 fournissant une puissance de 4800 ch, ou la Railton-Mobil Special de John Cobb, équipée de 2 Napier Lion V12 suralimentés de 1250 ch ; les pilotes sont désormais assis en avant du moteur, la structure du châssis se complexifie et supporte une carrosserie légère et profilée, dont les principes d'aérodynamisme sont empruntés à l'aviation (les vitesses de ces voitures sont en effet proches de celles des avions). La mise en œuvre de telles technologies, assez éloignées de celle des voitures de course de l'époque, permet à Cobb d'atteindre 563,5 km/h en septembre 1938, un record que lui reprend Eyston quelques jours plus tard en roulant à 575,2 km/h, et que Cobb et sa Railton-Mobil Special repoussent finalement en août 1939 à Bonneville à 594,8 km/h.

La plupart de ces chasseurs de records s'attaquent aussi à d'autres performances, certes de moindre importance, dans différentes classes de cylindrée, voire se lancent pour certains dans la construction de voitures avec lesquelles le public peut immédiatement s'identifier. En octobre 1935, John Cobb s'approprie, à 230,7 km/h, le record du tour du circuit de Brooklands dans sa monoplace Napier-Railton, équipée d'un moteur de 25 litres de cylindrée, et enregistre en même temps, à près de 244,6 km/h, la vitesse de pointe la plus élevée jamais atteinte sur la célèbre piste. George Eyston puis Goldie Gardner enregistrent tour à tour une série de remarquables performances sur différentes distances en ligne droite au volant des Magic Midget de MG. Gardner finit par s'imposer en 1939 en atteignant 326,6 km/h avec une voiture à moteur de 1100 cm³ (suralimenté) sur l'autoroute Francfort–Dessau.

L'autoroute, concept alors moderne de voie rapide reliant entre elles les grandes villes, est sans doute l'une des réalisations les plus positives du nouveau gouvernement national-socialiste allemand au début des années 1930. C'est l'Allemagne qui va introduire une autre novation dans les courses de Grand Prix de la seconde moitié des années 1930, lorsque les écuries Mercedes-Benz et Auto Union, soutenues et financées par le gouvernement, vont provoquer un bouleversement de la réglementation des Grand Prix et faire rentrer le sport automobile dans une période jamais vue jusque là.

La formule étant libre au début de cette décennie 1930, les constructeurs de voitures de Grand Prix, après avoir sorti des machines de 4 et 5 litres de cylindrée (4000–5000 cm³), se mettent à étudier et à produire, grâce au développement des alliages légers, des moteurs plus petits, plus légers et au rendement plus efficace, généralement d'une capacité de 3 litres et développant une puissance au frein de près de 200 ch. Les progrès réalisés dans le domaine de la course automobile bénéficient évidemment à la mécanique plus simple de la voiture de Monsieur Tout-le-monde. En 1934, les instances du sport automobile international introduisent une formule qui,

tout en libérant la cylindrée du moteur, limite le poids de la voiture à 750 kg maximum et élève à quatre le nombre de mécaniciens autorisés à travailler sur chaque voiture lors des arrêts au stand. Si cette formule encourage l'innovation technique, elle favorise également, de par sa nature même, les marques disposant des plus gros moyens. Le chancelier Adolf Hitler, comprenant alors tout l'intérêt politique et de propagande que peut représenter une victoire dans les compétitions internationales, fait en sorte que Mercedes-Benz et Auto Union deviennent rapidement les meilleures écuries nationales.

Disposant de budgets colossaux et bénéficiant d'extraordinaires installations de recherche et de développement, les deux constructeurs allemands n'ont plus à se préoccuper de choisir entre cylindrée et poids puisque, disposant de matériaux nouveaux, de carburants exotiques et de concepteurs inspirés, ils peuvent innover en tirant profit du meilleur des deux mondes : des moteurs volumineux et très puissants propulsant des voitures relativement légères sur des châssis employant la technologie la plus sophistiquée. En l'espace d'un an, les Auto Union – dessinées par Ferdinand Porsche avec le moteur en arrière du pilote – et Mercedes-Benz bénéficient d'une puissance au frein de 400 ch et de suspensions à roues indépendantes. Le temps qu'apparaisse une nouvelle formule, les voitures allemandes sont pourvues de moteurs à 12 cylindres (voire à 16 cylindres pour Auto Union) d'une cylindrée souvent supérieure à 6 litres, délivrant une puissance de près de 650 ch permettant d'atteindre 322 km/h. Si ces bolides se révèlent délicats à conduire, des pilotes de génie comme Caracciola, Nuvolari, Rosemeyer, Lang ou Dick Seaman réduisent à néant toute opposition, malgré les efforts déployés par Alfa Romeo pour les battre. La lutte acharnée entre latines et allemandes fera de cette période la plus exceptionnelle qu'aura connue le sport automobile européen.

Lorsqu'une modification de la formule, en 1938, introduit une dégressivité du poids de la voiture en fonction de sa cylindrée, la plupart des constructeurs reviennent à une volumétrie de 3 litres pour un poids minimum de 850 kg. Cette réduction n'empêche pourtant pas d'atteindre des puissances en sortie de 500 ch, qu'autorisent de plus les récents développements sur le châssis, la suspension, la transmission, les pneumatiques et l'aérodynamique. Alors que les « flèches d'argent » de Mercedes-Benz et Auto Union deviennent presque imbattables en course, la guerre mondiale que déclenche leur principal promoteur met brutalement fin à leur règne spectaculaire.

To many people, Tazio Nuvolari, the former motorcycle racer from Mantua, was the greatest racing driver of all. In the 1930s he was both an Auto Union team member and, in other makes of car, one of the German teams' toughest challengers.

Wenn man nach dem größten Rennfahrer aller Zeiten fragte, würden viele Tazio Nuvolari nennen, der in Mantua zur Welt kam und seine Karriere auf Motorrädern begann. In den dreißiger Jahren gehörte er zur Auto-Union-Werksmannschaft, fuhr aber auch für andere Marken und trat dann als zähester Herausforderer seiner deutschen Teamkollegen auf.

Tazio Nuvolari, ancien coureur motocycliste de Mantoue, était pour beaucoup le plus grand pilote de tous. Dans les années 1930, il fut successivement pilote à Auto Union et l'un des plus rudes adversaires des écuries allemandes lorsqu'il conduisait pour d'autres marques.

The Bentley Le Mans legend

Its successes at Le Mans in the late 1920s and
early 1930s established Bentley as one
of the great sporting marques, and made
the race forever popular with the English.
Nineteen thirty brought the team's fifth and
final win, led by Glen Kidston and Woolf
Barnato (below). Clément's and Watney's
Bentley receives attention in the pits (above)
on its way to second place.

Bentleys Le-Mans-Legende

Der Le-Mans-Erfolg in den späten zwanziger
und frühen dreißiger Jahren machte Bentley
zu einer der angesehensten Sportwagenmarken. Das Rennen wuchs den Engländern
besonders ans Herz. Das Jahr 1930 bescherte
der Mannschaft ihren fünften und letzten
Sieg, eingefahren von Glen Kidston und Woolf
Barnato (unten). Der Bentley von Clément
und Watney bei einem Boxenstopp (oben),
auf dem Weg zum zweiten Platz.

La légende de la Bentley Le Mans

Ses succès au Mans à la fin des années 1920
et au début des années 1930 placent Bentley
parmi les grands constructeurs de voitures
de sport et rendent cette course à jamais
populaire en Grande-Bretagne. L'année 1930
est marquée par la cinquième et dernière
victoire de l'écurie, obtenue par Glen
Kidston et Woolf Barnato (ci-dessous).
La Bentley de Clément et Watney, en route
pour la seconde place, fait l'objet de tous les
soins dans les stands (en haut).

W.O.'s doubts justified

One of the supercharged Speed Six Bentleys rushes past the
Le Mans pits during the 1930 race. Five Bentleys were entered –
three Speed Sixes from the factory and two of the 4.5-litre
Blower cars from the Birkin-Paget stable. W.O. Bentley disliked
the supercharged cars, and in the event both failed, though not
before Birkin had broken the lap record, at 89.7mph.

W. O. hatte Recht

Ein aufgeladener Bentley Speed Six passiert beim Rennen von
Le Mans im Jahr 1930 die Boxen. Fünf Bentleys traten an –
drei Speed-Six-Werkswagen und zwei aufgeladene 4,5-Liter-
Modelle aus dem Birkin-Paget-Stall. W. O. Bentley mochte die
Kompressorwagen nicht, und beide fielen schließlich aus –
allerdings erst nachdem Birkin mit 144,3 km/h einen neuen
Rundenrekord aufgestellt hatte.

Les doutes de W. O. justifiés

L'une des Bentley Speed Six à moteur suralimenté passe
devant les stands du Mans lors de l'édition 1930 de l'épreuve.
Cinq Bentley étaient engagées dans la course : trois Speed Six
d'usine et deux Blower 4,5 litres de l'écurie Birkin-Paget.
W. O. Bentley n'aimait pas les moteurs suralimentés et ses
deux voitures abandonnèrent, après toutefois que Birkin a
pulvérisé le record de vitesse du circuit à 144,3 km/h.

Conflicting opinions

'Tim' Birkin in one of the 4.5-litre supercharged Bentleys (left), here in single-seater form for the 1931 Brooklands 500-mile race. Just four of the racing Blower cars were built (below, right) with backing from the Hon. Dorothy Paget, and they became the most famous Bentleys of them all, but they were never really successful in racing, and W.O. Bentley disliked them for their complexity. Bentley's arch rival Ettore Bugatti (below left, in bowler hat) was dismissive of all the heavyweight Bentleys.

Ansichtssache

»Tim« Birkin in einem 4,5-Liter-Kompressor-Bentley (links), hier als Einsitzer für das 500-Meilen-Rennen von Brooklands, 1931. Nur vier Kompressor-Rennwagen wurden mit finanzieller Unterstützung von Dorothy Paget gebaut (unten rechts), doch die »Blower-Bentleys« sollten Legende werden, auch wenn sie nie wirklich erfolgreich in Rennen waren und W. O. Bentley stets eine Abneigung gegen sie hatte, weil sie ihm zu kompliziert waren. Bentleys Erzrivale Ettore Bugatti (unten links, mit Melone) hatte für die wuchtigen Bentleys nur Verachtung übrig.

Des opinions contraires

« Tim » Birkin et l'une des Bentley à moteur 4,5 l suralimenté (à gauche), ici en version monoplace pour les 500 Miles de Brooklands. Les quatre seules Blower qui furent construites (en bas à droite), avec l'appui financier de Dorothy Paget, furent les plus célèbres Bentley de toutes, sans obtenir toutefois de véritable succès en course. W. O. Bentley ne les aimait pas en raison de leur complexité et son grand rival, Ettore Bugatti (en bas à gauche, en chapeau melon), se moquait de leur lourdeur.

The lighter approach

Bentley had been an engineer with the railways; Bugatti had no formal engineering training at all, but he had a superb eye for line and a natural instinct for strong and lightweight shapes. His cars were quite the opposite of the heavily-built Bentleys, and typified by the elegant simplicity and compact size of R.L. Bowes's car seen here at Brooklands in 1933.

Das Leichtgewicht

Bentley war ursprünglich Eisenbahningenieur; das Naturtalent Bugatti hatte auch ohne formelle Ausbildung einen sicheren Blick für elegante Linien und Gespür für leichte und trotzdem stabile Strukturen. Seine Wagen waren das genaue Gegenteil der bulligen Bentleys, und das Exemplar von R. L. Bowes, hier in Brooklands 1933, ist ein typisches Beispiel für den kompakten Aufbau und die schlichte Eleganz der Bugattis.

Une approche plus légère

Si Bentley avait été ingénieur des chemins de fer, Bugatti n'avait aucune formation technique mais possédait un coup d'œil remarquable pour la ligne et l'instinct des formes légères et puissantes. Ses voitures, à l'opposé des lourdes Bentley, se caractérisaient par leur élégante simplicité et leur compacité, à l'exemple de celle que pilotait R.L. Bowes à Brooklands en 1933.

Under starter's orders

The start of the Swiss Grand Prix (left) at Berne in 1936, with the grid dominated by the near invincible Mercedes and Auto Union Silver Arrows. This time Auto Union finished 1-2-3, led by Bernd Rosemeyer. The first international race at London's Crystal Palace circuit (above right), the Imperial Trophy, in October 1937, and Bugattis dominate the line-up behind a start at Avus, Berlin's famous track (below right).

Auf die Plätze!

Das Feld, das zum Start des Schweizer Grand Prix 1936 in Bern Aufstellung genommen hat (links), wird von den fast unschlagbaren Silberpfeilen von Mercedes und Auto Union beherrscht. In diesem Falle endete das Rennen mit einem Auto-Union-Dreifachsieg, mit Bernd Rosemeyer an der Spitze. Als erste internationale Veranstaltung auf dem Crystal-Palace-Kurs in London fand im Oktober 1937 die Imperial Trophy statt (rechts oben); beim Start auf der berühmten Berliner Avus (rechts unten) dominieren die Bugattis.

Aux ordres du starter

La grille de départ du Grand Prix de Suisse (à gauche), organisé à Berne en 1936, est dominée par les quasi invincibles Flèches d'argent de Mercedes et Auto Union, qui prennent les trois premières places, Bernd Rosemeyer en tête. La première course internationale sur le circuit du Crystal Palace de Londres, l'Imperial Trophy, est organisée en octobre 1937 (en haut à droite). Les Bugatti s'apprêtent à prendre le départ de l'épreuve suivante sur le circuit d'Avus, la célèbre piste de Berlin (en bas à droite).

Fresh from the workshop

In February 1932 George Eyston (in white racing overalls) went to MG's Abingdon factory to collect his newly-finished Midget record-breaker, EX127, watched by almost the entire workforce. He would take the supercharged 750cc car to Pendine Sands a few days later to attack various class records, and to achieve 118.4mph – a big step on the way to MG's target of 120mph.

Frisch von der Werkbank

Im Februar 1932 kam George Eyston (im weißen Renndress) zu den MG-Werken in Abingdon, um seinen Midget-Rekordwagen abzuholen, den EX127, wobei ihn die Belegschaft begrüßte. Kurz darauf begann er auf der Strandpiste von Pendine mit dem 750-ccm-Kompressorwagen seine Rekordjagd und kam mit 118,4 mph (190,5 km/h) der angestrebten 120-Meilen-Marke schon sehr nah.

Fraîchement sorties de l'atelier

En février 1932, George Eyston (en combinaison blanche) vient à l'usine MG d'Abingdon prendre livraison sous les yeux de presque tous les ouvriers de sa toute nouvelle Midget, la EX127. C'est avec cette voiture à moteur suralimenté de 750 cm³ de cylindrée qu'il allait s'attaquer, à Pendine Sands quelques jours plus tard, à différents records de vitesse et atteindre 190,5 km/h, une première grande étape vers l'objectif des 193 km/h.

Record-breakers and racers

Eyston (left, showing off the 1932 record-breaker's engine) was a large man, and EX127 was designed to be the most compact shape that MG could build around him (above left). That involved offsetting the driver slightly from the centre line, so the transmission could pass alongside rather than below him. The 6-cylinder MG Magnette, which Eyston raced in 1934 (above right), was a rather more conventional shape, but just as successful in its own field.

Renn- und Rekordwagen

Eyston (der hier, links, den Motor des Rekordwagens von 1932 präsentiert) war ein Hüne, und der EX127 war maßgeschneidert, sodass er in die kompakte Form gerade noch hineinpaßte (oben links). Der Fahrer musste ein wenig seitlich versetzt sitzen, damit die Kardanwelle an ihm vorbei statt unter ihm hindurch geführt werden konnte. Im Vergleich dazu war der MG-Magnette-Sechszylinder, in dem Eyston 1934 zu Rennen antrat (oben rechts), eine konventionelle Konstruktion, doch auf ihrem Feld nicht minder erfolgreich.

Briseurs de records et bolides

Eyston (en bas à gauche, montrant le moteur de la EX127 de 1932 avec laquelle il battit plusieurs records) étant très grand, il fallut que MG conçoive une voiture en fonction de sa taille qui reste la plus compacte possible (en haut à gauche). Il fallait alors notamment décaler légèrement le pilote par rapport à l'axe central pour que la transmission puisse passer à côté du siège et non dessous. La Magnette MG six cylindres avec laquelle Eyston courut en 1934 (en haut à droite), malgré une silhouette plus conventionnelle, eut également du succès dans sa catégorie.

A speeding bullet

Kaye Don in the cockpit of the Silver Bullet, designed by Louis Coatalen and built by Sunbeam. The 2,000hp aero-engined car was a very sophisticated design, and one of the most expensive record challengers built up to that time, but it never fulfilled its promise. Don reached only 183mph at Daytona in 1930, when the record was already 231.4mph, and the car never ran again.

Das silberne Geschoss

Kaye Don im Cockpit des Silver Bullet, entworfen von Louis Coatalen und gebaut von Sunbeam. Der Wagen mit seinem 2000-PS-Flugzeugmotor war äußerst aufwändig konstruiert und zählte zu den teuersten Rekordfahrzeugen seiner Zeit, doch er hielt nie, was er versprach. Don erreichte mit ihm 1930 in Daytona nur 294,4 km/h, zu einer Zeit, als der Weltrekord schon bei 372,3 Stundenkilometern stand. Der Wagen trat nie wieder an.

Rapide comme une balle

Kaye Don dans le cockpit de sa Silver Bullet, dessinée par Louis Coatalen et construite par Sunbeam. Pourvue d'un aéromoteur de 2000 ch, cette voiture d'une conception très sophistiquée fut l'une des prétendantes au titre de champion du monde de vitesse les plus chères construites à cette époque. Elle ne remplit jamais ses promesses. Si Don atteignit bien 294,4 km/h à Daytona en 1930, le record était déjà établi à 372,3 km/h. La voiture ne courut jamais plus.

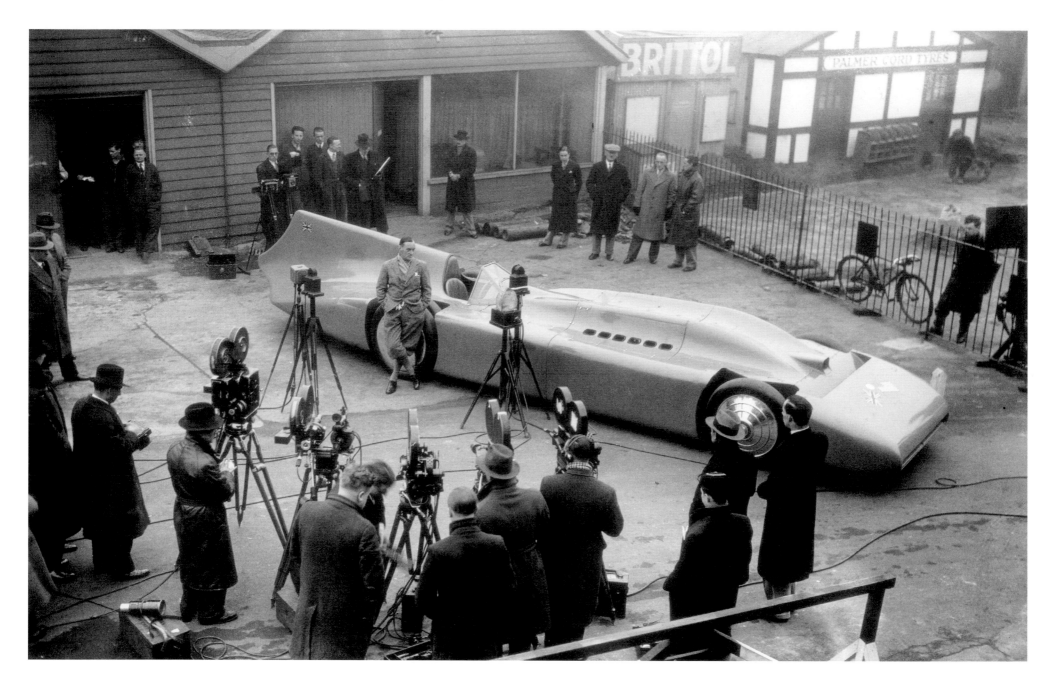

A more successful challenger

Malcolm Campbell poses for the cameras in January 1935 with
his new Bluebird, outside his base at Brooklands, where the
Rolls-Royce-powered car was built by Thomson and Taylor.
It was Campbell's final land speed record challenger and he
used it first at Daytona, then at Bonneville, to take the record to
276.9mph, and then for the first time past 300, to 301.1mph.

Ein erfolgreicherer Kandidat

Im Januar 1935 präsentiert Malcolm Campbell den Kameras
seinen neuen Bluebird. Er steht vor seiner Werkstatt in Brooklands, wo Thomson and Taylor den von einem Rolls-Royce-
Motor getriebenen Boliden gebaut hatte. Es war Campbells
letzter Weltrekordwagen, und er brachte den Rekord damit
in Daytona, später in Bonneville, zunächst auf 445,5 km/h,
dann auf 484,5 km/h oder 301,1 mph – die 300-Meilen-Grenze
war durchbrochen.

Un candidat plus heureux

Malcolm Campbell pose en janvier 1935 avec sa nouvelle
Bluebird devant ses ateliers de Brooklands, où la voiture
équipée d'un moteur Rolls-Royce avait été construite par
Thomson et Taylor. Ce fut la dernière voiture de record de
vitesse sur terre de Campbell, qui la pilota à Daytona puis à
Bonneville où il porta d'abord le record à 445,5 km/h avant
de dépasser pour la première fois les 300 miles/h (483 km/h)
à 484,5 km/h.

Speed on the track

In April 1932 Brooklands ran what was labelled the world's fastest car race. It was a match race for the fastest cars of the day and brought together John Cobb's V12 Delage and Birkin's single-seat Blower Bentley, which ultimately lapped at 158mph, for a purse of 100 sovereigns. Birkin and the Bentley (number 46) won the challenge by just one fifth of a second.

Geballtes Tempo

Im April 1932 kündigte Brooklands das schnellste Rennen der Welt an. Es war eine Wettfahrt zwischen den damals besten Rennwagen, bei der Größen wie John Cobbs V12-Delage und Birkins einsitziger Blower-Bentley gegeneinander antraten; dem Sieger winkte ein Preis von 100 Sovereigns. Birkin und der Bentley (Nummer 46) gewannen das Rennen mit einer schnellsten Runde von 222 km/h und einem Vorsprung von nur einer Fünftelsekunde.

Vitesse sur piste

Brooklands organisa en avril 1932 ce qui a été appelé la course des voitures les plus rapides du monde. Elle réunissait notamment la Delage V12 de John Cobb et la monoplace Blower Bentley de Birkin (numéro 46) qui, remportant l'épreuve d'un cinquième de seconde, boucla finalement le tour de circuit à 222 km/h et toucha la prime de 100 souverains.

Creating a monster

In August 1937 the car which would become George Eyston's sensational Thunderbolt was under construction in conditions of great secrecy. The huge car had six wheels, with four of them steering, and two Rolls-Royce V12 aero-engines, giving a total of 4,800hp. Thunderbolt took its first record at Bonneville in November 1937, at 312.0mph, and by September 1938, after a duel with John Cobb, had raised it to 357.5mph.

Ein Ungeheuer entsteht

Im August 1937 nahm unter großer Geheimhaltung George Eystons sensationeller Thunderbolt Gestalt an. Das monströse Gefährt hatte sechs Räder, vier davon lenkbar, und zwei Rolls-Royce-V12-Flugzeugmotoren mit zusammen 4800 PS. Im November 1937 errang der Thunderbolt in Bonneville mit 502 km/h seinen ersten Rekord. Im Duell mit John Cobb steigerte Eyston den Spitzenwert im September 1938 bis auf 575,2 Stundenkilometer.

La création d'un monstre

En août 1937, la voiture qui allait devenir la sensationnelle Thunderbolt de George Eyston est en cours de construction dans le plus grand secret. Cet énorme bolide disposait de six roues, dont quatre directrices, et de deux aéromoteurs Rolls-Royce V12 fournissant 4800 ch. C'est en novembre 1937 à Bonneville que la Thunderbolt s'adjuge son premier record à la vitesse de 502 km/h avant d'atteindre 575,2 km/h en septembre 1938, après un duel face à John Cobb.

Close to the action

S.C.H. 'Sammy' Davis races through the streets during the 1935 Tourist Trophy, where the buildings were rather better protected than some of the spectators. Davis was a motoring writer and a technical illustrator as well as a very fine racing driver, but this time his luck was out. His Singer crashed out of the race when its steering failed; his team-mates had similar problems.

An vorderster Front

S. C. H. »Sammy« Davis braust auf der Tourist Trophy von 1935 durch die Straßen, in denen die Häuser besser geschützt waren als manche Zuschauer. Davis war nicht nur ein begabter Rennfahrer, sondern dazu Motorsportjournalist und technischer Illustrator; diesmal hatte er allerdings kein Glück. Nach einem Lenkungsschaden baute er mit seinem Singer einen Unfall und musste aufgeben; seine Stallgefährten hatten ähnliche Schwierigkeiten.

Proche de l'action

Lors du Tourist Trophy de 1935, S. C. H. « Sammy » Davis traverse les rues d'un village, dont les immeubles semblent presque mieux protégés que certains spectateurs. Écrivain automobile et illustrateur technique, Davis était aussi un très bon pilote de course. La chance n'était pas avec lui cette fois-ci car, à l'instar de ses coéquipiers, il perdit le contrôle de sa Singer à la suite d'une rupture de direction et abandonna.

In Dublin's fair city

Ireland was not only home to the Tourist Trophy in the 1920s and 1930s, it also hosted other major races, including the Irish Grand Prix, and the Saorstát Cup which supported it, in this case the 1930 event on a circuit in Phoenix Park, Dublin. The 1930 Cup was won by Victor Gillow's Riley, the Grand Prix by Caracciola's Mercedes, in another wet-weather *tour de force*.

Stippvisite in Dublin

Irland richtete in den zwanziger und dreißiger Jahren nicht nur viele Tourist-Trophy-Rennen aus, sondern auch andere, darunter den Großen Preis von Irland und in dessen Rahmenprogramm den Saorstát Cup, hier 1930 auf einer Strecke im Dubliner Phoenix Park. Das Rennen gewann Victor Gillow auf Riley, den Grand Prix Mercedes-Pilot Caracciola, der wieder einmal seine Talente als Regenmeister zeigen konnte.

Dans la belle ville de Dublin

L'Irlande a accueilli non seulement le Tourist Trophy dans les années 1920 et 1930 mais aussi d'autres grandes courses, dont le Grand Prix d'Irlande et la coupe Saorstát, dont les éditions 1930 furent disputées sur un circuit aménagé dans Phoenix Park à Dublin. Cette épreuve fut remportée par Victor Gillow avec une Riley et le Grand Prix par Caracciola sur Mercedes, réussissant un tour de force de pilotage par temps pluvieux.

England versus Italy

The start of the 1930 Tourist Trophy at Ards, Belfast, saw four 4.5-litre Bentleys (including three of the supercharged cars) lined up against three supercharged 1750cc Alfa Romeos, which enjoyed a one-lap handicapping advantage. The Alfa trio of Campari, Nuvolari and Varzi promised to dominate the race and did so – but was challenged hard by Birkin's Bentley. Birkin crashed heavily in the wet; Nuvolari, Campari and Varzi finished 1-2-3.

England kontra Italien

Der Start zur 1930er Tourist Trophy in Ards, Belfast, wo vier 4,5-Liter-Bentleys (darunter drei mit Kompressor) gegen drei Alfa Romeos antraten, die mit ihren aufgeladenen 1750-ccm-Motoren beim Handicap mit einer Runde Vorsprung angesetzt wurden. Die drei Alfa-Fahrer Campari, Nuvolari und Varzi gingen als Favoriten ins Rennen, doch Birkin machte ihnen mit seinem Bentley das Leben schwer, bis er auf nasser Strecke schwer verunglückte. Nuvolari, Campari und Varzi belegten die ersten drei Plätze.

L'Angleterre contre l'Italie

Le départ du Tourist Trophy de 1930 à Ards, près de Belfast, voit s'aligner des Bentley de 4,5 litres (dont trois à moteur suralimenté) contre trois Alfa Romeo à moteur suralimenté de 1750 cm³, qui bénéficiaient d'un handicap d'un tour d'avance. Le trio Alfa – Campari, Nuvolari et Varzi – domina la course comme prévu malgré la forte concurrence de la Bentley de Birkin. Birkin subit un grave accident sous la pluie, laissant Nuvolari, Campari et Varzi terminer aux trois premières places.

Heroes of the age

The Tourist Trophy races attracted most of the finest drivers in the world. After his 1930 victory, Nuvolari is held aloft by a group which includes his Alfa Romeo team-mates Achille Varzi (front row with cigarette) and Giuseppe Campari (in overalls on the right). The trio had dominated both the 2-litre class and the race overall, to take the first three places.

Helden ihrer Zeit

Die Tourist-Trophy-Rennen lockten die weltweit besten Fahrer an. Nach seinem Sieg von 1930 wird Nuvolari auf die Schultern gehoben, im Vordergrund seine Alfa-Romeo-Teamkollegen Achille Varzi (mit Zigarette) und Giuseppe Campari (rechts, im Overall). Das Trio hatte die Zweiliterklasse und das gesamte Rennen beherrscht und die ersten drei Plätze erobert.

Les héros d'une époque

Les courses du Tourist Trophy attiraient la plupart des plus grands pilotes du monde. Après sa victoire de l'édition 1930, Nuvolari est porté sur les épaules de ses coéquipiers chez Alfa Romeo : Achille Varzi (au premier plan, avec une cigarette) et Giuseppe Campari (en combinaison à droite). Le trio a dominé non seulement toute la course, s'emparant des trois premières places, mais également la catégorie des voitures à moteur 2 l.

Mercedes' rainmaster

Whatever the weather, Rudi Caracciola was a hard man to beat, but when it rained he was virtually uncatchable, and earned the nickname 'Der Regenmeister' – 'the Rainmaster'. In 1930 he won the Irish Grand Prix (above) in his Mercedes SSK after a fine battle with Birkin's Bentley in the rain – supported by his wife Charly (on pit counter, right), who sadly died in a skiing accident soon after this photograph was taken.

Mercedes' Regenmeister

Rudi Caracciola war auch bei gutem Wetter nicht leicht zu schlagen, doch sobald der Regen kam, fuhr er allen anderen davon und erwarb sich so seinen Spitznamen »der Regenmeister«. 1930 siegte er mit seinem Mercedes SSK nach einem dramatischen Rennen im Regen gegen Birkins Bentley im Großen Preis von Irland (oben) – angefeuert von seiner Frau Charly (rechts, auf der Werkbank der Boxen), die leider kurz darauf bei einem Skiunfall ums Leben kam.

Mercedes et le maître de la pluie

Rudi Caracciola était déjà un homme difficile à battre quel que soit le temps mais, dès qu'il pleuvait, il devenait pratiquement invincible, ce qui lui valait le surnom de « Regenmeister » – le « maître de la pluie ». En 1930, il remporte le Grand Prix d'Irlande (ci-dessus) dans sa Mercedes SSK après une belle bataille sous la pluie contre la Bentley de Birkin – soutenu par son épouse Charly (assise au bord des stands, à droite), qui mourut dans un accident de ski peu après que cette photographie a été prise.

Challenging the men

Kay Petre (opposite, right) was badly injured in an accident at Brooklands in September 1937 but by March 1938 she was back in action, testing in her Riley (opposite, above) before her return to competition. Fay Taylour (opposite, below) raced an Alfa Romeo Monza in 1938, and Margaret Allan is airborne on the banking in 1936 with Richard Marker's Bentley (above).

Die Herausforderinnen

Kay Petre (gegenüber, rechts) trug bei einem Unfall in Brooklands im September 1937 schwere Verletzungen davon, doch im März 1938 war sie wieder dabei und trainierte in ihrem Riley (gegenüber, oben), bevor sie ins Renngeschehen zurückkehrte. Fay Taylour (gegenüber, unten) startete 1938 mit einem Alfa Romeo Monza; Margaret Allan (oben) hebt 1936 mit Richard Markers Bentley in der Steilkurve ab.

Défier les hommes

Kay Petre (ci-contre à droite), gravement blessée dans un accident à Brooklands en septembre 1937, revient dès mars 1938 pour essayer sa Riley (ci-contre en haut) avant de reprendre la compétition. Margaret Allan s'envole en 1936 sur un virage dans la Bentley de Richard Marker (ci-dessus) alors que Fay Taylour court en 1938 sur une Alfa Romeo Monza (ci-contre en bas).

Raising the dust
Stripped Austin Seven Specials (above) racing on a dirt track laid out on the plains in the shadow of Table Mountain, near Cape Town, in 1932; and England's slightly cruder version of an American icon – midget racing cars (below) on a dirt oval at Lea Bridge Stadium in east London, where English and French drivers contested a series of short circuit races in 1935.

Ordentlich Staub aufwirbeln
Abgemagerte Rennversionen des Austin Seven (oben) 1932 nahe Kapstadt auf einer Staubpiste im Schatten des Tafelbergs; und Englands ein wenig gröbere Variante eines typisch amerikanischen Vergnügens – Miniaturrennwagen (unten) auf einem unbefestigten Oval im Ostlondoner Lea-Bridge-Stadion, wo englische und französische Fahrer sich 1935 in einer Reihe kurzer Rundstreckenrennen maßen.

Dans la poussière
Ces Austin Seven Special assez dépouillées courent sur une piste en terre aménagée dans la plaine à l'ombre de la montagne de la Table, près du Cap, en 1932 (en haut). En Angleterre, c'est sur une version légèrement plus rudimentaire d'une icône américaine – la Midget de course (en bas) – que pilotes anglais et français s'affrontent en 1935 sur un ovale en terre créé dans le Lea Bridge Stadium, à l'est de Londres.

Mystery motor...

The period is the early 1930s, the track is undoubtedly one of America's many ovals, and the original caption says only 'a rocket car shows its paces on a race track with smoke billowing from the exhaust.' Whoever was at the wheel and whatever the car was, both seem to have disappeared from the records, leaving no more than that cloud of vapour.

Rätsel auf vier Rädern

Das Bild stammt aus den frühen Dreißigern und dürfte auf einem der vielen amerikanischen Rundkurse aufgenommen sein; die ursprüngliche Legende lautet: »Ein Raketenwagen zeigt auf der Rennstrecke, was er kann, und der Rauch quillt ihm nur so aus dem Auspuff«. Wer am Steuer saß und um was für einen Wagen es sich handelte, weiß offenbar niemand mehr – Motorsportgeschichte, die in einer großen Qualmwolke verpufft.

Une mystérieuse voiture ...

Si nous sommes au début des années 1930 et sur une piste qui est indubitablement un des nombreux ovales des États-Unis, la légende originale indique seulement : « une voiture fusée, le pot d'échappement fumant, procède à des essais sur une piste de course. » Le pilote au volant et le nom de sa voiture semblent avoir disparu des archives en ne laissant qu'un nuage de vapeur.

Around the houses

No form of motor sport is more dramatic than street racing. (Opposite, clockwise from top left) Bugatti leads Alfa in the Monaco Grand Prix, 1934; Piero Taruffi leads Luigi Fagioli in the Coppa Acerbo, Pescara, 1933; Prince Bira, with Frazer-Nash in the 1936 Tourist Trophy; and winning for ERA on the Isle of Man in 1937. (Above) Dick Seaman's Delage, an Isle of Man winner in 1936.

Zwischen den Häusern

Die dramatischste Form des Motorsports ist das Straßenrennen. (Gegenüber, im Uhrzeigersinn von oben links) Bugatti in Führung vor Alfa, Großer Preis von Monaco, 1934; Piero Taruffi vor Luigi Fagioli bei der Coppa Acerbo, Pescara, 1933; Prinz Bira bei der Tourist Trophy auf der Isle of Man, 1936 auf Frazer-Nash und 1937 im siegreichen ERA. (Oben) Dick Seaman mit seinem Delage, mit dem er die TT von 1936 gewann.

Autour des maisons

La course en ville est le type d'épreuve automobile le plus spectaculaire. (Ci-contre, dans le sens des aiguilles d'une montre à partir du haut à gauche) Bugatti mène devant Alfa lors du Grand Prix de Monaco de 1934 ; Taruffi devance Fagioli dans la Coppa Acerbo, 1933 ; le prince Bira, avec sa Frazer-Nash lors du Tourist Trophy de 1936, et vainqueur sur ERA sur l'île de Man en 1937. (Ci-dessus) La Delage de Seaman, vainqueur à Man en 1936.

Bringing motor racing into the home

Crystal Palace, in the south-eastern suburbs of London, took its name from the famous landmark which overlooked the area until it was destroyed by fire in 1936, creating the opportunity for a race circuit on the site of an earlier motorcycle speedway track. The new Crystal Palace circuit held its first car races in April 1937, and its first international race in October 1937 – which the BBC chose for its first motor racing outside broadcast.

Motorsport fürs Wohnzimmer

Die Rennstrecke von Crystal Palace in den südöstlichen Vororten von London war nach dem berühmten Glaspalast benannt, der die Gegend geprägt hatte, bis er 1936 abbrannte – was die Möglichkeit schuf, das vorhandene Motodrom zu einem größeren Rundkurs auszubauen. Im April 1937 fanden die ersten Automobilrennen auf dem neuen Crystal-Palace-Kurs statt, das erste internationale Rennen im Oktober 1937, und erstmals übertrug die BBC live von einer Motorsportveranstaltung.

Ramener la course automobile chez soi

Le circuit de Crystal Palace, dans la banlieue sud-est de Londres, doit son nom au célèbre bâtiment qui dominait l'endroit jusqu'à sa destruction dans un incendie en 1936. L'espace laissé vacant permit alors de créer un circuit automobile à l'emplacement d'une précédente piste pour motoclettes. Les premières épreuves s'y déroulèrent en avril 1937 et la première course internationale en octobre 1937 – occasion pour la BBC de réaliser sa première diffusion télévisée d'une compétition automobile en extérieur.

Wide open spaces

One thing Brooklands had in abundance was room for very large grids, in this case for the 'Double Twelve' in May 1930 (opposite). The Double Twelve format – of two twelve-hour 'heats' – was Brooklands' alternative to the true twenty-four-hour race. Night racing was not allowed and the track's proximity to residential areas also demanded special silencers on even the most serious racing cars. The Bentley team were out in force for the race (above and below right), were prominent from the start, and Woolf Barnato's (number 2) won the race.

Freiheit und Abenteuer

Ein besonderer Vorteil von Brooklands war, dass es nie an Platz für sehr große Startfelder mangelte, wie hier (gegenüber) beim Start zum »Doppelzwölf-Rennen« von 1930. Dieser Typ – zwei Läufe zu jeweils zwölf Stunden – war Brooklands' Alternative zu den 24-Stunden-Rennen. Nachtrennen waren verboten, und wegen der Nähe zu Wohngebieten mussten selbst die schweren Rennwagen mit Schalldämpfern fahren. Die Bentley-Mannschaft war bei dem Rennen zahlreich vertreten (rechts oben und unten) und dominierte es von Anfang an, und Woolf Barnato (Nummer 2) ging als Sieger ins Ziel.

De grands espaces ouverts

Brooklands avait l'avantage d'offrir beaucoup de place sur la grille de départ, souvent très remplie comme lors de l'épreuve du « Double Twelve » de mai 1930 (ci-contre). Le format de cette compétition – deux épreuves « éliminatoires » de douze heures – était l'alternative à la véritable course de 24 heures que proposait Brooklands. L'interdiction de courir en nocturne et la proximité de quartiers résidentiels nécessitaient également la pose de silencieux spéciaux sur les voitures de course. L'écurie Bentley, sortie en force (en haut et en bas à droite), domina dès le départ une course remportée par Woolf Barnato (numéro 2).

Sporting variations

International racing aside, motor sport has always had other opportunities. L.F. Robson's MG (above) on a test during a British rally in the mid-1930s; H. Hodgson and R.H.G. Robinson (opposite, above) both in Rileys on Southport Sands in 1937; John Bolster's Bloody Mary Special (opposite, below right) at Crystal Palace, and racing in a blizzard (opposite, below left) for a Talbot and an Austin on Birkdale Sands in 1931.

Sportliche Vielfalt

Neben internationalen Rennen hatte der Motorsport seit jeher viele Varianten zu bieten. L. F. Robsons MG (oben) bei einer Rallye um 1935; H. Hodgson und R. H. G. Robinson (gegenüber, oben) in zwei Rileys am Strand von Southport, 1937; John Bolster in seiner Bloody Mary Special (gegenüber, unten rechts), Crystal Palace; (gegenüber, unten links) ein Talbot und ein Austin im Schneesturm am Strand von Birkdale, 1931.

Variations sportives

Le sport automobile a toujours trouvé des lieux où s'exprimer en dehors des courses internationales : la MG de L. F. Robson lors d'un rallye vers 1935 (ci-dessus) ; H. Hodgson et R. H. G. Robinson, sur Riley, à Southport Sands en 1937 (ci-contre, en haut) ; la Bloody Mary Special de John Bolster à Crystal Palace (ci-contre, en bas à droite), et une Talbot et une Austin dans le blizzard à Birkdale Sands en 1931 (ci-contre, en bas à gauche).

Safety Fast

MG, with the motto 'Safety Fast', became one of Britain's most accessible sporting marques in the 1920s and 1930s, and its motor sport successes created a world-wide market that lasted many decades beyond that. MG's sports cars were at home in every level of motor sport from club trial to full international, including (above) the Midget against an Austin Special at the Brighton Speed Trials in 1932, and (below) T.L. Moss's Magna, winning the 15-mile race at Southport Sands in 1933.

Safety Fast

Mit seinem Wahlspruch »Safety Fast« entwickelte MG sich in den zwanziger und dreißiger Jahren zu einer der beliebtesten britischen Sportwagenmarken, und die Sporterfolge eröffneten ihr einen weltweiten Markt, der noch über Jahrzehnte florierte. MGs traten in allen Kategorien an, vom Amateurwettbewerb bis zum internationalen Rennen; zwei Beispiele sind der Midget (oben) im Wettstreit mit einem Austin Special bei den Brighton Speed Trials von 1932 und (unten) T. L. Moss' Magna, Sieger im 15-Meilen-Rennen von Southport Sands im Jahr 1933.

Safety Fast

C'est dans les années 1920-1930 que MG, dont la devise est la « Safety Fast » (« Vitesse Sûre »), devint l'une des marques britanniques de voitures de sport les plus abordables, dont les succès en sport automobile lui ouvrirent pendant plusieurs décennies le marché mondial. Les MG étaient à l'aise dans toutes les catégories, depuis les concours de club jusqu'aux compétitions internationales, comme le démontrent cette Midget opposée à une Austin Special lors des Brighton Speed Trials de 1932 (en haut), ou la Magna de T. L. Moss gagnant l'épreuve des 24 km de Southport Sands en 1933 (en bas).

The man behind the marque

Cecil Kimber, the man who created MG, was a great supporter of its motor sporting activities. In 1931 (above) he congratulates the Earl of March and co-driver Chris Staniland (nearest camera) after they had won the Brooklands Double Twelve in their C-Type MG Midget. MG attracted some fine drivers, including future Mercedes Grand Prix star Dick Seaman (below) who won his class and finished tenth overall with this MG Magnette in the 1935 Tourist Trophy.

Der Mann hinter der Marke

Cecil Kimber, der Mann, der MG groß machte, unterstützte das Rennengagement der Firma mit Begeisterung. 1931 (oben) gratuliert er dem Earl of March und seinem Kopiloten Chris Staniland (vorne) zum Sieg im Brooklands Double Twelve, den sie mit einem MG Midget Typ C errangen. MG konnte eine Reihe erstklassiger Fahrer verpflichten, darunter den späteren Mercedes-Grand-Prix-Star Dick Seaman (unten), der bei der Tourist Trophy von 1935 mit der MG Magnette seine Klasse gewann und Zehnter in der Gesamtwertung wurde.

L'homme de la marque

Cecil Kimber, le fondateur de MG, soutenait particulièrement l'activité sportive de sa firme. On le voit ainsi féliciter le comte de March et son copilote Chris Staniland (le plus proche de la caméra) après leur victoire dans l'édition 1931 du Double Twelve de Brooklands avec leur MG Midget Type C (en haut). MG engagea plusieurs bons pilotes, dont Dick Seaman (en bas), le futur pilote vedette de Mercedes en Grand Prix, qui remporta sa catégorie et termina dixième au classement général avec sa MG Magnette lors du Tourist Trophy de 1935.

High diving and low flying

Brooke's supercharged single-seater (opposite, far left) and
George Abecassis's Alta (opposite, above) came close to taking
a dip in the Crystal Palace lake in 1937 and 1938 respectively.
Freddie Dixon's Riley (opposite, below) flies through a hedge,
without great harm to either, during the 1932 Tourist Trophy,
but Sammy Davis was badly injured after crashing his Invicta
at Brooklands (above) in 1931.

Kopfsprung und Tiefflug

Brookes einsitziger Kompressorwagen (gegenüber, ganz links)
und George Abecassis' Alta (gegenüber, oben) entgingen 1937
bzw. 1938 nur knapp einem Bad im See von Crystal Palace.
Freddie Dixons Riley (gegenüber, unten) nimmt bei der Tourist
Trophy von 1932 eine Hecke im Flug, beide überstanden es ohne
größeren Schaden – anders als Sammy Davis, der mit seinem
Invicta (oben) 1931 in Brooklands einen schweren Unfall hatte.

Envols et plongeons

La monoplace suralimentée de Brooke (ci-contre, extrême
gauche) et l'Alta de George Abecassis (ci-contre, en haut) ont
manqué de peu leur plongeon dans le lac du Crystal Palace en
1937 et 1938. Si la Riley de Freddie Dixon survole une haie, sans
grand mal, lors du Tourist Trophy de 1932 (ci-contre, en bas),
Sammy Davis se blessa grièvement à Brooklands en 1931 dans
l'accident de son Invicta (ci-dessus).

The talented Prince from Siam
Raymond Mays congratulates fellow ERA driver B. Bira who had beaten him into second place in the Brooklands International Trophy in May 1936. B. Bira was the racing name of Prince Birabongse, a nephew of the King of Siam, who took up racing after his older cousin, Chula, presented him with an MG Magna in the early 1930s – and he raced into the 1950s.

Ein begabter Prinz aus Siam
Raymond Mays gratuliert seinem ERA-Teamkollegen B. Bira, der ihn beim Rennen um die Brooklands International Trophy vom Mai 1936 auf den zweiten Platz verwiesen hatte. B. Bira war der Rennname von Prinz Birabongse, einem Neffen des Königs von Siam, der Geschmack am Motorsport fand, als sein älterer Vetter Chula ihm Anfang der dreißiger Jahre einen MG Magna schenkte – er fuhr bis in die fünfziger Jahre Rennen.

Le talentueux prince de Siam
Raymond Mays félicite B. Bira, son coéquipier chez ERA, qui lui a ravi la seconde place lors du Trophée International de Brooklands en mai 1936. B. Bira est le nom en course du prince Birabongse, neveu du roi de Siam, qui entra dans la carrière de pilote au début des années 1930 après que son cousin Chula lui a présenté une MG Magna et ne prit sa retraite que dans les années 1950.

Campbell's other life

Away from his prolific land speed record activities, Malcolm Campbell was a very busy racing driver, and a regular competitor at Brooklands from 1911 to 1935. While he sat at the wheel of his Bugatti at the track in March 1930 (above), he may have been formulating his plan to claim the record back from Henry Segrave, which he managed to do in February 1931.

Campbells Doppelleben

Wenn er einmal keine Rekordfahrten unternahm, war Malcolm Campbell ein engagierter Rennfahrer, der zwischen 1911 und 1935 regelmäßig in Brooklands startete. Hier (oben) im März 1930 am Steuer seines Bugatti mag er Pläne geschmiedet haben, wie er Henry Segrave den Weltrekord wieder abjagen konnte, was ihm im Februar 1931 auch gelang.

L'autre vie de Campbell

En dehors de ses prolifiques activités de recordman de vitesse sur terre, Malcolm Campbell menait une vie très active de pilote de course et participa régulièrement aux épreuves de Brooklands entre 1911 et 1935. Assis au volant de sa Bugatti en mars 1930 (ci-dessus), il pense peut-être déjà à reprendre le record de vitesse détenu par Henry Segrave, ce qu'il réussira d'ailleurs en février 1931.

The international brigade
(Opposite, clockwise from top left) Luigi Villoresi
of Italy, fellow Italian Giuseppe Campari (on right),
English co-drivers John Cobb and T.E. Rose-Richards,
and Raymond Mays talking to German star Manfred
von Brauchitsch (seated on the pit counter).
(Left) The first international race at London's
Crystal Palace brought an Italian contingent which
included Count Carlo Felice Trossi, Signor Rovere,
Count Johnny Lurani and Villoresi together in the
Maserati squad.

Die internationale Brigade
(Gegenüber, im Uhrzeigersinn von oben links)
Luigi Villoresi aus Italien, sein Landsmann
Giuseppe Campari (rechts), das englische Gespann
John Cobb und T. E. Rose-Richards und Raymond
Mays im Gespräch mit dem deutschen Fahrer-Ass
Manfred von Brauchitsch (auf der Werkbank der
Boxen). (Links) Beim ersten internationalen Rennen
auf dem Londoner Crystal-Palace-Kurs waren die
Italiener zahlreich vertreten, darunter die Maserati-
Equipe, bestehend aus Graf Carlo Felice Trossi,
Signor Rovere, Graf Johnny Lurani sowie Villoresi.

La brigade internationale
(Ci-contre, dans le sens des aiguilles d'une montre
à partir du haut à gauche) les Italiens Luigi Villoresi
et Giuseppe Campari (à droite), les Anglais John Cobb
et T. E. Rose-Richards, et Raymond Mays parlant à
la vedette allemande Manfred von Brauchitsch (assis
sur le comptoir des stands). Toute l'écurie Maserati,
avec le comte Carlo Felice Trossi, Signor Rovere, le
comte Johnny Lurani et Villoresi, participe à la
première compétition internationale organisée au
Crystal Palace de Londres (à gauche).

Ambitions to improve

In the 1930s, while Italy and France fought for Grand Prix glory and German domination loomed, British motor racing was mostly a lower key affair, typically involving cars like the Austin and MG Specials (above). Raymond Mays (opposite, left) had an ambition to revive Britain's Grand Prix fortunes, and he helped create English Racing Automobiles, and the ERA (opposite, right).

Ehrgeizige Pläne

In den dreißiger Jahren, als Italien und Frankreich um Grand-Prix-Ehren fochten und die Deutschen dominierten, spielte der britische Motorsport mit Wagen wie Austin und MG Specials (oben) keine große Rolle. Raymond Mays (gegenüber, links) wollte Großbritannien wieder zu mehr Ruhm im Renngeschehen verhelfen und gründete mit anderen die Firma English Racing Automobiles, die mit ihren ERAs (gegenüber, rechts) antrat.

Des ambitions à confirmer

Dans les années 1930, tandis que l'Italie et la France s'affrontent en Grand Prix et que la domination allemande s'accentue, la course automobile reste à un niveau inférieur en Grande-Bretagne, avec les Austin et les MG Special (ci-dessus). R. Mays (ci-contre, à gauche), qui nourrissait l'ambition de faire renaître le Grand Prix en Grande-Bretagne, participa à la création de l'ERA, English Racing Automobiles (ci-contre à droite).

Approaching the end of an era
Dudley Froy's Bugatti speeds through the sunlight in 1933 (above), and Penn Hughes's similar car attempts to go around the outside of Malcolm Campbell, high on the banking in 1931 (left). Sights like this were the joy of Brooklands, but in August 1939, with war only weeks away, Brooklands held its last race. During the war it was taken over by the military, and after it by the aircraft industry. It never reopened for racing.

Das Ende einer Epoche
Dudley Froys Bugatti 1933 bei voller Fahrt im Sonnenlicht (oben) und Penn Hughes auf einem Schwestermodell 1931 bei dem Versuch, Malcolm Campbell hoch oben in der Steilkurve zu überholen – solche Bilder waren das Schönste an Brooklands. Doch im August 1939, wenige Wochen vor Kriegsausbruch, startete in Brooklands das letzte Rennen. Im Zweiten Weltkrieg wurde die Strecke für das Militär requiriert, später ging sie an die Flugzeugindustrie. Rennen wurden darauf nie wieder gefahren.

Vers la fin d'une époque
Des images comme celles de Penn Hughes, dans une Bugatti, tentant de faire l'extérieur à Malcolm Campbell dans le haut du virage en 1931 (à gauche) ou de Dudley Froy courant au soleil dans une voiture similaire en 1933 (ci-dessus) faisaient la joie de Brooklands, dont la dernière course fut disputée en août 1939, à quelques semaines du déclenchement de la Seconde Guerre mondiale. Le circuit sera alors occupé par l'armée puis par l'industrie aéronautique et ne sera jamais rouvert à la compétition.

Preparing for action

Motor races can be won and lost before a wheel has ever turned. Mechanics work on Bira's stable of racing cars in his garage in west London, making final preparations for the 2.9-litre Maserati single-seater he was due to drive in a few days time in the Coronation Trophy at Brooklands in 1938. In the foreground are two of his ERAs.

Die letzten Vorbereitungen

Ein Autorennen kann schon gewonnen oder verloren sein, bevor das erste Rad sich dreht. Mechaniker in Biras Rennstall in West-london legen letzte Hand an den 2,9-Liter-Maserati-Monoposto, mit dem er ein paar Tage darauf, 1938 in Brooklands, zum Rennen um die Coronation Trophy antreten sollte. Im Vorder-grund zwei seiner ERAs.

Préparation à l'action

Une course automobile peut se gagner ou se perdre avant même le premier tour de roue. Ces mécaniciens travaillent sur les voitures de course de Bira dans son garage à l'ouest de Londres, s'occupant des derniers préparatifs de la monoplace Maserati 2,9 litres qu'il va piloter quelques jours plus tard lors du Coronation Trophy à Brooklands en 1938. On reconnaît deux de ses ERA au premier plan.

All shapes and sizes

The big car is an Alfa Romeo, but the small one is, in its way, more interesting. It was powered by a small two-stroke engine, could reach just over 50mph, had four-wheel brakes and independent suspension. It was built in 1935 by Charles Cooper for his son John – who went on to become world champion constructor with the mid-engined Coopers of the 1950s and 1960s...

Die Großen und die Kleinen

Interessanter als der große Alfa Romeo ist in vielerlei Hinsicht der Zwerg, der neben ihm steht. Als Antrieb diente ein kleiner Zweitakter, mit dem er über 80 km/h schnell war. Er verfügte über Vierradbremsen und Einzelradaufhängung. Charles Cooper baute den Flitzer 1935 für seinen Sohn John – der später mit den Mittelmotor-Coopers der fünfziger und sechziger Jahre Wagen für Weltmeister konstruieren sollte ...

De toutes formes et de toutes tailles

La petite voiture est, à sa manière, plus intéressante que la grosse Alfa Romeo qu'elle côtoie. Propulsée par un petit moteur deux temps, capable d'atteindre à peine plus de 80 km/h, disposant de freins et d'une suspension indépendante sur les quatre roues, elle fut construite en 1935 par Charles Cooper pour son fils John – le futur constructeur champion du monde avec ses Cooper à moteur central des années 1950 et 1960 ...

An age of contrasts

By 1938, British and French cars included the Alta (opposite, below right), designed and driven by George Abecassis, and the Delahaye (opposite, below left), driven by René Dreyfus. The German teams, with massive funds and brilliant engineers, had moved on, with cars like the Mercedes W125 of 1937, driven by Dick Seaman (opposite, above), and the mid-engined V16 Auto Union of 1938, driven by Achille Varzi (above).

Eine Zeit der Gegensätze

Engländer und Franzosen traten 1938 mit Wagen wie dem von George Abecassis entworfenen und pilotierten Alta (gegenüber, unten rechts) und dem Delahaye mit René Dreyfus am Steuer an (gegenüber, unten links). Doch dank großzügiger finanzieller Unterstützung und erstklassiger Ingenieure waren die Deutschen schon weit überlegen, mit Modellen wie dem 1937er Mercedes W125, den Dick Seaman fuhr (gegenüber, oben), und Achille Varzis Auto Union von 1938 mit V16-Mittelmotor (oben).

Une époque de contrastes

Vers 1938, on distingue du côté britannique l'Alta, conçue et pilotée par George Abecassis (ci-contre, en bas à droite), et du côté français la Delahaye, pilotée par René Dreyfus (ci-contre, en bas à gauche). Les écuries allemandes, disposant d'un important financement et de brillants ingénieurs, ont évolué différemment avec des voitures comme la Mercedes W125 de 1937, pilotée par Dick Seaman (ci-contre, en haut) et l'Auto Union à moteur V16 central de 1938, pilotée par Achille Varzi (ci-dessus).

Sponsor and results

Later he would become Porsche's team manager, but in 1938 Huschke von Hanstein (opposite, left) raced a BMW 328 in the German hillclimb championship, and wore the insignia of the SS. In the late 1930s, Hitler's ambitions to dominate world motor sport helped create masterpieces of design like the Mercedes W154 (opposite, right) and the Auto Union (above), driven here by Nuvolari in 1938.

Auf den Sponsor kommt es an

Bevor er Rennleiter bei Porsche wurde, nahm Huschke von Hanstein 1938 (gegenüber, links) mit einem BMW 328 als Fahrer an der deutschen Bergmeisterschaft teil und trug dabei die Abzeichen der SS. In den späten dreißiger Jahren finanzierte Hitler in seinem Ehrgeiz, weltweit das Renngeschehen zu beherrschen, Meisterwerke wie den Mercedes W154 (gegenüber, rechts) und den Auto Union (oben), hier 1938 mit Nuvolari.

Sponsor et résultats

Avant de devenir le directeur d'écurie de Porsche, Huschke von Hanstein, portant l'insigne SS, participa en 1938 au championnat d'Allemagne de courses de côte sur une BMW 328 (ci-contre, à gauche). À la fin des années 1930, les ambitions de Hitler de dominer le sport automobile mondial permirent de créer des chefs-d'œuvre comme la Mercedes W154 (ci-contre, à droite) ou l'Auto Union, ici pilotée par Nuvolari en 1938 (ci-dessus).

They came, they saw, they conquered
When the State-sponsored German teams with their fabulously sophisticated Grand Prix cars and impeccably managed racing organisations
came to the British Grand Prix in 1937, they put on a display of superiority rarely equalled. Bernd Rosemeyer won for Auto Union. This is one
of the Mercedes, cresting the rise from Donington's hairpin.

Sie kamen, sahen und siegten
Die staatlich finanzierten deutschen Grand-Prix-Wagen waren Wunder-
werke, die Rennställe bis ins kleinste organisiert. Als sie 1937 zum
Großen Preis von England kamen, siegten sie mit einer Überlegenheit,
wie man sie selten gesehen hat. Bernd Rosemeyer auf Auto Union
ging als erster ins Ziel. Hier ein Mercedes, wie er über die Kuppe der
Haarnadelkurve von Donington kommt.

Veni, vidi, vici
Lorsque les écuries allemandes, largement financées par l'État, vinrent
participer au Grand Prix de Grande-Bretagne de 1937, elles affichèrent
une supériorité rarement égalée grâce à de fabuleuses voitures de
Grand Prix, comme cette Mercedes prise au sommet de la côte de
l'épingle de Donington, et une organisation en course exemplaire.
Cette édition fut remportée par Bernd Rosemeyer sur Auto Union.

—5—
Post-War Revival:
Return of the Grands Prix

When motor sport came back to life again after the interruption of war, there was never any possibility, in the short term at least, that it would reach the levels it had achieved with the State-financed German Grand Prix teams immediately before the conflict. That was a mixed blessing. It meant the end of an era of exceptional racing car technology, of undreamed of performance, of almost military-style team organisation and race discipline, and of perhaps the most perfect combination of the world's greatest drivers – of whatever nationality – in unquestionably the world's fastest Grand Prix racing cars. But it also meant an end to the Silver Arrows' crushing domination of the sport, and a return to more open competition.

Nor would the German cars reappear, as would many of their European rivals, once the fighting was over. For many years they would remain lost to the motor racing world, either destroyed during the war, or in a few cases salted away in secret hiding places, several of them in what became the Soviet sector of Germany and beyond. Their re-emergence would come many years later, which would at least mean that later generations could eventually see what the legend had been all about. But as motor racing began again in Europe, the majority of the machinery available was that which had chased the pre-war German teams for the minor places. In the absence of the German titans the rest had once again become the fastest racing cars in the world.

In America, racing had not suffered nearly the same disruptions as it had in Europe over the past years, and in one way American racing took a step forward, as servicemen returning from Europe took back with them a new passion for European-type sports cars, and European-type racing, on 'road' circuits, as opposed to the more traditional oval tracks. American racing also made use of one thing that was not in short supply after the war – disused and abandoned wartime airfields, whose long runways and wide perimeter roads were the perfect basis for a new kind of race venue. Britain had its share of disused airfields, too, and used them in the same way, including one which became the most famous British airfield circuit of them all – Silverstone. The track hosted its first Grand Prix race in 1948, and, in the absence of the leading Alfas and Ferraris, it was won by Luigi Villoresi's Maserati with team-mate Ascari second and Bob Gerard a patriotic third in the ERA. That set the scene for a far more fully supported Grand Prix at the same venue in 1949, this time won by

Baron Emmanuel de Graffenried's Maserati and starting a long Grand Prix history for the former airfield. But the aeroplane had cost Britain one other part of its motor racing heritage, Brooklands.

The famous track had been taken over by the military during the war, for aircraft development and construction, and as the place where Barnes Wallis did much of his research and development. It was at Brooklands that he worked on the Wellington bomber, the 'grand slam' bombs and his best-known invention, the 'bouncing bomb' made famous by the RAF Dambusters, from an office in what used to be the Clubhouse, in the centre of the old racing paddock. Sadly, the track and its facilities were badly treated by their supposedly temporary residents, who in any case stayed on long after the war ended, precluding any possibility of the historic venue ever returning to its former racing glories. It was the end of an important and evocative chapter in motor sporting history, but the motor racing world would move on.

For Europe, the revival was not easy. As well as losing its erstwhile German heroes, in the early days after the war the racing fraternity was short of several other important necessities, including fuel, tyres and many other specialised components; and, not least, most teams were also short of finance. Nonetheless, within months of the end of the war in Europe, there was a race meeting in Paris, in the Bois de Boulogne – ostensibly to celebrate the city's liberation but remembered now as the first return to international motor sport. Appropriately, it was won by a pre-war French star in a pre-war French car – Jean-Pierre Wimille in a 1939 Bugatti. Sadly, some of the great pre-war drivers would not return, but alongside Wimille the early post-war grids had some familiar heroes, including Achille Varzi, Taruffi, Louis Chiron, Raymond Sommer, Philippe Etancelin, even Tazio Nuvolari.

By the late 1940s Nuvolari was a sick man. Having survived numerous serious accidents in his pre-war career on both two and four wheels, he contracted severe lung problems after breathing alcohol-fuel fumes during a race in 1946. His doctors told him he should never race again, but he continued to take whatever drives he could find, even though he sometimes finished his races coughing blood, as the fumes from the front engines and acrid fuels of the day made his condition worse. In 1947 he entered the Mille Miglia in a tiny Cisitalia, intending to drive the race non-stop. Some thought he was intent on suicide: he had said many times that he would prefer to die in a racing car rather than in bed. By sheer driving ability he took the lead against far bigger and faster cars but was delayed by electrical problems and eventually finished second; at the end of the race he had to be lifted, exhausted and chronically ill, from his car. But a year later he was back, in one of the new cars recently launched by his old Alfa Romeo team manager Enzo Ferrari. Again he led; again he had mechanical problems. This time he lost the bonnet, his seat broke loose (he replaced it with a sack of oranges), the suspension collapsed, and almost within sight of the finish his brakes failed, finally forcing the skidding Nuvolari to admit defeat.

His final race was in April 1950 – a minor sports car race which he won. His health now deteriorated rapidly, and he died in August 1953, at the age of sixty. He was buried in his familiar racing clothes, pale blue trousers, a yellow jersey with his good luck charm of a tortoise, and his pale blue leather helmet. The words on his gravestone translate as, 'You will travel faster still upon the highways of heaven'.

With the death of Nuvolari the motor racing world lost one of its greatest, but in his place, and alongside those famous names from the past, were emerging the first of a new generation, including Farina, Villoresi and a second-generation Ascari, Alberto, son of Antonio. As the sport became re-established, many more would join them, and soon they would be racing another new breed of racing car, as the technical evolution began again.

A new Grand Prix formula was introduced in 1947, based on engine capacities of 4.5 litres unsupercharged or 1.5 litres supercharged, but with no weight restrictions and few other technical complications. It was a clever piece of rule-making which made way for the kind of cars the rest of Europe had been concentrating on in the immediate pre-war years while the German teams had dominated the top levels of the sport. So the first great Grand Prix cars of the late 1940s were directly descended from the big-engined racing sports cars and the 'voiturettes' of the immediate pre-war years – the smaller capacity, single-seater racing cars which had latterly backed the Grand Prix giants in the European motor sporting calendar. It was a formula which lasted for the rest of the decade, and, in spite of its apparently apologetic origins, it led to some fascinating racing between cars like the relatively simple 4-litre French Talbots and Delahayes, the old-fashioned but still fairly effective English ERAs and Altas, and the

supercharged 1.5-litre Alfa Romeos and Maseratis – a rivalry eventually dominated by the Alfa 158s, descendants of Alfa's pre-war 'voiturettes'. Their ultimate speed, even their lap speeds, was considerably inferior to that of the pre-war German giants, and would remain so for years to come, but their engine and chassis technology were all pushing forwards in new directions, and once again racing was reborn.

Enthusiasm for the sport was as great as ever, but so, sadly, were its dangers, and the remaining years of the 1940s saw the deaths of Alfa's Grand Prix star Varzi, at Berne in 1948, their former driver Wimille, who was killed while practising for the 1949 Buenos Aires Grand Prix in a Simca-Gordini, and Trossi, who died of cancer in the same year, to temper Alfa's period of virtual invincibility.

Finally, towards the end of the 1940s two other famous names also came to Grand Prix racing, one a driver, the other a team manager turned constructor – Juan Manuel Fangio and Enzo Ferrari. Both men would score their first Grand Prix victories before the end of the 1940s, and both would lead the sport through much of the 1950s, in so doing establishing themselves as legends of the track.

Some things had not changed. Motor racing was still about extracting maximum performance and reliability from the most exotic machinery – in this case from a Maserati and Bira's ERA, before the Jersey road races in 1947.

Manches war aber auch noch wie vor dem Krieg. Nach wie vor ging es darum, den exotischsten Maschinen ein Maximum an Leistung und Verlässlichkeit zu entlocken – hier einem Maserati und Biras ERA, die vor dem Straßenrennen von Jersey im Jahr 1947 den letzten Schliff erhalten.

Certaines choses n'ont pas changé. L'objectif de la course automobile reste d'obtenir les performances et la fiabilité maximum de la machine la plus étrange – ici d'une Maserati et d'une ERA de Bira avant les courses de Jersey en 1947.

Louis Chiron was born in Monaco,
one of motor sport's most famous
venues, in 1900, had a successful
Grand Prix career between the
wars, and resumed it in the 1940s.

Louis Chiron kam im Jahr 1900
in Monaco zur Welt, wo eine
der berühmtesten Strecken des
Motorsports lockte, begann seine
erfolgreiche Grand-Prix-Karriere
zwischen den Kriegen und knüpfte
in den vierziger Jahren an seine
Vorkriegserfolge an.

Né en 1900 à Monaco, l'un des plus
célèbres circuits automobiles du
monde, Louis Chiron connut une
grande carrière de pilote de Grand
Prix entre les deux guerres, qu'il
interrompit dans les années 1940.

Als der Motorsport nach der Unterbrechung durch den Krieg wieder zum Leben erwachte, gab es, zumindest auf lange Zeit, kaum die Chance, dass noch einmal solch Schwindel erregende Höhen erreicht wurden, wie sie die staatliche Unterstützung der deutschen Mannschaften unmittelbar vor Kriegsbeginn möglich gemacht hatten. Doch das hatte auch sein Gutes. Zwar war damit die Zeit der perfekten Rennwagentechnik vorbei, der unerhörten Leistungen, der geradezu militärischen Organisation der Rennställe und der Disziplin auf den Strecken, der vielleicht perfektesten Kombination von Fahrern – aller Nationalitäten – und der schnellsten Grand-Prix-Wagen, die die Welt je gesehen hatte. Doch dafür beherrschten nun auch nicht mehr die Silberpfeile den Sport, und der Wettbewerb war wieder offen.

Anders als viele ihrer europäischen Rivalen sollten die deutschen Wagen nach Kriegsende nicht wieder antreten. Die meisten kehrten nicht in die Motorsportwelt zurück – sie waren entweder verloren gegangen oder schlummerten in Verstecken, viele davon in der sowjetisch besetzten Zone oder noch weiter im Osten. Einige tauchten später wieder auf, sodass spätere Generationen zumindest die Fahrzeuge bestaunen konnten, die längst Legende waren. Doch was nun auf die Rennstrecken ging, waren im wesentlichen die Wagen, die sich vor dem Krieg hinter den Deutschen um die weiteren Plätze gestritten hatten. Nun, wo die deutschen Titanen begraben waren, waren sie von neuem die schnellsten Rennwagen der Welt.

Anders als in Europa hatte es in Amerika in den Kriegsjahren keine Unterbrechung des Rennbetriebs gegeben, der nun noch durch die zurückkehrenden Soldaten angefeuert wurde, die in Europa die dortigen Sportwagen und die Rennen auf Straßenstrecken statt auf den traditionellen Rennkursen kennen gelernt hatten. Die Amerikaner machten sich auch jene Einrichtungen zunutze, die es nach dem Krieg im Überfluss gab – stillgelegte Militärflugplätze, deren lange Startbahnen und umlaufenden Straßen die ideale Grundlage für eine neue Form von Rennstrecke boten. Auch in Großbritannien gab es solche Plätze, auch dort fuhr man Rennen darauf, und einer dieser britischen Flugplatzkurse sollte es zu Berühmtheit bringen – Silverstone. Das erste Grand-Prix-Rennen fand dort 1948 statt, und da die führenden Alfas und Ferraris nicht antraten, ging Luigi Villoresi auf Maserati als Sieger ins Ziel, gefolgt von seinem Teamgefährten Ascari,

und Bob Gerard belegte auf ERA einen patriotischen dritten Platz. Damit war die Bühne für den schon weitaus besser besetzten Großen Preis von 1949 bereit – diesmal siegte Baron Emmanuel de Graffenried, wiederum auf Maserati, und dies war der eigentliche Beginn der langen Grand-Prix-Tradition auf dem alten Flugplatz. Eine andere britische Motorsportlegende war allerdings dem Flugzeugbau zum Opfer gefallen – Brooklands.

Die berühmte Rennstrecke war im Krieg für Entwicklung und Bau von Flugzeugen requiriert worden, und der Konstrukteur Barnes Wallis richtete im ehemaligen Clubhaus seine Versuchswerkstatt ein. In Brooklands entwickelte er den Wellington-Bomber, die »Grand Slam«-Bombe und die berühmten hüpfenden Bomben, mit denen die R.A.F. deutsche Staudämme sprengte. Leider nahmen die Gäste, die zudem bis lange nach dem Krieg blieben, keinerlei Rücksicht auf Strecke und Einrichtungen, und am Ende war Brooklands so verfallen, dass es keine Hoffnung mehr gab, dass dort je wieder Rennen gefahren würden. Damit war eins der wichtigsten und ruhmreichsten Kapitel der Motorsportgeschichte zu Ende – doch der Sport hatte seinen Blick bereits in die Zukunft gerichtet.

Der Neubeginn in Europa war nicht leicht. Der Rennbetrieb hatte nicht nur seine deutschen Helden verloren, sondern es fehlte am Notwendigsten, darunter an Brennstoff, Reifen und vielen Ersatzteilen – und nicht zuletzt mangelte es bei den meisten Teams an Geld. Trotzdem richtete Paris schon wenige Monate nach Kriegsende ein Rennen im Bois de Boulogne aus; offiziell war es eine Feier zur Befreiung der Stadt, doch in die Geschichte ist es als Neubeginn des internationalen Motorsports eingegangen. Es war nur angemessen, dass der Sieger eine französische Vorkriegsgröße in einem französischen Vorkriegswagen war – Jean-Pierre Wimille in einem 1939er Bugatti. Manche großen Fahrer des vergangenen Jahrzehnts waren leider nicht mehr dabei, doch etliche alte Kämpen traten neben Wimille wieder an, darunter Achille Varzi, Taruffi, Louis Chiron, Raymond Sommer, Philippe Etancelin und auch Tazio Nuvolari.

In den späten vierziger Jahren war Nuvolari schon ein kranker Mann. Im Laufe seiner Vorkriegskarriere auf zwei und vier Rädern hatte er zahlreiche schwere Unfälle überstanden, doch nun zerfraßen ihm die Dämpfe von Alkoholbrennstoff, die er 1946 bei einem Rennen eingeatmet hatte, die Lunge. Die Ärzte hatten ihm von weiteren Fahrten abgeraten, doch er ging bei jeder Gelegenheit an den Start, auch wenn er am Ende mancher Rennen Blut spuckte, so schwer setzten ihm die Abgase und die ätzenden Dämpfe der damaligen Treibstoffe zu. 1947 erschien er zur Mille Miglia in einem winzigen Cisitalia und kündigte an, er werde das Rennen ohne Zwischenstopp fahren. Manche verstanden es als Absicht, sich das Leben zu nehmen. Er hatte oft genug gesagt, er wolle lieber in einem Rennwagen sterben als im Bett. Durch schieres fahrerisches Können setzte er sich vor weitaus größeren und schnelleren Wagen an die Spitze, dann fiel er durch einen Schaden an der Elektrik zurück, kam aber doch noch als Zweiter ans Ziel; am Ende musste man ihn, elend und erschöpft, aus dem Cockpit heben. Doch im Jahr darauf war er wieder dabei, in einem der neuen Modelle, die sein einstiger Alfa-Romeo-Teamleiter Enzo Ferrari vorgestellt hatte. Wieder lag er vorn, und wieder warfen ihn mechanische Mängel zurück. Diesmal verlor er die Motorhaube, sein Sitz löste sich (er setzte sich stattdessen auf einen Sack Apfelsinen), die Federung brach, und fast schon in Sichtweite des Ziels versagten die Bremsen; Nuvolari schlitterte noch weiter, aber er musste sich geschlagen geben.

Sein letztes Rennen fuhr er im April 1950 – ein kleineres Sportwagenrennen, das er gewann. Doch nun ging es sichtlich mit ihm zu Ende, er starb im August 1953 mit sechzig Jahren. Er wurde in dem Renndress begraben, in dem ihn alle gekannt hatten, mit hellblauer Hose, dem gelben Pullover mit seinem Glücksbringer, einer Schildkröte, und mit dem hellblauen Lederhelm. Die Worte auf seinem Grabstein lauten: »Auf den Straßen des Himmels wirst du schneller fahren denn je.«

Mit Nuvolari verlor die Motorsportwelt einen ihrer Größten, doch neben jenen aus der alten Garde, die noch fuhren, traten die ersten einer neuen Generation seine Nachfolge an, Fahrer wie Farina, Villoresi und Ascari junior: Alberto, der Sohn Antonios. Weitere kamen hinzu, als der Sport sich wieder erholte, und auch die Techniker nahmen ihre Arbeit wieder auf und stellten die ersten Neukonstruktionen auf die Räder.

1947 wurde eine neue Formel festgesetzt, die für nicht aufgeladene Motoren ein maximales Volumen von 4,5 Litern, für Kompressormotoren von 1,5 Litern vorsah, jedoch ohne Gewichtsbegrenzung und fast ohne weitere technische Einschränkungen. Es war eine kluge Entscheidung, denn damit konnten die übrigen Europäer dort anknüpfen, wo sie in den Vorkriegsjahren stehen geblieben waren, als die Deutschen

die höheren Ränge des Sports dominierten. Die ersten Grand-Prix-Wagen der späten vierziger Jahre waren also direkte Nachfolger der großmotorigen Rennsportwagen und der »Voiturettes« der Vorkriegszeit – der kleineren Einsitzer, die in den Rennen der Dreißiger oft neben den schwereren Grand-Prix-Wagen an den Start gegangen waren. Die Formel hielt sich für den Rest des Jahrzehnts, und auch wenn sie ursprünglich eine Verlegenheitslösung gewesen war, brachte sie doch einige faszinierende Rennwagen hervor, etwa die recht einfach gebauten 4-Liter-Talbots und Delahayes aus Frankreich, die technisch konservativen, aber noch immer leistungsstarken englischen ERAs und Altas sowie die Alfa Romeos und Maseratis mit 1,5-Liter-Kompressormotoren – deren Wettstreit am Ende der Alfa 158 für sich entscheiden konnte, ein Nachfahr von Alfas leichteren Vorkriegswagen. Ihre Höchstgeschwindigkeiten und auch die Rundenzeiten lagen deutlich unter denen der deutschen Giganten der späten Dreißiger, und es sollte noch Jahre dauern, bis solche Zeiten wieder erreicht wurden; doch in Motoren- und Fahrwerkstechnik wiesen diese Wagen den Weg in die Zukunft, und wieder einmal wurde der Rennsport neu geboren.

Die Sportbegeisterung war ungebrochen, doch leider blieben die Rennen auch gefährlich wie eh und je. 1948 ließ Alfas Grand-Prix-Star Varzi in Bern sein Leben, 1949 kam der ehemalige Alfa-Pilot Wimille beim Training zum Großen Preis von Buenos Aires in einem Simca-Gordini um, und als Trossi im selben Jahr an Krebs starb, waren die Zeiten, als die Alfas beinahe unschlagbar waren, vorüber.

Zwei große neue Namen tauchten dafür am Ende der vierziger Jahre auf, der eine ein Grand-Prix-Fahrer, der andere ein ehemaliger Teamleiter, der nun als Konstrukteur seinen eigenen Rennstall aufgemacht hatte – Juan Manuel Fangio und Enzo Ferrari. Beide sollten ihre ersten Triumphe feiern, bevor die Vierziger vorüber waren, und beide sollten bis weit in die Fünfziger hinein an der Spitze des Sportes stehen und zu Legenden der Rennpisten werden.

The ERA, built by English Racing Automobiles, was conceived in the 1930s as Britain's most serious Grand Prix challenger, and until something more modern came along was again a Grand Prix stopgap into the late 1940s.

Der in den dreißiger Jahren konzipierte ERA war Großbritanniens erfolgreichster Grand-Prix-Wagen, und da nichts Moderneres verfügbar war, erfüllte er seinen Zweck noch bis in die späten Vierziger hinein.

L'ERA, acronyme de English Racing Automobiles, était considérée dans les années 1930 comme l'une des plus sérieuses concurrentes britanniques en Grand Prix mais ne joua qu'un rôle de faire-valoir vers la fin des années 1940 en attendant qu'arrive une voiture un peu plus moderne.

The final fling

The first major race of the 1940s was also the last before war called a complete halt to the sport. The Brescia Grand Prix replaced the Mille Miglia and took place in April 1940, after war had been declared. It was dominated by German and Italian entries and convincingly won by the BMW team, which included the roadster of Brudes and Roese, seen here passing the Brescia scoreboard.

Die letzte Runde

Das erste große Rennen der vierziger Jahre war zugleich auch das letzte, bevor der Rennbetrieb durch den Krieg zum Erliegen kam. Der Grand Prix von Brescia fand im April 1940 als Ersatz für die Mille Miglia statt und wurde von deutschen und italieni-schen Mannschaften beherrscht. BMW – hier der Wagen von Brudes und Roese vor der Anzeigentafel von Brescia – lieferte einen überzeugenden Sieg.

La dernière aventure

La première grande course des années 1940 fut également la dernière, le déclenchement des hostilités obligeant à tout arrêter. Le Grand Prix de Brescia, qui est organisé en avril 1940, juste après la déclaration de guerre, en remplacement des Mille Miglia, est dominé par les voitures allemandes et italiennes et remporté de manière éclatante par l'écurie BMW, qui aligne notamment ce roadster de Brudes et Roese.

From victory to reparation

The victorious BMW team (below) was led home by Baron Huschke von Hanstein (second from right) and Walter Baumer, while Alfa Romeo were allowed second place. After the war, BMW began to rebuild, while the English Bristol company took over production of the BMW 328 engine, heart of the very BMW-like Frazer-Nash High Speed models which appeared in the 1949 Mille Miglia, including (right) this car driven by Peter Richard.

Vom Sieg zur Reparation

Das siegreiche BMW-Team wurde angeführt von Baron Huschke von Hanstein (Zweiter von rechts) und Walter Baumer; den zweiten Platz ließ man Alfa Romeo. Nach dem Krieg baute BMW wieder auf, doch der 328-Motor ging als Reparationsleistung an die englische Firma Bristol und war das Herzstück der Frazer-Nash-Rennwagen, die 1949 zur Mille Miglia kamen und eine große Ähnlichkeit mit den BMWs hatten – hier (rechts) mit Peter Richard am Steuer.

De la victoire à la réparation

L'écurie BMW (en bas) est emmenée à la victoire par le baron Huschke von Hanstein (le deuxième à partir de la droite) et Walter Baumer, Alfa Romeo s'attribuant la seconde place. BMW se reconstruisit après la guerre tandis que la société anglaise Bristol reprenait la production du moteur BMW 328, le cœur des Frazer-Nash High Speed (très semblables à la BMW) engagées dans les Mille Miglia de 1949, dont cette voiture pilotée par Peter Richard (à droite).

Social climbing

Hillclimbing was one of the earliest forms of motor sport. In Europe it gravitated to long, often very fast mountain climbs, in Britain on to shorter, less extreme hills – but the pursuit of the perfect climb was just as intense. Shelsley Walsh is one of Britain's oldest climbs, and one of the fastest, for cars like the single-seat Special (above) and the twin rear-wheel Bugatti (right) in 1947.

Es geht aufwärts

Bergfahrten zählen zu den ältesten Formen des Motorsports. Auf dem Kontinent entwickelten sich daraus lange, oft äußerst schnelle Bergrennen, während die Briten sanftere Hügel bevorzugten – auch wenn sie sie nicht mit weniger Elan in Angriff nahmen. Shelsley Walsh, hier 1947, war eine der ältesten Strecken des Landes und auch eine der schnellsten, für Wagen wie diesen Einsitzer (oben) und den Bugatti (rechts) mit den hinteren Zwillingsreifen.

Une ascension sociale

La course de côte est l'un des premiers types de compétition automobile. En Europe, il s'agissait de longues ascensions souvent très rapides tandis qu'en Grande-Bretagne les épreuves se déroulaient dans des collines moins pentues sans que la course ne soit moins intense pour autant. Shelsley Walsh comptait parmi les plus anciennes courses de côte britanniques, et l'une des plus rapides, pour des voitures de 1947 comme cette monoplace Special (ci-dessus) ou la Bugatti à roues jumelées à l'arrière (à droite).

Beside the seaside

Brighton's annual speed trials, along the long promenade of
the town's Madeira Drive, was a head-to-head test of straight-
line acceleration and outright speed for cars in a huge variety
of classes racing against each other in pairs. It was first held,
over a one-mile course, in 1905. In 1947 it attracted competitors
from America, France, Belgium, Italy and Finland.

Ein Tag an der See

Einmal im Jahr fanden in Brighton die Geschwindigkeits-
prüfungen am Madeira Drive entlang der Seepromenade statt,
ein reiner Beschleunigungs- und Tempowettbewerb in einer
Vielzahl von Klassen, in denen die Wagen jeweils paarweise
gegeneinander antraten. Das Rennen über eine Distanz von
einer Meile fand erstmals 1905 statt; 1947 zog es Teilnehmer aus
Amerika, Frankreich, Belgien, Italien und Finnland an.

Au bord de la mer

Le concours annuel organisé à Brighton le long de la promenade de Madeira Drive était une course d'accélération et de
vitesse pure en ligne droite ouverte à des voitures d'un grand
nombre de catégories s'affrontant deux par deux. La 1ʳᵉ édition
eut lieu pour la première fois en 1905 sur un parcours de 1 mile
(1,6 km). En 1947, il attirait des concurrents venus des États-
Unis, de France, de Belgique, d'Italie et de Finlande.

Off-shore assets

Like the Isle of Man and Ireland, the Channel Islands were not affected by Britain's reluctance to allow racing on public roads. This is the start of the international road race in Jersey in May 1947, with a large crowd very close to the action as the upright ERAs are led away by the Maserati Grand Prix cars, by far the quickest entries.

Zuflucht auf der Insel

Wie Irland und die Isle of Man waren auch die Kanalinseln nicht von dem britischen Verbot für Rennen auf öffentlichen Straßen betroffen. Hier sehen wir den Start zum internationalen Straßenrennen von Jersey im Mai 1947, wo eine große Menschenmenge die Maserati-Grand-Prix-Wagen, die bei weitem schnellsten Teilnehmer, bestaunt, wie sie den wackeren ERAs davonfahren.

Les atouts de l'off-shore

Les îles anglaises de la Manche, ainsi que l'Irlande et l'île de Man, ne sont pas frappées par l'interdiction britannique des courses sur route. Une foule très proche de l'action assiste au départ de l'épreuve internationale sur route de Jersey en mai 1947, alors que les ERA à haut capot sont devancées par les Maserati Grand Prix, de loin les concurrents les plus rapides.

British winner in an Italian car

Reg Parnell (above) was thirty when he won the 1947 Jersey race, and was described by the newspapers as 'a little-known British driver in a pre-war privately owned Maserati'. Within a few years, the businessman from Derby would be rather more famous for his associations with the new BRM marque. Refuelling Parnell's car (below) and cooling the rear axle.

Britischer Sieger, italienisches Gefährt

Reg Parnell (oben) war dreißig, als er das 1947er Rennen in Jersey gewann, und die Zeitungen schrieben von einem »kaum bekannten britischen Fahrer in einem privat gemeldeten Vorkriegs-Maserati«. In den nächsten Jahren, als er für den neu gegründeten BRM-Rennstahl fuhr, sollte der Name des Geschäftsmanns aus Derby bekannter werden. (Unten) Beim Auftanken von Parnells Wagen wird auch die Hinterachse gekühlt.

Un vainqueur britannique sur une voiture italienne

Reg Parnell (en haut), qui remporta la course de Jersey de 1947 à l'âge de trente ans, était décrit par les journaux comme « un pilote britannique méconnu dans une Maserati privée datant d'avant-guerre ». Cet homme d'affaires de Derby allait se rendre célèbre en quelques années en pilotant les voitures de la nouvelle firme BRM. La voiture de Parnell au stand pour un ravitaillement et le refroidissement de l'essieu arrière (en bas).

The racing car of choice
The pre-war Maseratis were out in considerable force in the Jersey road race, as the line-up in the pits (above) shows, with the number 1 car driven by Louis Chiron in the foreground and Parnell's winning car (7), in the distance. Parnell is garlanded and chaired through the pits by his mechanics (right) after his popular win against the continental drivers.

Das Beste auf dem Markt
Vorkriegs-Maseratis traten beim Straßenrennen von Jersey in Scharen an, wie dieser Blick in die Boxen beweist (oben), mit Louis Chirons Nummer 1 im Vordergrund und Parnells Siegerwagen (7) in der Ferne. Parnell wurde für seinen Triumph über die Konkurrenz vom Kontinent gefeiert, hier (rechts) auf den Schultern der Mechaniker bei der Parade durchs Fahrerlager.

Une voiture de choix
Nombre de Maserati d'avant-guerre furent engagées dans la course sur route de Jersey, comme on le constate sur la grille de départ des stands (ci-dessus) où l'on distingue la numéro 1 de Louis Chiron, au premier plan, et la numéro 7 victorieuse de Parnell, tout au fond. Parnell, la guirlande de fleurs du vainqueur autour du cou, est porté dans les stands sur les épaules de ses mécaniciens après sa victoire sur les pilotes du continent (à droite).

Battles resumed

Alberto Ascari, son of the great Antonio Ascari, had his first experience of Grand Prix racing as war approached. Luigi Villoresi, born nine years before Ascari, in 1909, also raced in the 1930s. After the war the two became rivals, but in 1948 they were team-mates at Maserati, and here for the RAC Grand Prix at Silverstone. Luigi (on the right) won, Alberto was second.

Auf in den Kampf

Alberto Ascari, Sohn des großen Antonio Ascari, fuhr seine ersten Grand-Prix-Rennen, als der Krieg sich ankündigte. Auch der neun Jahre ältere Luigi Villoresi, Jahrgang 1909, war in den Dreißigern schon gefahren. Nach dem Krieg wurden sie Rivalen, doch 1948 waren sie als Stallgefährten bei Maserati wieder vereint, hier beim Großen Preis des RAC in Silverstone. Luigi (rechts) eroberte den ersten, Alberto den zweiten Rang.

La reprise de la lutte

Alberto Ascari, le fils du grand Antonio Ascari, a fait ses premières armes en Grand Prix peu avant la guerre. Luigi Villoresi, né neuf ans avant lui, en 1909, courut également dans les années 1930. D'abord grands rivaux, ils entrèrent tous deux chez Maserati en 1948. On les voit ici réunis lors du Grand Prix du RAC disputé à Silverstone, remporté par Luigi (à droite) devant Alberto, second.

Men at the top

Experienced drivers dominated the major races of the late 1940s, until the new generation gained experience in its turn. (Left to right) Achille Varzi (facing camera) after winning the 1946 'Lottery' race at Monza for Alfa; Bira, not quite into the Simca after finishing second in Geneva in 1948; Giuseppe Farina (standing) and Juan Manuel Fangio, Silverstone 1948.

Spitzenfahrer

Ältere Fahrer beherrschten die großen Rennen der späten vierziger Jahre, bis die junge Generation herangereift war. (Von links nach rechts) Alfa-Pilot Achille Varzi (mit Blick zur Kamera) nach seinem Sieg im 1946er »Lotterie«-Rennen von Monza; Bira, Zweiter in Genf 1948, beim kniffligen Einstieg in den Simca; Giuseppe Farina (stehend) und Juan Manuel Fangio, Silverstone 1948.

Des hommes au sommet

Les grandes courses de la fin des années 1940 furent dominées par des pilotes d'expérience jusqu'à l'arrivée d'une nouvelle génération : (de gauche à droite) Achille Varzi, de face, après avoir remporté la course de la « Loterie » à Monza pour Alfa en 1946 ; Bira, à moitié installé dans sa Simca après avoir terminé second à Genève en 1948 ; Giuseppe Farina (debout) et Juan Manuel Fangio à Silverstone en 1948.

The start of great things

In the 1920s, Enzo Ferrari had been a racing driver; by the 1930s he was a team manager, for Alfa Romeo. When, in 1946, he became a racing car constructor in his own right, one of the most famous of all racing marques was born. This is Raymond Sommer's Ferrari leading Villoresi's Maserati in the 1948 Italian Grand Prix, where they finished third and second behind Wimille's Alfa.

Große Ereignisse kündigen sich an

In den zwanziger Jahren war Enzo Ferrari selbst Rennfahrer gewesen, in den Dreißigern leitete er das Alfa-Romeo-Team. Als er 1946 seinen ersten eigenen Wagen konstruierte, schlug die Geburtsstunde einer der größten Rennwagenmarken aller Zeiten. Hier sehen wir Raymond Sommers Ferrari, gefolgt von Villoresi auf Maserati, beim Großen Preis von Italien 1948, wo sie als Dritter und Zweiter hinter Wimilles Alfa ins Ziel kamen.

Le début de grandes choses

Enzo Ferrari fut pilote dans les années 1920 puis directeur d'écurie chez Alfa Romeo dans les années 1930. L'une des marques les plus célèbres naît en 1946 lorsqu'il se met à construire des voitures de course. On voit ici la Ferrari de Raymond Sommer devancer la Maserati de Villoresi lors du Grand Prix d'Italie de 1948, où ils terminèrent troisième et second derrière l'Alfa de Wimille.

An old Italian rivalry

Before Ferrari made it a three-cornered fight, Alfa Romeo and Maserati had long disputed the role of Italy's leading Grand Prix contender. This is the 1947 Italian Grand Prix, run on a street circuit in Milan, with a stripped Delage sports car trailing the leading group, comprising Achille Varzi's and Count Trossi's Alfa 158s sandwiching one of the Maseratis. Trossi went on to win, as the glorious super-charged Alfettas usually did in this period.

Italienische Rivalen

Bevor Ferrari auftauchte und einen Kampf zwischen drei Kontrahenten entfachte, wetteiferten Alfa Romeo und Maserati lange um den Ruhm der führenden italienischen Grand-Prix-Marke. Beim Großen Preis von Italien, der 1947 auf einem Straßenkurs in Mailand ausgetragen wurde, folgt ein abgemagerter Delage-Sportwagen der führenden Dreiergruppe, in der Achille Varzi und Graf Trossi mit ihren Alfa 158 einen Maserati in die Zange nehmen. Trossi siegte, und dass einer der prachtvollen Kompressor-Alfettas auf den ersten Platz kam, gehörte damals bei den Rennen beinahe dazu.

Une vieille rivalité italienne

Avant que Ferrari ne devienne le troisième larron, Alfa Romeo et Maserati se disputèrent longtemps le rôle de leader italien en Grand Prix. Dans cette édition du Grand Prix d'Italie de 1947, disputé sur le circuit urbain de Milan, on reconnaît une Delage à rayures suivant le groupe de tête formé par les glorieuses Alfa 158 à moteur suralimenté d'Achille Varzi et du comte Trossi, futur vainqueur, encadrant une des Maserati.

Wide open spaces and narrow confines
David Murray's Maserati (opposite) leaving the line in an individually timed sprint on one of Britain's newly-popular airfield venues, at a meeting of the Nottingham Sports Car Club in June 1949. The Jersey road race course in 1947 (above) offered rather less open space and considerably more solid objects to make life interesting for the drivers of Grand Prix machinery in 1947.

Weite Flächen, enge Straßen
David Murrays Maserati (gegenüber) beim Einzelstart zu einem Rennen des Nottingham Sports Car Club, das im Juni 1949 auf einer der neuen populären Flugplatz-Strecken stattfand. Der Kurs des Jersey-Straßenrennens von 1947 (oben) bot weniger offene Flächen, dafür sorgten umso mehr massive Objekte dafür, dass den Fahrern der Grand-Prix-Wagen nicht langweilig wurde.

Grands espaces et circuits étroits
Le tracé de l'épreuve sur route de Jersey en 1947 (ci-dessus), offrant moins d'espace et des obstacles plus consistants, rendait le pilotage plus intéressant pour les pilotes des machines de Grand Prix de 1947. La Maserati de David Murray (ci-contre) s'élance de la ligne de départ pour un sprint individuel sur l'un des nouveaux circuits aménagés sur un aérodrome britannique lors d'une réunion du Nottingham Sports Car Club, organisée en juin 1949.

Classic circuits, mixed futures

Formula 2 cars at the Nürburgring (above). The road circuit in the Eifel Mountains was part of the pre-Hitler period's legacy to the motor industry and motor sport, and it became one of motor racing's greatest venues. Talbot-Lagos dominate the grid for the Grand Prix de Paris (right) on the banked track at Montlhéry, which lost its status as a major venue as the Nürburgring's grew.

Klassische Strecken, ungewisse Zukunft

Formel-2-Wagen auf dem Nürburgring (oben). Den Straßenkurs in der Eifel hatten Industrie und Motorsport aus der Zeit vor Hitler geerbt, und er sollte sich zu einem Rennplatz entwickeln, der bis heute zu den größten des Sports zählt. Talbot-Lagos beherrschten das Feld beim Großen Preis von Paris (rechts) auf dem Steilkurs von Montlhéry, doch im Gegensatz zum Nürburgring sollte diese Strecke ihren Rang bald verlieren.

Circuits classiques, avenirs mélangés

Le Nürburgring accueille une course de voitures de Formule 2 (ci-dessus). Aménagé dans le massif de l'Eifel, ce circuit faisait partie de l'héritage laissé à la fin des années 20 à l'industrie et au sport automobiles et devint l'une des plus grandes scènes de compétition mécanique. Le célèbre circuit de Montlhéry, qui perdit beaucoup de son importance à mesure qu'augmentait celle du Nürburgring, accueillait le Grand Prix de Paris, où dominent les Talbot-Lago (à droite).

British successes and failures

In December 1949, Raymond Mays
(left, in the car) revealed the new BRM,
the Grand Prix challenger he had
conceived as a successor to the ERA.
At first, the vastly complex car was an
embarrassing failure, but BRM improved.
In the same year 'Goldie' Gardner drove
MG EX135 (above), which eventually took
records at up to 202mph. The 500cc
Cooper (below), as driven here by
Sir Francis Samuelson at Goodwood
in September 1948, turned racing car
design around, with the engine behind
the driver.

Britische Triumphe,
britische Blamagen

Im Dezember 1949 stellte Raymond Mays
(links, am Steuer) den von ihm als
Nachfolger des ERA entworfenen BRM
vor, der die Grand-Prix-Konkurrenz
herausfordern sollte. Anfangs erwies
sich der viel zu komplizierte Wagen als
peinlicher Versager, doch die BRMs
wurden besser. Im selben Jahr startete
»Goldie« Gardner mit dem MG EX135
(rechts oben), mit dem er Rekord-
geschwindigkeiten von bis zu 325 km/h
fuhr. Der 500-ccm-Cooper, hier (rechts
unten) im September 1948 in Goodwood
mit Sir Francis Samuelson, revolutio-
nierte den Rennwagenbau, denn der
Motor befand sich nun hinter dem
Fahrer.

Succès et échecs britanniques

Raymond Mays (à gauche, dans la
voiture) présente en décembre 1949 la
nouvelle BRM, la voiture de Grand Prix
plutôt complexe qu'il a conçue pour
remplacer l'ERA et qui fut tout d'abord
un échec retentissant. Après les améliorations qui y furent apportées, « Goldie »
Gardner s'arrogea finalement la même
année le record de vitesse en atteignant
325 km/h avec la MG EX135 (en haut). La
conception de la Cooper 500 cm³, pilotée
ici par sir Francis Samuelson à Goodwood en septembre 1948, a révolutionné
la voiture de course en installant le
moteur en arrière du pilote (en bas).

The supreme stylist

Giuseppe Farina (opposite) was one of the giants of the immediate postwar era, and widely regarded as the driver who set the relaxed, arms-forward style of modern race driving. When the new World Championship was inaugurated, in 1950, he was its first champion, for Alfa. In 1946 the Alfa Romeo team with its 158 Alfettas had dominated the Circuit of Milan, but Farina (above) had to watch team-mates Trossi, Varzi and Sanesi take the first three places.

Der große Stilist

Giuseppe Farina war einer der ganz Großen der unmittelbaren Nachkriegsära. Er wurde weithin begrüßt als der Fahrer, der die entspannte Armhaltung in den modernen Autorennsport einführte. Bei der feierlichen Eröffnung der neuen Weltmeisterschaft 1950 war er der erste Sieger – für Alfa. Noch 1946, als Alfa Romeo mit 158 Alfettas die Rennstrecke von Milano beherrschte, hatte Farcina das Nachsehen und musste Trossi, Varzi und Sanesi die ersten drei Plätze überlassen.

Styliste par excellence

Giuseppe Farina (ci-contre) comptait parmi les pilotes les plus prisés de la course automobile à l'issue de la Deuxième Guerre mondiale. Il fut le pionnier d'un style de conduite moderne et détendu. Avec son Alfa, il ressortit vainqueur de la course en 1950, année de l'inauguration du nouveau Championnat du Monde. En 1946, l'équipe Alfa Romeo avait dominé le Circuit de Milan avec ses Alfetta 158, mais Farina (ci-dessus) dût laisser les trois premières places à ses collègues Trossi, Varzi et Sanesi.

Britain's new generation

Motor sport flourished in Britain in the late 1940s as the 500cc Formula 3 led to a new breed of rear-engined cars, alongside new manufacturers and a new generation of young drivers. Stirling Moss joined the 500 class, supported as at Silverstone in October 1948 by his father Alfred (right), and often won with his Cooper – as at Goodwood just two weeks earlier (opposite, above). In the larger formulae, George Abecassis contested the British Empire Trophy Race on the Isle of Man in May 1948 in the Alta (opposite, below), designed by Geoffrey Taylor to be sold to a broad range of racing customers.

Die jungen Briten

In Großbritannien blühte der Motorsport in den späten Vierzigern auf. Die 500-ccm-Klasse der Formel 3 ließ einen neuen Typ von Rennwagen mit hinten liegenden Motoren entstehen, die von neuen Herstellern gebaut und von einer neuen Fahrergeneration gefahren wurden. Stirling Moss sammelte seine ersten Erfahrungen in der 500er Klasse, unterstützt – wie hier im Oktober 1948 in Silverstone – von seinem Vater Alfred (rechts), und kam auf seinem Cooper oft genug als Erster ins Ziel, zum Beispiel zwei Wochen zuvor in Goodwood (gegenüber, oben). In der größeren Klasse nahm George Abecassis im Mai 1948 auf der Isle of Man mit seinem Alta am Rennen um die British Empire Trophy teil (gegenüber, unten); der von Geoffrey Taylor konstruierte Alta wurde an eine Vielzahl von Privatfahrern verkauft.

Une nouvelle génération britannique

Le sport automobile se développe en Grande-Bretagne à la fin des années 1940 grâce à la Formule 3, pour moteurs de 500 cm³, qui conduit à développer un nouveau type de voitures à moteur arrière et permet l'émergence de constructeurs et de jeunes pilotes d'une nouvelle génération. Stirling Moss s'engage dans la catégorie 500, soutenu par son père Alfred à Silverstone en octobre 1948 (à droite), dans des épreuves qu'il remporte souvent avec sa Cooper, notamment à Goodwood à peine deux semaines plus tôt (ci-contre, en haut). Dans une formule supérieure, George Abecassis dispute la British Empire Trophy Race sur l'île de Man en mai 1948 avec son Alta (ci-contre, en bas), conçue par Geoffrey Taylor et destinée à une clientèle sportive.

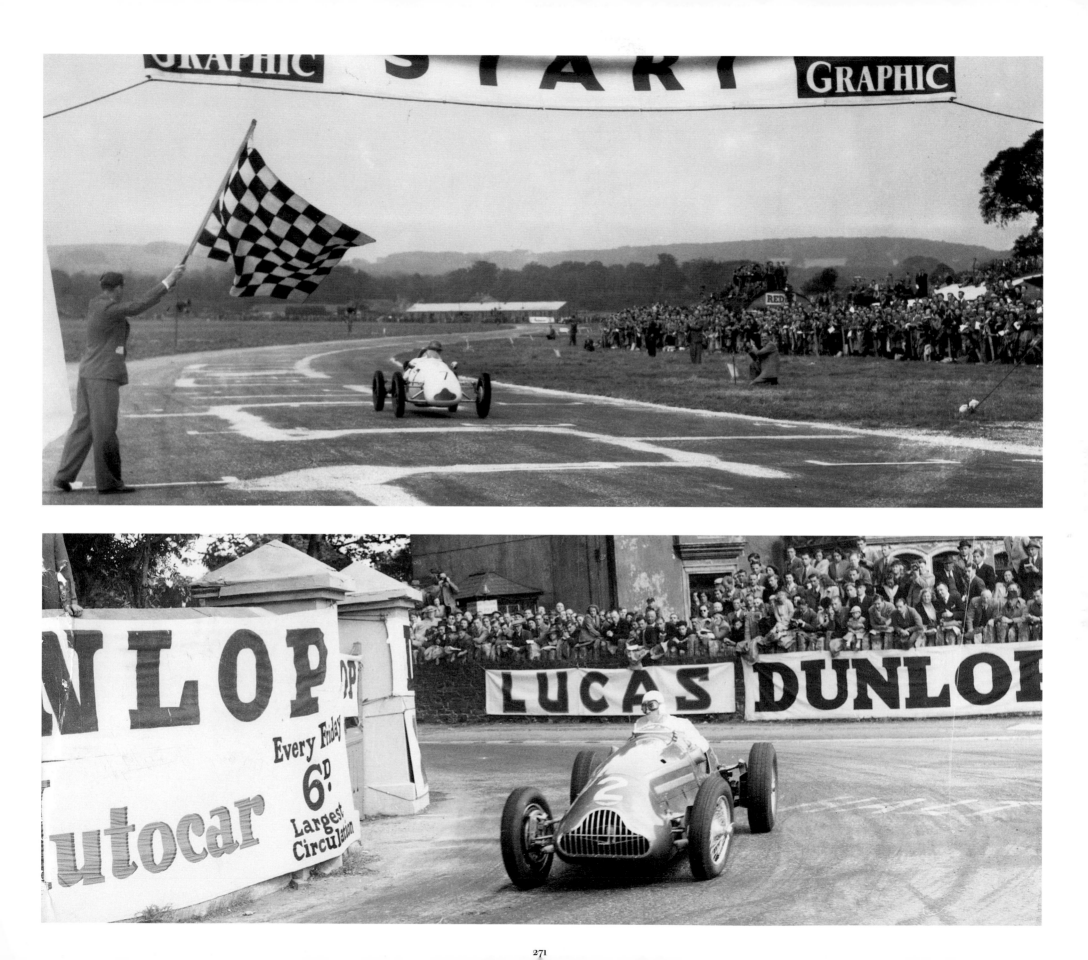

Back to business
Luigi Villoresi (above and opposite, above) won the RAC Grand Prix for Maserati when international racing first came to Silverstone in October 1948. The updated ERA (opposite, below left) and the French Talbot-Lago driven by Philippe Etancelin, wearing his familiar reversed cap (opposite, below right), were among Villoresi's opposition in the first Grand Prix race held in Britain since the late 1920s.

Wieder im Geschäft
Luigi Villoresi (oben und gegenüber, oben) siegte auf Maserati im Großen Preis des RAC, den ersten internationalen Rennen in Silverstone im Oktober 1948. Der überarbeitete ERA (gegenüber, unten links) und der Talbot-Lago (gegenüber, unten rechts) – am Steuer Philippe Etancelin mit seiner falsch aufgesetzten Kappe – waren Villoresis Konkurrenten bei diesem ersten Grand Prix auf britischem Boden seit den späten Zwanzigern.

Retour aux affaires
Luigi Villoresi (en haut et ci-contre en haut) remporte pour Maserati le Grand Prix RAC, à Silverstone, en 1948. La nouvelle ERA (ci-contre, en bas à gauche) et la Talbot-Lago française pilotée par Philippe Etancelin, portant son habituelle casquette à l'envers (ci-contre, en bas à droite), furent les principaux adversaires de Villoresi lors de ce Grand Prix organisé pour la première fois en Grande-Bretagne depuis la fin des années 1920.

France's fastest roads

The start of the Coupe des Petites Cylindrées for smaller
engined single-seater cars at Reims in July 1947. The race
supported the French Grand Prix on the superfast, roughly
triangular road circuit just outside the city, a course defined by
its long flat-out straights. This 'voiturette' race was dominated
by the Simca-Gordinis, and won by Bira's version.

Frankreichs schnellste Straßen

Der Start zum Coupe des Petites Cylindrées für Wagen mit
kleineren Motoren, Reims, Juli 1947. Das Rennen lief als
Nebenveranstaltung zum Großen Preis von Frankreich auf
dem ultraschnellen, fast dreieckigen Straßenkurs vor den Toren
der Stadt, der berühmt war für seine langen, flachen Geraden.
Das Voiturette-Rennen beherrschten die Simca-Gordinis, und
auch Sieger Bira fuhr Simca.

Les routes les plus rapides de France

Le départ de la Coupe des Petites Cylindrées, réservée aux
monoplaces à moteur de faible capacité, est donné à Reims en
juillet 1947. La course, organisée en complément du Grand Prix
de France, se déroulait sur le circuit ultra-rapide situé aux
environs immédiats de la ville. Cette course de « voiturettes » fut
dominée par les Simca-Gordini et remportée par Bira sur un
modèle personnel.

The airfield's new role

A new era for British motor racing started when the former wartime airfield at Silverstone was adapted into a race circuit, and given international status when the RAC held its Grand Prix there in October 1948. This is Louis Chiron, who led the opening laps of this forerunner to the post-war series of British Grands Prix in his Talbot-Lago, before Villoresi took victory.

Neues Leben auf dem alten Platz

Für den britischen Motorsport begann eine neue Ära, als der ehemalige Militärflugplatz Silverstone als Rennstrecke hergerichtet wurde, und mit dem Großen Preis des RAC erhielt sie im Oktober 1948 internationalen Status. Hier sehen wir Louis Chiron auf Talbot-Lago, der bei diesem Vorläuferrennen zu den britischen Grand Prix der Nachkriegszeit zunächst in Führung lag; als Sieger ging jedoch Villoresi ins Ziel.

Le nouveau rôle des aérodromes

Une nouvelle ère s'annonce pour le sport automobile britannique lorsque l'ancien aérodrome militaire de Silverstone est transformé en circuit automobile et obtient une reconnaissance internationale avec l'organisation du Grand Prix du RAC, précurseur des Grand Prix de Grande-Bretagne, en 1948. Louis Chiron (ci-dessus) mena les premiers tours dans sa Talbot-Lago avant que Villoresi ne s'empare de la victoire.

Flirting with disaster

Rex Mays was one of America's greatest dirt track racers but even he had crashes, like the one at Del Mar, California (opposite, above), and one of them finally claimed his life at Milwaukee Fairgrounds in 1947. Pedro Adames injured two marshals and a mechanic (opposite, below) in a race in Buenos Aires, and Ansell's ERA (above) made a spectacular exit at Silverstone in the 1948 Grand Prix.

Auge in Auge mit der Katastrophe

Rex Mays war ein Star auf den amerikanischen Sandpisten, doch auch für ihn gingen die Rennen nicht immer glücklich aus, wie hier (gegenüber, oben) im kalifornischen Del Mar, und bei einem Unfall auf den Milwaukee Fairgrounds ließ er 1947 schließlich sein Leben. Pedro Adames verletzte zwei Streckenposten und einen Mechaniker (gegenüber, unten) bei einem Rennen in Buenos Aires, und Ansells ERA (oben) verließ beim Grand Prix von 1948 in Silverstone spektakulär die Strecke.

Frôler le désastre

S'il était l'un des plus grands pilotes sur piste en terre des États-Unis, Rex Mays n'échappait pas non plus à l'accident, comme ici à Del Mar (ci-contre, en haut) ou, plus tragiquement, au Milwaukee Fairgrounds, dans lequel il perdit la vie en 1947. Pedro Adames blessa deux commissaires et un mécanicien lors d'une course à Buenos Aires (ci-contre, en bas). L'ERA de Ansell fait une sortie spectaculaire à Silverstone lors du Grand Prix de 1948 (ci-dessus).

The new star and the old champion

Ascari's Ferrari 125 (above) led the Grand Prix of Marseille in 1950, but the race was won by his team-mate Villoresi, confirming Ferrari's Grand Prix winning abilities just a couple of years after their debut. The cars everyone had to beat when Ferrari first arrived on the scene were the Alfa Romeo 158s, from the stable where Enzo Ferrari was once team manager. Trossi and Varzi scored an Alfa 1-2 in the Italian Grand Prix in Milan in 1947 (right).

Der neue Star und der alte Champion

Ascaris Ferrari 125 (oben) startete beim Großen Preis von Marseille im Jahr 1950 in vorderster Reihe, als erster ins Ziel kam sein Teamgefährte Villoresi, und damit war bewiesen, dass die Ferraris nur zwei Jahre nach ihrem Debüt bereits das Zeug zum Sieger hatten. Die Wagen, an denen alle anderen sich messen mussten, als Ferrari die Arena betrat, waren die Alfa Romeo 158 aus dem Stall, in dem Enzo Ferrari Rennleiter gewesen war. Beim Großen Preis von Mailand 1947 (rechts) sorgten Trossi und Varzi für einen Alfa-Doppelsieg.

La nouvelle star et l'ancien champion

Si la Ferrari 125 de Ascari (ci-dessus) mène dans le Grand Prix de Marseille de 1950, la course sera remportée par son coéquipier Villoresi, confirmant ainsi les capacités des Ferrari quelques années seulement après l'arrivée de la firme en Grand Prix. Jusqu'à présent, comme dans le Grand Prix d'Italie de 1947 à Milan, où Trossi et Varzi s'arrogent les deux premières places (à droite), les voitures à battre étaient les Alfa Romeo 158, l'écurie dont Enzo Ferrari avait été autrefois le directeur.

Giants of the track

Argentine Juan Manuel Fangio won the Monza Cup with his privately entered Formula 2 Ferrari (above) in 1949 as he began to establish his reputation in Europe. In the early days of post-war racing, the beautiful, supercharged 1.5-litre Alfa Romeo 158/159 Alfettas were in a class of their own in Grand Prix racing. This is Jean-Pierre Wimille's (below) at Reims in 1948.

Giganten der Rennstrecke

Der Argentinier Juan Manuel Fangio gewann den Pokal von Monza 1949 mit seinem privat gemeldeten Formel-2-Ferrari (oben), als er noch am Anfang seiner europäischen Karriere stand. In den ersten Nachkriegsrennen waren die prachtvollen Alfa Romeo 158/159-Alfettas mit 1,5-Liter-Kompressormotor bei den Grand-Prix-Wagen eine Klasse für sich. Hier (unten) mit Jean-Pierre Wimille am Steuer, Reims 1948.

Les géants de la piste

L'Argentin Juan Manuel Fangio remporte en 1949 la Coupe Monza avec sa Ferrari de Formule 2 engagée à titre privé (ci-dessus) alors qu'il commence à peine à se forger une réputation en Europe. À la reprise des courses après-guerre, les belles Alfetta 158/159 à moteur suralimenté de 1,5 litre construites par Alfa Romeo, comme celle de Jean-Pierre Wimille à Reims en 1948 (ci-dessous), formaient une catégorie en soi dans les courses de Grand Prix.

Against the elements

Appalling weather for Grand Prix cars at the start of the Italian Grand Prix in Turin in September 1948. The Ferrari has the advantage over the Alfas and Maseratis at the start, but the Alfettas were almost unbeatable during this season, and here Wimille's Alfa led Villoresi's Maserati and Raymond Sommer's Ferrari at the finish, with Wimille also setting fastest lap.

Die feindlichen Elemente

Entsetzliches Wetter für Grand-Prix-Wagen beim Start zum Großen Preis von Italien, Turin, September 1948. Der Ferrari hat die bessere Startposition vor den Alfa- und Maserati-Wagen, doch die Alfettas waren in dieser Saison kaum zu schlagen, und Wimille ging auf Alfa als erster ins Ziel, gefolgt von Villoresis Maserati und Raymond Sommers Ferrari; Wimille fuhr auch die schnellste Runde.

Contre les éléments

Un temps épouvantable accueille les concurrents du Grand Prix d'Italie, organisé à Turin en septembre 1948. La Ferrari prend dès le départ l'avantage sur les Alfa et les Maserati mais les Alfetta sont alors presque imbattables pendant cette saison. L'Alfa de Wimille, qui enregistre le tour le plus rapide, mène devant la Maserati de Villoresi et la Ferrari de Raymond Sommer.

A Prince and a schoolboy
Not long after the arrival of Mrs Anna Leonowens as a tutor at the Court of the Siamese royal family (the inspiration for the musical *The King and I*), the new King's nephew, Prince Bira, had come to Europe and become famous as a racing driver. Here Bira is pursued for his autograph during the Jersey races in 1947 by a schoolboy from a less exotic background.

Ein Prinz und ein Schuljunge
Kurz nach der Ankunft von Mrs. Anna Leonowens als Lehrerin am Hof der Königsfamilie von Siam (die Inspiration zum Musical *Anna und der König von Siam*) war der Neffe des neuen Königs, Prinz Bira, nach Europa gegangen und ein berühmter Rennfahrer geworden. Hier bittet ein Schuljunge von weniger exotischer Herkunft Bira bei den Jersey-Rennen von 1947 um ein Autogramm.

Un prince et un écolier
Peu de temps avant l'arrivée de Mrs Anna Leonowens comme préceptrice à la cour royale du Siam (elle inspira la comédie musicale *Le Roi et Moi*), le neveu du nouveau roi, le prince Bira, arrivait en Europe où il devint un pilote de course si célèbre que même les écoliers viennent lui demander des autographes, comme ici pendant l'édition 1947 des courses de Jersey.

A supporting role

There have been many famous and excellent female racing drivers through the history of the sport, and there have also been those women whose support has been a vital part in the success of the men. Signora Pagani (above left) on timekeeping duty for her husband in Jersey in 1947, and an observer's role for one team member (above right) at Shelsley Walsh in 1947.

Die Frau im Hintergrund

In der Geschichte des Sports hat es eine ganze Reihe berühmter und ausgezeichneter Fahrerinnen gegeben, hinzu kommen die Frauen, die mit ihrer Unterstützung entscheidend zum Erfolg der Männer beigetragen haben. Signora Pagani (oben links) stoppt 1947 in Jersey für ihren Mann die Zeit, während dieses Teammitglied in Shelsley Walsh (oben rechts), ebenfalls 1947, eher kontemplativ bleibt.

Un rôle de soutien

L'histoire du sport automobile a rendu célèbre nombre d'excellents pilotes féminins. Mais il ne faut pas oublier ces femmes de pilotes, dont le soutien a joué un rôle vital dans la réussite de leurs compagnons. La signora Pagani chronomètre son mari à Jersey en 1947 (à gauche) tandis que l'épouse d'un membre de l'écurie se cantonne dans un rôle d'observatrice à Shelsley Walsh en 1947 (à droite).

Legacies of pre-war ambitions
The Pertrix sports car, racing through the forests in around 1949, was the streamlined racer that Petermax Müller created around the simple mechanical components of the Volkswagen Beetle, the car that Ferdinand Porsche had created for Adolf Hitler before the war as a car for the people. The Pertrix was only one of many VW-based sports and racing cars – including the first Porsche.

Nicht im Sinne des Erfinders
Der Pertrix-Sportwagen, um 1949 auf einer Waldstrecke aufgenommen, war kaum mehr als Petermax Müllers Stromlinienkarosserie auf einem Volkswagen-Chassis – der Mechanik des Wagens, den Ferdinand Porsche für Adolf Hitler zur Motorisierung des deutschen Volkes konstruiert hatte. Neben dem Pertrix gab es eine Vielzahl von weiteren Sport- und Rennwagen auf VW-Basis – darunter auch den ersten Porsche.

Retour des ambitions d'avant-guerre
La Pertrix, que l'on aperçoit ici à travers les arbres vers 1949, était la barquette profilée qu'avait construite Petermax Müller sur la base de la Coccinelle Volkswagen, à la mécanique assez simple, la voiture du peuple imaginée par Ferdinand Porsche pour Adolf Hitler avant la guerre. Cette Pertrix n'était qu'un des nombreux exemples de voitures de sport, dont la première Porsche, créées à partir d'une VW.

Germany's Formula 3 forerunners
Huschke von Hanstein on his way to an easy win on 'the little Nürburgring', the Aachen Forest circuit, in June 1949 in the tiny rear-engined Condor. Designed for the under-750cc racing car class, cars like the Condor, designed by Helmut Hütten, flourished briefly before they were superseded by the more universally popular 500cc Formula 3 as the 1950s approached.

Deutsche Vorläufer der Formel 3
Huschke von Hanstein fährt im Juni 1949 auf dem »kleinen Nürburgring« im Wald von Aachen mit einem winzigen Mittelmotor-Condor dem sicheren Sieg entgegen. Wagen wie der von Helmut Hütten konstruierte Condor erlebten eine kurze Blütezeit in der Klasse bis 750 ccm, bevor Anfang der fünfziger Jahre die weltweit populäre Formel 3 mit 500 ccm aufkam.

Les précurseurs de la Formule 3 en Allemagne
En juin 1949, Huschke von Hanstein fonce vers la victoire sur le « petit Nürburgring », le circuit tracé dans la forêt d'Aix-la-Chapelle, dans sa Condor à moteur arrière dessinée par Helmut Hütten. Conçues pour courir dans la catégorie des moins de 750 cm³, des voitures comme la Condor, firent brièvement florès avant d'être dépassées par celles de Formule 3 (500 cm³), dont la popularité s'accrut vers la fin des années 1940.

The gruelling marathon

The Mille Miglia, a flat-out 1,000-mile road race through the heart of Italy, was one of the toughest tests in motor sport. Italian driver Clemente Biondetti leaves the start in his Ferrari (opposite, above) in 1948 and returns as the winner (opposite, below). In 1949 (opposite, right) the strain shows after his fourth win, his third in succession. Nuvolari (above) before the 1948 race.

Nichts für schwache Naturen

Die Mille Miglia, tausend Meilen auf Landstraßen durch Italien, gehörte zu den härtesten Rennen des Motorsports. Der Italiener Clemente Biondetti geht 1948 mit seinem Ferrari an den Start (gegenüber, links oben) und siegt (gegenüber, links unten). 1949 (gegenüber, rechts) ist ihm nach seinem vierten Sieg – drei davon in aufeinander folgenden Jahren – die Erschöpfung anzusehen. Nuvolari (oben) vor dem 1948er Rennen.

Un marathon éprouvant

Le rallye des Mille Miglia, une épreuve de 1600 km au cœur de l'Italie, était l'une des plus difficiles du sport automobile. Après Nuvolari (ci-dessus), le pilote italien Clemente Biondetti prend le départ dans sa Ferrari en 1948 (ci-contre, en haut) pour revenir en vainqueur (ci-contre, en bas). L'année suivante, en 1949, la fatigue se lit sur son visage après sa quatrième victoire, la troisième successive (ci-contre, à droite).

—6—
Once were Warriors:
Ferraris, Fangio and Moss

The 1950s started with the creation of one new motor racing institution, a new official world championship for Grand Prix cars and drivers, and ended with the last throes of another, the classic front-engined Grand Prix car. In between, it was a decade of superb rivalries, a new generation of front-running cars and drivers from both Europe and South America, the rise of Great Britain as a successful builder of Grand Prix cars, and a decade when motor sport continued to grow around the world.

Two of the biggest names of the decade were still relative newcomers in 1950, but in spite of only having been part of the scene for a couple of years both were already forces to be reckoned with. The first was a new sporting marque – Ferrari. It was only, of course, a new name as a car constructor in its own right, but it already had a substantial motor racing heritage which stretched back to the Twenties. Back then, Enzo Ferrari, born in 1898 the son of a prosperous metalworker in Modena in northern Italy, had first been a minor racing driver himself, then a hugely successful team manager for Alfa Romeo, whose cars he ran through the 1920s and 1930s, latterly under the prancing horse badge of his own Scuderia Ferrari. Shortly before the Second World War, Ferrari had returned to manage the official Alfa racing team, but rapidly fell out with the management and walked away, with a certain amount of cash compensation and a small group of important engineering colleagues. He set up a small engineering consultancy, Auto Avio Costruzioni, in Modena, and in 1940 he built two small 8-cylinder Fiat-engined sports cars. By the terms of his separation from Alfa he was forbidden, for a period of four years, to go racing in opposition to Alfa Romeo under his own name. So when he entered his new cars in the 1940 Mille Miglia (strictly speaking the Brescia Grand Prix) he simply called them 815s, by Auto Avio Costruzioni. Both led their class before being obliged to retire, after which motor racing was forced into its wartime break. When it returned post-war, Ferrari's four-year restriction on racing cars bearing his own name had expired, and in the dying months of 1946 a new make of sporting car appeared – the Ferrari.

The first Ferrari was a sports car, with an engine of only 1.5 litres but introducing the classic Ferrari layout of 12 cylinders in a vee. It was designed specifically for racing, as most of the early Ferraris would be – even if some had to be sold to pay for the racing programme. Almost immediately

Ferrari entered his sports cars in major races and by 1948 the first real Ferrari Formula 1 car had appeared in the Italian Grand Prix, in Turin. Raymond Sommer finished an encouraging third in the only one of the three Ferraris entered to finish, but the car won the next time out and in 1949 Ferrari won three Grands Prix, including the European Grand Prix at Monza. By the Fifties, and that first official world championship series, Ferrari was the biggest threat to the domination of Alfa Romeo, his former employers.

In 1948 the Argentine government headed by Juan Perón, a motor racing fanatic, financed a trip to America and Europe for a group of the top Argentine drivers. One of them was a driver who was already in his late thirties, and whose early racing experience had been mainly with home-built specials and American coupés. But it was clear that he had talent, and motor racing was about to find out how much talent. His name was Juan Manuel Fangio, and, after an almost unnoticed European debut with a Simca-Gordini at Reims in 1948, he returned to Europe late in 1949 and began to win important races, with a Maserati sponsored by the Argentine Automobile Club and running in their blue and yellow colours. Later in the season the Maserati was joined by a Ferrari and, when the official championship began in 1950, Fangio was a full-time Grand Prix driver, having been signed up by Alfa alongside Giuseppe Farina and Luigi Fagioli.

In that first official year, Alfa swept all before them, and Farina won the first driver's title – while Fangio won the Monaco, Belgian and French Grands Prix on his way to second place in his first championship year. Over the next seven years (in spite of missing the whole 1952 Grand Prix season after a major accident in a Formula 2 race), he won the drivers' championship five times, in 1951 (for Alfa), 1954 and 1955 (for Mercedes-Benz), 1956 (for Ferrari) and 1957 (for Maserati), a record still unbeaten in Grand Prix racing until Michael Schumacher won his sixth and seventh titles in 2003 and 2004.

Fangio had been a natural choice for Mercedes-Benz when they made their return to Grand Prix racing in the mid-1950s. They had begun their renewed onslaught on top-class motor racing earlier in the decade with a very advanced racing sports car, the 300SL, the forerunner of the 300SL 'Gullwing', one of the world's most famous production sports cars. They won Le Mans with the racing 300SL in 1952, on their return to the greatest sports car race in the world; and they won just as convincingly as soon as they came back to the Grand Prix arena, with both the conventionally open-wheeled W196 single-seaters and the controversial streamlined version, with its sleek, all-enveloping body.

But Mercedes' glorious comeback of the 1950s was tragically short-lived, and it was ended by the greatest disaster in motor racing history, at Le Mans in 1955. That year Fangio was leading the sports car team, and in the early hours of the Le Mans race was fighting for the lead with Mike Hawthorn's Jaguar D-Type, continuing a superb rivalry between the two marques at the highest level of sports car racing. But as dusk approached, tragedy struck. Approaching the starting-line grandstands, Fangio's team-mate Pierre Levegh in another Mercedes struck the back of Lance Macklin's Austin Healey, apparently as Macklin moved to avoid Hawthorn, who was himself moving quickly across his path into the pits. Levegh's car hit the low bank on the outside of the track, burst into flames and broke into several parts, many of which scythed through the crowded starting-line enclosures. Levegh and more than eighty spectators were killed, but the race continued. The remaining Mercedes were withdrawn. Hawthorn went on to win. It was by far the blackest day in the sport's history, and with motor racing immediately banned in some places it might have been the end of the sport completely; but it fought back.

It changed, too, and not only in response to new safety requirements, but as it always had to become ever more technically advanced and ever faster. Through much of the 1950s, one of Fangio's greatest rivals was a young Englishman who had first raced against him in rival marques and then with him as a team-mate at Mercedes-Benz. Famously, Stirling Moss never won the world championship, although he finished runner-up four times in the 1950s and was widely regarded as one of the few drivers who could genuinely give Fangio a hard time. Moss won the 1955 Mille Miglia for the German team, accompanied by *Motor Sport* magazine's famous bearded Grand Prix correspondent, Denis Jenkinson, who had created pace notes for the whole route, which he read to Moss from a long roll of paper wound by hand through a small box. Moss won Grands Prix for Mercedes, too, and for other marques in the 1950s, including Maserati and Vanwall.

He had started his single-seater racing career in the late 1940s in what was then a new kind of racing car, a Cooper-JAP, of the Formula 3 type. It was powered by a 500cc vee-twin motorcycle-type engine, and the engine was mounted behind

A moment of early morning calm for Jaguar mechanics at Le Mans during the 1953 race, where the Jaguars finished first, second and fourth, led home by Tony Rolt and Duncan Hamilton.

Ein wenig frühmorgendliche Ruhe für die Jaguar-Mechaniker beim Le-Mans-Rennen von 1953, wo Jaguar den ersten, zweiten und vierten Platz belegte, mit Tony Rolt und Duncan Hamilton an der Spitze.

Un moment de tranquillité au petit matin pour les mécaniciens de l'écurie Jaguar lors de l'édition 1953 des 24 Heures du Mans, où les Jaguar occupèrent les première, seconde et quatrième places, emmenées par Tony Rolt et Duncan Hamilton.

the driver, in a very light and compact tubular spaceframe chassis with independent suspension. The design was the first of a series of rear-engined racing cars, for sports car racing as well as for single-seater racing, by English designer John Cooper. Cooper became the latest in a line of British Grand Prix manufacturers which had included both BRM and Vanwall from 1950s to 1960s, and with far fewer resources than any of them he became the most successful of them all at the end of the 1950s and into the 1960s. And it was Cooper's rear-engined designs that both started that run of success and, with the end of this dramatic decade, brought the age of the front-engined Grand Prix car towards its close.

The changing face of Grand Prix racing. Stirling Moss's mid-engined Cooper leads Jo Bonnier's front-engined BRM in the Dutch Grand Prix at Zandvoort in 1959. Both led, but Moss retired twelve laps from the end, leaving Bonnier to win.

Das neue Gesicht des Grand-Prix-Sports. Stirling Moss' Mittelmotor-Cooper liegt 1959 beim Großen Preis von Holland in Zandvoort vor Jo Bonniers Frontmotor-BRM in Führung. Der Spitzenplatz war hart umkämpft, doch in der zwölftletzten Runde gab Moss auf, und Bonnier gewann das Rennen.

Le changement de visage des Grand Prix. La Cooper à moteur central de Stirling Moss mène devant la BRM à moteur avant de Jo Bonnier lors du Grand Prix de Hollande 1959 à Zandvoort. Après avoir occupé la tête, Moss abandonna à douze tours de la fin, laissant Bonnier triompher.

Die Schaffung einer neuen Motorsportinstitution, der offiziellen Weltmeisterschaft für Fahrer auf Grand-Prix-Wagen, markiert den Beginn der fünfziger Jahre, und am Ende der Dekade läutete die Ablösung der traditionellen Rennwagen mit Frontmotor eine neue Epoche des Sports ein. Die Jahre dazwischen waren ein Jahrzehnt der großen Rennen, ein Jahrzehnt, in dem sich britische Grand-Prix-Wagen erstmals die vordersten Plätze erkämpften und eine neue Generation erstklassiger Maschinen und Fahrer heranwuchs, nicht mehr nur aus Europa, sondern auch aus Südamerika, denn nicht zuletzt waren die Fünfziger auch die Dekade, in der der Motorsport sich zur wirklich weltumspannenden Disziplin entwickelte.

Zwei der größten Namen waren 1950 noch neu, doch auch wenn sie erst zwei oder drei Jahre zum Renngeschehen gehörten, waren sie doch bereits Kräfte, mit denen man rechnen musste. Der erste war ein neuer Rennstall – Ferrari. Genau genommen war natürlich nur die Marke neu, denn ihr Besitzer war schon seit den zwanziger Jahren aktiv. Enzo Ferrari kam 1898 als Sohn eines Metallindustriellen im norditalienischen Modena zur Welt, versuchte sich zunächst selbst als Rennfahrer, leitete dann mit großem Erfolg das Team von Alfa Romeo und gründete in den Dreißigern mit Alfa-Wagen unter dem Zeichen des springenden Pferdes seine eigene Scuderia Ferrari. Kurz vor dem Krieg kehrte er als Rennleiter zu Alfa Romeo zurück, zerstritt sich jedoch bald mit der Firmenleitung und machte sich mit einer Abfindung und einer Hand voll Konstrukteurskollegen selbstständig. Er richtete ein Ingenieursbüro in Modena ein, Auto Avio Costruzioni, und baute 1940 zwei kleine Sportwagen mit Achtzylindermotoren von Fiat. Die Vereinbarungen mit Alfa sahen vor, dass er vier Jahre lang nicht mit einem Rennstall unter seinem eigenen Namen gegen Alfa Romeo antreten durfte. So hießen die Wagen denn, als er sie bei der Mille Miglia von 1940 (dem Großen Preis von Brescia) an den Start brachte, lediglich »815«, von Auto Avio Costruzioni. Beide führten ihre Klasse an, bis sie ausfielen, und nach diesem Rennen kam der Motorsport während der Kriegszeit zum Erliegen. Als die ersten Nachkriegsrennen stattfanden, war die Vierjahresfrist um, und gegen Ende 1946 erblickte eine neue Sportwagenmarke das Licht der Welt – Ferrari.

Das erste Modell galt als Sportwagen, war aber wie die meisten frühen Ferraris ein reinrassiger Rennwagen, von dem auch nur ein paar Exemplare verkauft werden mussten, um die Rennen zu finanzieren. Der Motor war nur 1,5 Liter groß, jedoch schon nach dem klassischen Ferrari-Prinzip des V12-Zylinders gebaut. Die Ferraris gingen auf Anhieb bei allen großen Rennen an den Start, und 1948 trat beim Großen Preis von Italien in Turin der erste echte Formel-1-Ferrari an. Von drei Wagen fielen zwei aus, doch immerhin errang Raymond Sommer auf dem dritten einen achtbaren dritten Platz, und das nächste Rennen endete schon mit einem Ferrari-Sieg. 1949 war Ferrari dreimal Grand-Prix-Sieger, darunter im Großen Preis von Europa in Monza. Als die Fünfziger und die offiziellen Weltmeisterschaften begannen, galt Ferrari als heißester Kandidat, die Vorherrschaft seines ehemaligen Arbeitgebers Alfa Romeo zu brechen.

1948 schickte der rennsportbegeisterte argentinische Staatschef Juan Perón die besten Fahrer des Landes auf Tournee durch die Vereinigten Staaten und Europa. Einer unter ihnen war schon Ende dreißig und hatte seine Erfahrungen bisher in selbstgebauten Wagen und amerikanischen Coupés gesammelt. Aber er war ein talentierter Mann, und die Motorsportwelt sollte bald erkennen, was in ihm steckte. Er hieß Juan Manuel Fangio und gab sein kaum beachtetes Europadebüt kaum beachtet 1948 in Reims auf einem Simca-Gordini; doch Ende 1949 war er wieder dabei und gewann die ersten großen Rennen mit einem Maserati, der vom argentinischen Automobilclub finanziert wurde und in dessen blau-gelben Farben Fangio antrat. Später im selben Jahr kam ein Ferrari hinzu, und als 1950 die offiziellen Weltmeisterschaftsläufe begannen, trat Fangio neben Giuseppe Farina und Luigi Fagioli als dritter Werksfahrer für Alfa an.

In jenem ersten Meisterschaftsjahr konnte keiner mit Alfa mithalten, und der erste Weltmeistertitel ging an Farina – doch mit Siegen in den Großen Preisen von Monaco, Belgien und Frankreich kam Fangio auf Anhieb auf den zweiten Platz. In den folgenden sieben Jahren gewann er (obwohl er nach einem schweren Formel-2-Unfall das ganze Jahr 1952 aussetzen musste) den Meistertitel fünfmal, 1951 für Alfa, 1954 und 1955 für Mercedes-Benz, 1956 für Ferrari und 1957 für Maserati – ein Triumph, der im Grand-Prix-Sport ungeschlagen war, bis Michael Schumacher 2003 und 2004 sein sechstes und siebtes Rennen gewann

Es lag nahe, Fangio zu verpflichten, als Mercedes-Benz Mitte der fünfziger Jahre wieder Einzug in die Grand-Prix-Arena hielt. Schon zu Anfang des Jahrzehnts hatten sich die Stuttgarter mit dem 300SL zurückgemeldet, einem hoch entwickelten Rennsportwagen, dessen zivile Version, der 300SL-Flügeltürer, zu einem der berühmtesten Seriensportwagen aller Zeiten werden sollte. Mit der Rennausführung siegten sie 1952 in Le Mans bei ihrer Rückkehr zum größten Sportwagenrennen der Welt, und genauso folgte Sieg auf Sieg, als Mercedes wieder zu den Großen Preisen antrat, ob nun mit dem konventionelleren W196 oder mit der viel diskutierten Stromlinienversion, deren Verkleidung auch die Räder abdeckte.

Doch der triumphale Neuanfang währte nur kurze Zeit und endete 1955 in Le Mans mit der größten Tragödie in der Geschichte des Motorsports. In jenem Jahr führte Fangio die Sportwagenmannschaft an und rang in den ersten Stunden des Rennens mit Mike Hawthorn auf dem Jaguar D-Type erbittert um die Führung – eine neue Runde im Wettstreit der beiden Marken, die sich schon eine ganze Reihe spannender Wettkämpfe geliefert hatten. Doch als die Abenddämmerung hereinbrach, kam es zur Katastrophe. Als Fangios Stallgefährte Pierre Levegh sich in einem weiteren Mercedes den Tribünen an der Start- und Ziellinie näherte, kollidierte er mit dem Heck von Lance Macklins Austin-Healey; Macklin hatte Hawthorn ausweichen wollen, der ihn schnitt, um an die Boxen zu gehen. Leveghs Wagen prallte gegen die äußere Einfassung der Strecke, fing Feuer und zerbrach in mehrere Teile, und Trümmer flogen in die dicht gedrängten Zuschauermassen. Levegh und über achtzig Zuschauer fanden den Tod, doch das Rennen ging trotzdem weiter. Die übrigen Mercedes zogen sich zurück, Hawthorn gewann. Für den Rennsport war es der schwärzeste Tag überhaupt; es schien sogar, als sei sein Schicksal damit besiegelt, denn vielerorts wurden Rennen daraufhin verboten. Aber der Sport überstand auch diese Krise.

Und er veränderte sich, nicht nur als Reaktion auf neue Sicherheitsbestimmungen, sondern auch durch technische Neuerungen, die immer schnellere Wagen möglich machten. Die ganzen Fünfziger hindurch zählte zu Fangios größten Rivalen ein junger Engländer, der zuerst bei konkurrierenden Marken gegen ihn angetreten war, dann als Teamgefährte bei Mercedes-Benz. Stirling Moss brachte es nie zum Weltmeistertitel, auch wenn er in jenem Jahrzehnt viermal den zweiten Platz belegte und als einer der ganz wenigen galt, die Fangio wirklich Paroli bieten konnten. 1955 gewann Moss auf Mercedes die Mille Miglia. Als Kopilot fuhr der bärtige Denis Jenkinson mit, legendärer Rennreporter der britischen

Froilan 'Pampas Bull' Gonzalez argues a point with Raymond Mays in 1952.

Froilan Gonzales, »der Stier aus der Pampa«, und Raymond Mays sind 1952 nicht ganz einer Meinung.

Froilan «Pampas Bull» Gonzalez discute avec Raymond Mays en 1952.

Zeitschrift *Motor Sport*, der sich Aufzeichnungen über die Strecke auf einer langen Papierrolle gemacht hatte, die er auf der Fahrt abwickelte und dabei Moss vorlas. Auch Grand-Prix-Rennen gewann Moss in den Fünfzigern für Mercedes und für andere Marken, darunter Maserati und Vanwall.

Zum ersten Mal hatte er Ende der Vierziger in einem Monoposto gesessen, in einem Cooper-JAP der damals neu geschaffenen Formel 3. Als Antrieb diente ein 500-Kubikzentimeter-Zweizylinder aus dem Motorradbau. Der Motor saß in der ultraleichten Gitterrohrkonstruktion mit Einzelradaufhängung hinter dem Fahrer. Es war der Erste einer neuen Generation von Rennwagen des englischen Konstrukteurs John Cooper – Sport- und Formelwagen, bei denen der Motor in die Mitte hinter den Fahrersitz gerückt war. Cooper war damit der jüngste in der wachsenden Schar von britischen Rennwagenbauern, die sich mit BRM und Vanwall in den fünfziger und sechziger Jahren etabliert hatte, und obwohl er von allen die geringsten Ressourcen hatte, ließ er Ende der fünfziger und Anfang der sechziger Jahre alle anderen weit hinter sich. Seinen Erfolg verdankte Cooper dem Mittelmotor, der am Ende der Dekade die traditionellen Frontmotorwagen verdrängte – womit eine Ära des Motorsports zu Ende ging.

Les années 1950 débutent avec l'institution d'une nouvelle organisation du sport automobile et la création d'un championnat du Monde officiel en Grand Prix pour s'achever sur les derniers avatars des bolides à moteur avant. Dans l'intervalle, alors que le sport automobile continue de se développer dans le monde entier, on assiste à des rivalités magnifiques entre pilotes, qu'ils soient européens ou sud-américains, à la naissance d'une nouvelle génération de voitures et à l'arrivée distinguée des constructeurs britanniques en Grand Prix.

Mais cette première décennie d'après-guerre va surtout être marquée par l'inscription au fronton du sport automobile de deux des noms les plus illustres de son histoire, connus seulement de quelques initiés en 1950 et dont les débuts resteront modestes pendant quelques années. Le premier est celui d'une marque d'automobiles : Ferrari. S'il s'agit d'un nouveau constructeur en tant que tel, la firme hérite toutefois de l'expérience substantielle en course acquise depuis les années 1920 par son fondateur, Enzo Ferrari. Né en 1898, ce fils d'un prospère ferronnier de Modène, dans le Nord de l'Italie, a d'abord été un pilote de course moyen avant de devenir l'artisan de la réussite d'Alfa Romeo, autant comme directeur de cette écurie dans les décennies 1920–1930 que sous l'écusson au cheval cabré de sa propre Scuderia Ferrari. Revenu diriger l'écurie Alfa Romeo officielle peu avant la Seconde Guerre mondiale, Ferrari entre en conflit avec sa direction et quitte le constructeur avec une forte indemnité et un petit groupe d'ingénieurs. Il crée alors à Modène une petite société de conseil en ingénierie, Auto Avio Costruzioni, et construit en 1940 deux petites voitures de sport à moteur 8 cylindres Fiat. Suivant les termes de l'accord conclu avec Alfa Romeo lors de leur séparation, il lui est interdit de courir sous son nom contre Alfa Romeo pendant quatre ans. Aussi, lorsqu'il engage deux de ses nouvelles voitures dans les Mille Miglia de 1940 (en réalité le Grand Prix de Brescia), les appelle-t-il simplement 815S par Auto Avio Costruzioni ; elles vont prendre la tête de leur catégorie avant d'être contraintes à l'abandon. Mais, après l'interruption des courses automobiles due à la guerre, le délai de quatre ans imposé à Ferrari est écoulé et il peut donc créer fin 1946 une nouvelle marque portant son nom et dont les voitures courront sous ses couleurs.

Cette première Ferrari, équipée d'un moteur de 1,5 litres de cylindrée seulement mais qui inaugure la conception traditionnelle du 12 cylindres en V, est une voiture de sport conçue spécifiquement pour la course comme la plupart des premières Ferrari – même s'il fallut en vendre certaines à des privés pour financer les engagements. Ferrari engage presque immédiatement ses voitures dans les principales compétitions et c'est en 1948 que la première véritable Ferrari de Formule 1 apparaît au Grand Prix d'Italie, organisé à Monza, près de Turin. Raymond Sommer finit à une encourageante troisième place au volant de la seule des trois Ferrari engagées à terminer cette épreuve. La Ferrari gagne la course suivante puis remporte trois Grands Prix en 1949, dont le Grand Prix d'Europe à Monza. La Scuderia devient ainsi la plus grande menace pour l'écurie Alfa Romeo, dont elle conteste la suprématie dans le premier championnat du monde officiel de Formule 1.

Le deuxième patronyme à marquer de son empreinte la course automobile dans les années 1950 (et les suivantes) est celui de Juan Manuel Fangio. En 1948, le gouvernement argentin dirigé par Juan Perón, un fanatique de la compétition automobile, finance le voyage aux États-Unis et en Europe d'un groupe de pilotes argentins émérites. Parmi eux se trouve Fangio, alors âgé d'une quarantaine d'année, qui a fait ses premières armes en course essentiellement sur des coupés américains et des machines bricolées par lui-même. Son talent naturel apparaît vite évident après des débuts discrets à Reims en 1948 au volant d'une Simca Gordini. Lorsqu'il revient en Europe fin 1949, il commence à remporter des courses importantes avec une Maserati aux couleurs bleu et jaune de l'Automobile Club d'Argentine qui la finance, bientôt rejointe, un peu plus tard dans la saison, par une Ferrari. Mais c'est en 1950, l'année du premier championnat du Monde officiel, que Fangio entame sa véritable carrière de pilote de Grand Prix en entrant dans l'écurie Alfa Romeo aux côtés de Giuseppe Farina et Luigi Fagioli.

Alfa Romeo balaie tout devant elle dès cette première année de championnat, Farina remportant le titre mondial des pilotes alors que Fangio, second au classement général pour sa première participation, gagne les Grands Prix de Monaco, de Belgique et de France. Bien qu'il manque toute la saison 1952 à cause d'un grave accident en Formule 2, il remportera cinq fois le championnat du Monde des pilotes au cours des sept années suivantes : en 1951 avec Alfa Romeo, en 1954 et 1955 avec Mercedes-Benz, en 1956 avec Ferrari et en 1957 avec Maserati. Le record fut inégalé en Grand Prix jusqu'à ce que Michael

Schumacher remporte sa 6ᵉ et 7ᵉ course en 2003 et 2004.

Fangio est à l'évidence le pilote qu'il faut à Mercedes-Benz pour le retour de l'Allemagne sur la scène des Grand Prix au milieu des années 1950. La firme allemande a déjà tenté de revenir dans la course automobile de haut niveau quelques années auparavant grâce à une voiture de sport très moderne, la 300SL, qui annonce la 300SL « Gullwing », l'une des voitures de sport de production les plus célèbres au monde et dont la première participation, en 1952, à l'épreuve reine de l'endurance, les 24 Heures du Mans, se solde par la victoire. Mercedes gagne de manière tout aussi convaincante dès que le constructeur engage sur le plateau des Grand Prix la W196, qu'il s'agisse de la monoplace classique à roues apparentes ou de sa version aérodynamique à carrosserie enveloppante.

Mais le glorieux come-back de Mercedes dans les années 1950 s'interrompt tragiquement par la plus grande catastrophe que connaît l'histoire du sport automobile. En 1955, au Mans, Fangio est en tête de l'écurie Mercedes et lutte depuis les premières heures de la course contre la Jaguar Type D de Mike Hawthorn, illustrant la magnifique rivalité qui oppose les deux marques au niveau le plus élevé. La tragédie éclate en début de soirée lorsque Pierre Levegh, le camarade d'écurie de Fangio, heurte l'arrière de l'Austin Healey de Lance Macklin, vraisemblablement au moment où il déboîte pour éviter Hawthorn qui se rabat pour rentrer aux stands. La voiture de Levegh heurte le muret bordant la piste, prend feu et se disloque en projetant des morceaux de ferraille, dont plusieurs vont faucher la foule massée dans les gradins de la ligne de départ. Levegh et plus de quatre-vingts spectateurs sont tués. Mercedes retire aussitôt toutes ses voitures mais la course n'est pas arrêtée et Hawthorn remporte une bien amère victoire. La conséquence de cet accident est l'interdiction ou l'annulation immédiate de certaines épreuves, voire la menace d'un arrêt définitif du sport automobile.

La compétition change alors de visage non seulement à cause d'une modification de la réglementation, qui renforce désormais la sécurité, mais aussi grâce aux progrès techniques réalisés et à l'augmentation de la vitesse atteinte par les voitures. Pendant une grande partie des années 1950, l'un des plus grands adversaires de Fangio est un jeune pilote anglais qui a d'abord couru contre lui au volant de voitures de marques rivales puis est devenu son compagnon d'écurie chez Mercedes-Benz. Stirling Moss doit une partie de sa

célébrité au fait qu'il n'a jamais remporté le championnat du monde bien qu'il ait terminé quatre fois second dans les années 1950 et soit considéré comme l'un des rares pilotes capables de rivaliser à armes égales avec Fangio. En 1955, Moss donne la victoire à l'écurie allemande dans les Mille Miglia, où il a pour copilote Denis Jenkinson, célèbre spécialiste des Grand Prix du magazine *Motor Sport*, qui lit à Moss ses notes de course inscrites sur un rouleau de papier qu'il déroule à la main.

Moss va également remporter quelques Grand Prix pour Mercedes et d'autres marques, dont Maserati et Vanwall, dans les années 1950.

Il commence sa carrière de pilote monoplace à la fin des années 1940 au volant d'une Cooper-JAP, une voiture de Formule 3 d'un tout nouveau type, qui dispose d'un moteur de motocyclette en V de 500 cm³, installé derrière le pilote dans un châssis tubulaire compact et très léger à suspension indépendante. Cette monoplace, de conception résolument moderne due à l'ingénieur anglais John Cooper, est la première voiture de course à moteur arrière. Bien qu'il soit un nouveau venu parmi les constructeurs britanniques de voitures de Grand Prix, où s'illustreront BRM et Vanwall dans les années 1950, et qu'il dispose de ressources bien inférieures, Cooper va offrir à son écurie de formidables succès dans les années 1960 grâce notamment à cette révolution du moteur arrière qu'il a lancée et qui marque la fin définitive de l'ère des voitures à moteur avant.

Former French motorcycle racing champion Jean Behra took to four wheels immediately after the Second World War. Here he raises his arm in victory after winning the Pau Grand Prix in a Maserati, in 1955.

Der ehemalige französische Motorradmeister Jean Behra stieg nach dem Zweiten Weltkrieg auf vier Räder um. Hier hebt er triumphierend den Arm, als er 1955 beim Großen Preis von Pau mit seinem Maserati als Sieger über die Ziellinie geht.

L'ancien champion motocycliste français Jean Behra passe à la course automobile après la Seconde Guerre mondiale. On le voit ici dans sa Maserati saluant sa victoire dans l'édition 1955 du Grand Prix de Pau.

Britain's Grand Prix hope

Raymond Mays, leaning on the table (opposite), studies the new BRM Grand Prix car with some of his collaborators in 1950. The complex car with its supercharged V16 engine appeared in December 1949, after many delays, and in its early years it proved fast, occasionally even a winner, but fragile. (Right, top to bottom) Mays preparing for a demonstration run at Silverstone in 1950; Peter Walker's car at Silverstone in 1951; and another failure at Dundrod in 1952.

Die britische Grand-Prix-Hoffnung

Raymond Mays (gegenüber, auf den Tisch gestützt) mustert mit einigen Mitarbeitern 1950 den BRM-Grand-Prix-Wagen. Das aufwändig konstruierte Fahrzeug mit V16-Kompressormotor war nach zahlreichen Verzögerungen im Dezember 1949 fahrbereit und erwies sich in seinen ersten Jahren als schnell, bisweilen sogar für einen Sieg gut, doch störanfällig. (Rechts, von oben nach unten) Mays beim Start zu einer Vorführung in Silverstone, 1950; Peter Walkers Wagen 1951 in Silverstone; und noch ein Exemplar, das in die Boxen geschoben werden muss, 1952 in Dundrod.

L'espoir britannique en Grand Prix

Raymond Mays, appuyé sur la table, examine la nouvelle BRM Grand Prix avec quelques-uns de ses collaborateurs en 1950 (page précédente). Cette voiture complexe, équipée d'un moteur V16 suralimenté, sort en décembre 1949 après de nombreux retards, et se révèle à ses débuts rapide voire victorieuse mais assez fragile. (À droite, de haut en bas) Mays s'apprête à effectuer un tour de démonstration à Silverstone en 1950 ; la voiture de Peter Walker à Silverstone en 1951 ; nouvel échec à Dundrod en 1952.

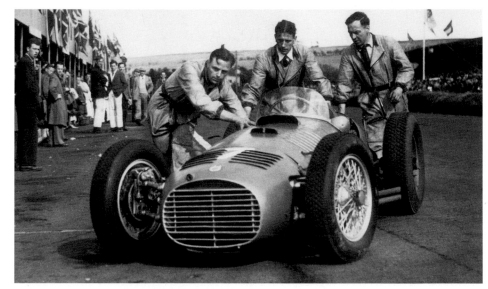

The long road to respectability

In spite of many embarrassingly public failures in its early years, the BRM developed into a race winner, as at Goodwood in 1954 (opposite, above), just in time for the formula to change. It was continuously developed (right) and showed its promise at Silverstone in the 1951 British Grand Prix, where Peter Walker (opposite, below) finished seventh, and Reg Parnell (opposite, right), finished fifth – after carrying out much of the test driving.

Der lange Weg zur Anerkennung

Anfangs war es peinlich, wie oft die BRMs bei Rennen ausfielen, doch nach und nach entwickelten sie sich zu Siegern, 1954 in Goodwood zum Beispiel (gegenüber, links oben), kurz bevor die Formel geändert wurde. Ständig arbeitete man an Verbesserungen (rechts), und schon 1951 beim Großen Preis von England in Silverstone zeigten die Wagen, was in ihnen steckte: Peter Walker (gegenüber, links unten) kam auf den siebten, Reg Parnell (gegenüber, rechts), der einen Großteil der Test-fahrten bestritten hatte, auf den fünften Rang.

La longue route vers la respectabilité

Améliorée en permanence (à droite), la voiture montra un potentiel prometteur à Silverstone lors du Grand Prix de Grande-Bretagne de 1951, où Peter Walker termina septième (ci-contre, en bas) et Reg Parnell termina cinquième après avoir mené une grande partie des essais (ci-contre, à droite). Malgré plusieurs échecs embarrassants à ses débuts, BRM renoue avec la victoire à Goodwood en 1954 (ci-contre, en haut), juste au moment du changement de formule.

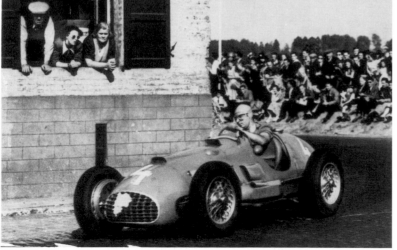

Ferrari, making their mark

Ferrari trio Fangio, Ascari and Villoresi (above) in the non-championship 1950 Argentine Grand Prix at Mar del Plata, which Ascari won after his two team-mates crashed out of the race. Ascari, again Ferrari-mounted (left), in the round-the-houses race at Ville de Mons in 1950, where he and Villoresi dominated.

Ferrari macht Eindruck

Das Ferrari-Trio Fangio, Ascari und Villoresi (oben) 1950 beim nicht zur Weltmeisterschaft zählenden Großen Preis von Argentinien in Mar del Plata; Ascari gewann, nachdem beide Stallgefährten durch Unfälle ausgeschieden waren. Er beherrschte, wiederum im Ferrari (links), zusammen mit Villoresi im selben Jahr auch das Stadtrennen von Mons.

Ferrari prend ses marques

Le trio Ferrari composé de Fangio, Ascari et Villoresi (ci-dessus) mène la danse dans le Grand Prix d'Argentine de 1950 (hors championnat) disputé à Mar del Plata et remporté par Ascari après l'abandon sur accident de ses deux coéquipiers. Ascari, encore sur Ferrari (à gauche) domine avec Villoresi la course sur circuit urbain de Mons en 1950.

Alfa Romeo's driving force

Alfa's drivers Felice Bonetto, Consalvo Sanesi, Giuseppe Farina and Juan Manuel Fangio wrapped up against the cold for the non-championship International Trophy race at Silverstone in May 1951. Fangio and Farina won the heats but a downpour took away their advantage and stopped the main race while Reg Parnell's Thinwall Special Ferrari was in the lead.

Die Alfa-Mannschaft

Die Alfa-Fahrer Felice Bonetto, Consalvo Sanesi, Giuseppe Farina und Juan Manuel Fangio beim nicht zur Meisterschaft zählenden Rennen um die International Trophy im Mai 1951 in Silverstone. Fangio und Farina gewannen die Vorläufe, doch im schweren Regen konnten sie sich nicht durchsetzen, und das Hauptrennen wurde schließlich mit Reg Parnell auf einem Thinwall-Special-Ferrari in Führung abgebrochen.

Les combattants d'Alfa Romeo

Felice Bonetto, Consalvo Sanesi, Giuseppe Farina et Juan Manuel Fangio, les pilotes de l'écurie Alfa Romeo lors de la course de l'International Trophy, hors championnat, à Silverstone en mai 1951. Fangio et Farina remportèrent les éliminatoires mais une violente averse leur fit perdre tout avantage en provoquant l'interruption de la course alors que la Ferrari Thinwall Special de Reg Parnell était en tête.

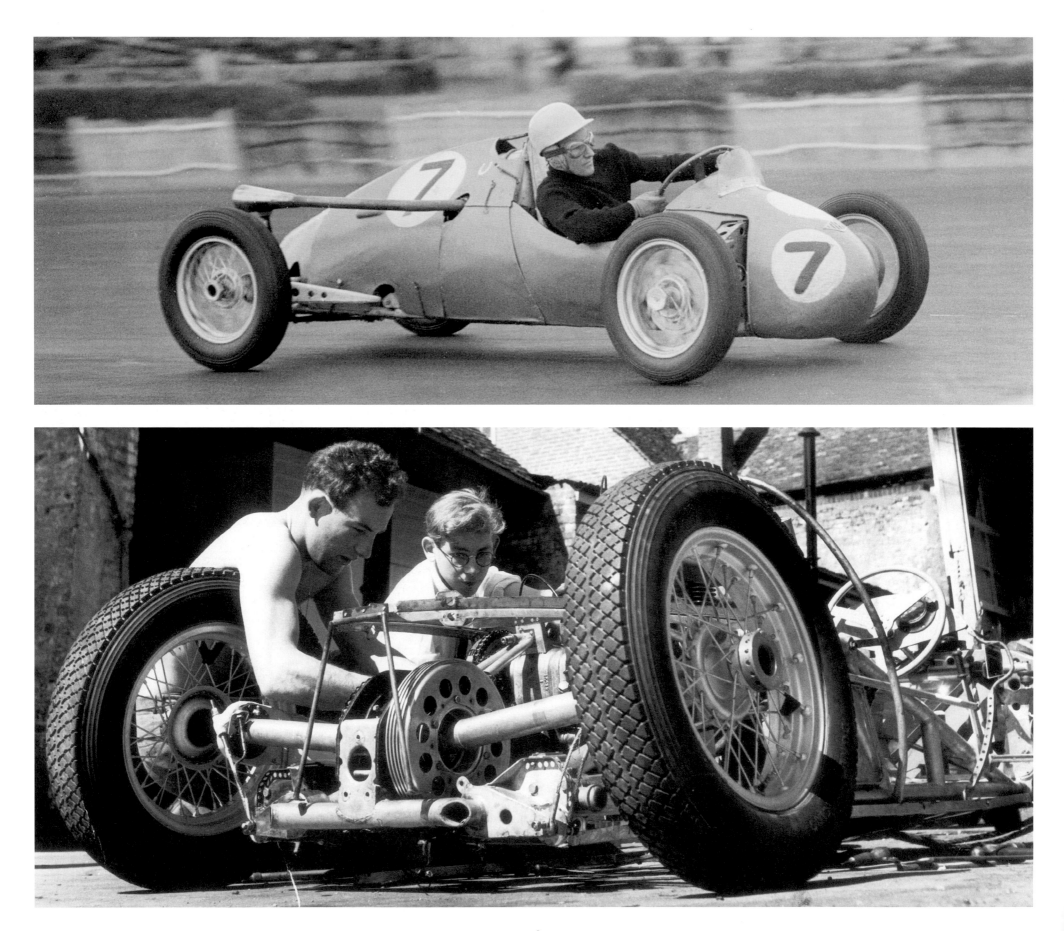

The rise of Stirling Moss

Stirling Moss made his competition debut in hillclimbs in 1948, at eighteen. He built his reputation in the 500cc Formula 3 and, although he had already raced in both sports cars and Formula 2 by 1952, he still raced, and won, with cars like the 500 Kieft (opposite, above and below). In 1954 he lined his privately entered Maserati (28) up against Ascari's Ferrari and winner Fangio's streamlined Mercedes in the Italian Grand Prix.

Stirling Moss' Aufstieg

Sein Renndebüt gab Stirling Moss 1948 mit achtzehn Jahren bei Bergprüfungen. Einen Namen machte er sich zuerst in der 500-ccm-Formel-3, und auch 1952, als er schon in Sportwagen- und Formel-2-Rennen gefahren war, trat er noch mit Wagen wie dem Kieft 500 an (gegenüber, oben und unten) und siegte. 1954 ging er (oben) beim Großen Preis von Italien mit seinem privat gemeldeten Maserati (28) gegen Ascaris Ferrari und den siegreichen Stromlinien-Mercedes von Fangio an den Start.

L'ascension de Stirling Moss

Stirling Moss fait ses débuts en course de côte en 1948, à l'âge de 18 ans puis se forge une réputation en Formule 3-500. Tout en participant en 1952 à des courses de Formule 2 et de grand tourisme, il continue de courir et de gagner avec des voitures comme la 500 Kieft (ci-contre, en haut et en bas). En 1954, il aligne sa Maserati privée (28) contre la Ferrari d'Ascari et la barquette Mercedes de Fangio, victorieuse dans le Grand Prix d'Italie.

Giants of the sport

(Opposite, far left) Alberto Ascari washes up after winning at Silverstone in 1952; (opposite, above) Enzo Ferrari with Mercedes team manager Alfred Neubauer in 1953; (opposite, below) Fangio and Moss in animated conversation after Moss had pipped his rival to the post to win the 1957 Italian Grand Prix at Monza. (Above) Villoresi and Ascari slake their thirsts at Monza in 1953.

Giganten des Motorsports

(Gegenüber, ganz links) Alberto Ascari greift 1952 nach seinem Sieg in Silverstone zur Seife; (gegenüber, rechts oben) Enzo Ferrari mit Mercedes-Rennleiter Alfred Neubauer, 1953; (gegenüber, rechts unten) Fangio und Moss im Gespräch, nachdem Fangio seinem Rivalen in der letzten Runde den Sieg im Großen Preis von Italien, Monza 1957, abgerungen hatte. (Oben) Villoresi und Ascari löschen 1953 in Monza ihren Durst.

Des géants du sport

Alberto Ascari fait sa toilette après sa victoire à Silverstone en 1952 (ci-contre, à l'extrême gauche). Enzo Ferrari avec Alfred Neubauer, le directeur d'écurie de Mercedes, en 1953 (ci-contre, en haut). Fangio et Moss en pleine conversation après que Moss a coiffé son rival au poteau lors du Grand Prix d'Italie de 1957 à Monza (ci-contre, en bas). Villoresi et Ascari étanchent leur soif à Monza en 1953 (ci-dessus).

Room for two

Alongside Grand Prix racing, the highest levels of sports car racing were among the most spectacular disciplines in motor sport in the 1950s, on both sides of the Atlantic. In the 1954 Carrera Panamericana (above), Porsche entered two racing Spyders, to score a dominant class win and third place overall, giving Porsche a famous model name in Carrera. Europe's classic long distance road race, the Mille Miglia, saw huge numbers of cars leave the Brescia start at one-minute intervals, in this case Giannino Marzotto's Ferrari (below), heading for victory in 1953.

Platz für zwei

Neben den Grand Prix gab es in den fünfziger Jahren Sportwagenrennen auf höchstem Niveau, spektakuläre Veranstaltungen auf beiden Seiten des Atlantiks. Bei der Carrera Panamericana von 1954 (oben) startete Porsche mit zwei Spyder-Rennversionen und errang damit einen souveränen Klassensieg sowie den dritten Platz in der Gesamtwertung – und fand seinen berühmten Modellnamen Carrera. Zur Mille Miglia, dem klassischen europäischen Langstreckenrennen, startete in Brescia eine lange Reihe von Wagen in Ein-Minuten-Intervallen, hier (unten) Giannino Marzottos Ferrari, der Sieger von 1953.

De la place pour deux

Parallèlement à la course de Grand Prix, les courses de voitures de grand tourisme comptent, à leur plus haut niveau, parmi les disciplines les plus spectaculaires du sport automobile des années 1950 des deux côtés de l'Atlantique. Lors de la Carrera Panamericana de 1954, Porsche engage deux Spyder et remporte une victoire écrasante dans sa catégorie et une troisième place au classement général (en haut); à la suite de cet exploit, Porsche donnera le nom de Carrera à l'un de ses plus célèbres modèles. Dans la course d'endurance classique en Europe, les Mille Miglia, les très nombreuses voitures prennent le départ de Brescia à une minute d'intervalle, comme la Ferrari de Giannino Marzotto, victorieuse de l'édition 1953 (en bas).

Different scenery, same dangers
Serious racing cars in different settings, thundering through the narrow streets of small-town Italy during the Mille Miglia (above left) and on the mountain roads of Central America in the Carrera Panamericana, the spectacular Mexican road race. These were magnificent events, but in the end both were outlawed because of their terrible records of accidents and fatalities.

Die Umgebung wechselt, die Gefahr bleibt
Rennwagen vor unterschiedlichsten Kulissen – links donnern sie auf der Mille Miglia durch die engen Straßen einer italienischen Kleinstadt, rechts winden sie sich auf der Carrera Panamericana, dem spektakulären mexikanischen Straßenrennen, durch die Berge Mittelamerikas. Beides waren großartige Ereignisse, aber am Ende wurden beide eingestellt, weil die Zahl der Unfälle und Todesopfer zu groß war.

Les mêmes dangers dans des décors différents
Les voitures de sport courent dans des décors variés : fonçant à travers les rues étroites d'une petite ville d'Italie lors des Mille Miglia (ci-dessus à gauche) ou sur les routes montagneuses d'Amérique centrale lors de la Carrera Panamericana, la spectaculaire route mexicaine. Il s'agissait de deux épreuves magnifiques mais qui durent être interdites en raison du grand nombre d'accidents et de blessés qu'elles provoquèrent.

Mercedes variations – the Grand Prix car…
Juan Manuel Fangio at full speed on the ultra-fast Reims circuit in the 1954 French Grand Prix, which he won with the streamlined version of Mercedes' superb W196 Grand Prix car. Enclosed wheels were a rarity in Grand Prix racing, highly desirable for the fastest circuits, hard to position precisely on tighter courses – so Mercedes ran both closed and open wheelers, depending on the circuit.

Zweimal Mercedes – als Grand-Prix-Wagen …
Juan Manuel Fangio auf der ultraschnellen Piste von Reims, 1954 beim Großen Preis von Frankreich, den er mit dieser Stromlinienversion des Mercedes W196 gewann. Karosserien, die die Räder einbezogen, waren bei Grand-Prix-Wagen selten, sie sorgten für noch mehr Tempo auf den schnellen Strecken, waren aber nicht so präzise zu fahren, wenn es eng zuging; so fuhr Mercedes mit beiden Varianten, je nach Austragungsort.

Variations Mercedes – la voiture de Grand Prix …
Juan Manuel Fangio sur le circuit ultra-rapide de Reims lors du Grand Prix de France 1954, qu'il remporta avec la version profilée de la Mercedes W196 Grand Prix. Les roues carrossées, encore une rareté en Grand Prix, pouvaient avantager le pilote sur les circuits rapides mais le gênaient pour se placer avec précision en virage sur des tracés étroits ; Mercedes proposait alors selon les circuits des voitures avec ou sans roues carrossées.

...and the sports racer

Fangio in a streamlined Mercedes again: this time the two-seater 300SLR sports car at Le Mans in 1955. Technically brilliant, the car would have disputed the race all the way with arch rivals Jaguar, but the Mercedes team withdrew its remaining cars after the accident involving one of its cars and French driver Pierre Levegh in the early hours of the race.

... und als Rennsportwagen

Wiederum Fangio in einem Stromlinien-Mercedes: diesmal im zweisitzigen 300 SLR-Sportwagen, 1955 in Le Mans. Die technisch brillanten Wagen hätten das Rennen allein zwischen sich und den Erzrivalen von Jaguar entscheiden können, wäre es nicht schon bald nach dem Start zum Unfall mit dem Mercedes-Fahrer Pierre Levegh gekommen, woraufhin die Mannschaft sich vom Rennen zurückzog.

... et la voiture de sport

Fangio dans sa Mercedes 300 SLR biplace profilée au Mans en 1955. Techniquement brillante, elle aurait pu disputer toute la course contre sa grande rivale Jaguar mais l'écurie Mercedes retira toutes ses voitures après l'accident fatal ayant impliqué le pilote français Pierre Levegh dans les premières heures de la course.

Before the catastrophe

Chasing the Ferrari which led the early stages, Mike Hawthorn's D-Type Jaguar heads the Mercedes shared by Fangio and Moss through the Esses at Le Mans in 1955 – the Jaguar with the advantage of disc brakes, the Mercedes counter-attacking with a moveable air-brake behind the cockpit. Hawthorn and Ivor Bueb won the race after the Mercedes team's withdrawal.

Vor der Katastrophe

1955 in den S-Kurven von Le Mans: Mike Hawthorn jagt mit seinem Jaguar D-Type den Ferrari, der zunächst in Führung lag, gefolgt von Fangios und Moss' Mercedes. Jaguar hatte seinen Konkurrenten die Scheibenbremsen voraus, Mercedes konterte mit einer ausklappbaren Luftbremse hinter dem Cockpit. Hawthorn und Ivor Bueb gewannen das Rennen, nachdem sich das Mercedes-Team zurückgezogen hatte.

Avant la catastrophe

Poursuivant la Ferrari qui mène le bal dans les premiers tours, la Jaguar Type D de Mike Hawthorn devance les Mercedes de Fangio et Moss dans la chicane du Mans en 1955. Si la Jaguar bénéficiait de freins à disque, la Mercedes disposait d'un aéro-frein mobile en arrière du cockpit. Hawthorn et Ivor Bueb gagnèrent la course après le retrait de Mercedes.

The darkest moment

Barely two hours into the 1955 Le Mans race, Hawthorn's Jaguar passed Macklin's Austin Healey near the start–finish line, then cut across his line towards the pits. Macklin swerved to avoid the Jaguar and Levegh's Mercedes hit the tail of the Healey. The Mercedes hit the barriers, Levegh died instantly, and debris from the disintegrating car killed more than eighty spectators. The race went on.

Der schwärzeste Augenblick

Das Le-Mans-Rennen von 1955 war noch nicht zwei Stunden alt, als Hawthorns Jaguar den Austin Healey von Macklin überholte und dann schnitt, um an die Boxen zu gehen. Macklin versuchte dem Jaguar auszuweichen, und Leveghs Mercedes kollidierte mit dem Healey. Der Mercedes prallte gegen die Absperrung, Levegh war auf der Stelle tot, und Trümmerteile erschlugen über achtzig Zuschauer. Das Rennen ging trotzdem weiter.

Les plus noirs moments

Deux heures après le début de l'édition 1955 des 24 Heures du Mans, la Jaguar de Hawthorn dépasse l'Austin Healey de Macklin dans la ligne droite puis coupe la ligne centrale pour rentrer aux stands. Macklin tente d'éviter la Jaguar et Levegh vient le heurter avant de partir dans les barrières de sécurité. Levegh meurt dans le choc. Les débris de la voiture blessent et tuent plus de 80 spectateurs. Mais la course doit continuer.

Advantage compromised

The aerodynamic advantage of the fully-bodied Mercedes was a significant factor on the high-speed Silverstone circuit for the 1954 British Grand Prix, but even Fangio found that the enclosed wheels made it difficult to place the car accurately through tighter corners. Gonzalez and Hawthorn (9 and 11) took first and second for Ferrari, while Fangio could only manage fourth.

Ein zweifelhafter Vorzug

Die aerodynamische Verkleidung war für den Mercedes beim 1954er Großen Preis von England auf dem schnellen Kurs von Silverstone vorteilhaft, doch selbst Fangio konnte die engen Kurven nicht exakt nehmen, wenn er die Räder nicht sah. Gonzales und Hawthorn (9 und 11) eroberten für Ferrari den ersten und zweiten Platz, Fangio musste sich mit dem vierten begnügen.

Un avantage compromis

Lors du Grand Prix de Grande-Bretagne de 1954, la silhouette aéro-dynamique de la Mercedes lui donne un net avantage sur le circuit rapide de Silverstone, bien que Fangio trouve que le carrossage des roues complique le placement précis de la voiture dans les virages les plus serrés. Gonzalez et Hawthorn (numéros 9 et 11) prennent les première et seconde places tandis que Fangio ne parvient qu'à se classer en quatrième position.

Moss and Mercedes: a fine partnership

After proving his abilities in 1954, Stirling Moss tested the prototype W196
Mercedes at Hockenheim in January 1955 (opposite, above left) and soon
agreed terms with team manager Neubauer (opposite, below left). As well
as winning the British Grand Prix at Aintree (right), Moss was magnificent
in the sports cars, and took a famous victory in the 1955 Mille Miglia
for Mercedes (opposite, right). He was partnered by journalist Denis
Jenkinson (above).

Moss und Mercedes: eine gute Partnerschaft

Nachdem er 1954 sein Talent unter Beweis gestellt hatte, fuhr Stirling Moss
im Januar 1955 auf dem Hockenheimring den Mercedes W196-Prototyp zur
Probe (gegenüber, links oben) und war sich bald mit Rennleiter Neubauer
einig (gegenüber, links unten). Moss gewann den Großen Preis von
England in Aintree (rechts) und feierte Erfolge in Sportwagenrennen;
berühmt wurde sein Sieg für Mercedes in der Mille Miglia von 1955
(gegenüber, rechts) mit dem Journalisten Denis Jenkinson als Beifahrer
(oben).

Moss et Mercedes : un bon partenariat

Ayant fait la preuve de ses capacités en 1954, Stirling Moss procède
aux essais du prototype Mercedes W196 à Hockenheim en janvier 1955 (ci-
contre, en haut à gauche) et accepte bientôt de signer avec le directeur
d'écurie Neubauer (ci-contre, en bas à gauche). En même temps qu'il
remporte le Grand Prix de Grande-Bretagne à Aintree (à droite), Moss
poursuit une belle carrière en grand tourisme et signe pour Mercedes une
victoire restée célèbre dans les Mille Miglia de 1955 (ci-contre, à droite).
Son copilote était le journaliste Denis Jenkinson (ci-dessus).

Britain's Grand Prix winners

In the 1950s, Vanwall put Britain on the Grand Prix map. The Vanwall and Thinwall Specials (opposite, below left and right, on the Monza grid and winning at Goodwood in 1951) were modified Ferraris, sponsored by bearing maker Tony Vandervell (above right, with Stirling Moss). They were the forerunners of the Vanwall proper, in which Tony Brooks won the 1958 Italian Grand Prix (above left) and which Stirling Moss raced in 1957 (opposite, above), to take second place in the world championship.

Britische Grand-Prix-Erfolge

In den fünfziger Jahren wurde Großbritannien mit den Vanwall-Wagen (gegenüber, unten links und rechts am Start in Monza und beim Sieg in Goodwood, 1951) ein ernst zu nehmender Konkurrent im Grand-Prix-Sport. Die Vanwall- und Thinwall-Specials waren modifizierte Ferraris, die der Kugellager-Hersteller Tony Vandervell finanzierte (oben rechts, mit Stirling Moss). Sie waren die Vorläufer der Vanwall-Eigenkonstruktionen, mit denen Tony Brooks 1958 den Großen Preis von Italien gewann (oben links) und Stirling Moss 1957 (gegenüber, oben) den zweiten Platz der Weltmeisterschaft errang.

Les vainqueurs des Grand Prix de Grande-Bretagne

Vanwall remet la Grande-Bretagne dans la course aux Grand Prix dans les années 1950. Les Vanwall et les Thinwall Specials (page suivante, en bas à gauche et à droite, sur la grille de départ de Monza et lors de leur victoire à Goodwood en 1951) étaient des Ferrari modifiées, financées par le fabricant de roulements Tony Vandervell (en haut à droite, avec Stirling Moss). Elles annonçaient les précurseurs de ces Vanwall avec lesquelles Stirling Moss prit la deuxième place au championnat du monde en 1957 (ci-contre en haut) et Tony Brooks remporta le Grand Prix d'Italie de 1958 (en haut à gauche).

A true drivers' circuit

Prince Bira points to the track during the drivers' briefing for the French Grand Prix at Reims in 1954 (above), with Maurice Trintignant looking pensive alongside. Reims was a public road course, one of the fastest on the Grand Prix calendar and a daunting challenge for any driver. The long main straight stretches into the distance as one of the Ferraris is pushed past the Mercedes pit (left), and seated team manager Neubauer, whose legendary organisational skills contributed to a Mercedes 1-2 in 1954.

Eine Fahrerstrecke

Bei der Fahrerbesprechung zum Großen Preis von Frankreich, Reims 1954, weist Prinz Bira auf die Strecke (oben), und Maurice Trintignant schaut nachdenklich zu. Reims war ein Straßenkurs, unter den Grand-Prix-Strecken einer der schnellsten und für die Fahrer eine große Herausforderung. Die lange Gerade (links) reicht bis an den Horizont; hier wird ein Ferrari an den Mercedes-Boxen vorbeigerollt, und vorn sitzt Rennleiter Neubauer, der mit seinem legendären Organisationstalent 1954 seinen Teil zum Mercedes-Doppelsieg beitrug.

Un vrai circuit de pilotes

Le prince Bira montre le circuit du Grand Prix de France à Reims en 1954 pendant le briefing des pilotes, sous le regard pensif de Maurice Trintignant (ci-dessus). Le circuit de Reims, utilisant des portions de voie publique, était l'un des plus rapides du calendrier des Grand Prix et un défi pour tout pilote. Dans la longue ligne droite, une des Ferrari est poussée vers son stand en passant devant Mercedes (à gauche) et le directeur d'écurie Neubauer, dont les légendaires talents d'organisateur contribuèrent à l'obtention des deux premières places par Mercedes en 1954.

When the rains come

S. Coldham and George Wicken (above) splash through the puddles in their Formula 3 Coopers at a wet and slippery Goodwood in 1950, while spectators resort to raincoats and umbrellas to cheer on Biondetti's Jaguar XK120 (right) in the 1950 Mille Miglia. Biondetti survived the treacherous cobbles and the mountain roads to finish eighth in a race which saw victory for Giannino Marzotto – one of four Marzotto brothers in the race, all driving for Ferrari.

Wenn der Regen kommt

S. Coldham und George Wicken (oben) schlittern 1950 auf ihren Formel-3-Coopers durch die Pfützen von Goodwood, und die Zuschauer, die bei der Mille Miglia desselben Jahres Biondetti auf dem Jaguar XK120 anfeuern (rechts), brauchen Regenmäntel und Schirme. Biondetti überstand die Fahrt über tückisches Kopfsteinpflaster und gefährliche Bergstraßen und kam als Achter ins Ziel; Sieger wurde Giannino Marzotto – einer von vier Marzotto-Brüdern, die alle vier auf Ferrari antraten.

Lorsque vient la pluie

En 1950, S. Coldham et George Wicken (ci-dessus) foncent dans les flaques avec leur Cooper de Formule 3 sur le circuit humide et glissant de Goodwood, tandis que des spectateurs s'abritent sous les imperméables et les parapluies pour saluer le passage de la Jaguar XK120 de Biondetti engagée dans le rallye des Mille Miglia (à droite). Biondetti, déjouant les pièges des pavés et des routes de montagne, finit huitième dans cette course qui vit la victoire de Giannino Marzotto, l'un des quatre frères Marzotto engagés et tous pilotes chez Ferrari.

Appliance of science

When Mercedes returned to Grand Prix racing in 1954, after an absence of fifteen years since the days of the all-conquering pre-war Silver Arrows, they came back with the same aura of invincibility, of supreme organisation and technical mastery. These are the team cars in the pit garages at Reims in 1954, where Fangio and Karl Kling scored a dominant 1-2, a full lap ahead of Manzon's third-placed Ferrari.

Eine exakte Wissenschaft

Als Mercedes 1954 ins Renngeschehen zurückkehrte, waren 15 Jahre seit der Zeit der unschlagbaren Vorkriegs-Silberpfeile vergangen, doch die Aura der Unbesiegbaren, der organisatorischen und technischen Überlegenheit war geblieben. Hier sind die Werkswagen in der Boxenwerkstatt in Reims, 1954, wo Fangio und Karl Kling einen Doppelsieg einfuhren, mit einer ganzen Runde Vorsprung vor dem Ferrari des Drittplatzierten Manzon.

Une science exacte

Lorsque Mercedes revient en Grand Prix en 1954, après 15 ans d'absence depuis l'époque des Flèches d'argent d'avant-guerre, c'est avec la même aura d'invincibilité et de maîtrise technique. Les voitures de l'écurie sont en cours de préparation dans les stands du circuit de Reims, où Fangio et Karl Kling remportent les deux premières places du Grand Prix de 1954, avec un tour d'avance sur la Ferrari de Manzon, classée troisième.

Winning habits

In 1954 Reims was the first race for the new Mercedes team, and its first victory. Three more Mercedes wins for Fangio, plus two when he was driving for Maserati before the Mercedes return, gave him his second world championship. The Mercedes, which ran in streamlined form at Reims (above), were usually the fastest cars on the circuit but their success also owed much to the skill of the larger-than-life Alfred Neubauer (below), here supervising pit signals during the Reims comeback victory.

Gewohnheitssieger

Reims 1954 war das erste Rennen für das auf Anhieb erfolgreiche neue Mercedes-Team. Drei weitere Male kam Fangio in diesem Jahr auf Mercedes als Erster ins Ziel. Zusammen mit den zwei Siegen auf Maserati vor seiner Zeit bei Mercedes reichte das für den zweiten Weltmeistertitel. Die Mercedes, die in Reims mit der Stromlinienkarosserie antraten (oben), waren meist die schnellsten Wagen auf der Strecke, aber zum guten Teil verdankten sie ihren Erfolg auch dem Geschick des genialen Alfred Neubauer (unten), der hier beim großen Reims-Comeback die Boxensignale beaufsichtigt.

Des habitudes de vainqueur

La nouvelle écurie Mercedes disputa sa première épreuve en 1954 à Reims, et y enregistra sa première victoire. Fangio remporte son second titre de champion du monde en totalisant trois victoires sur Mercedes et deux autres lorsqu'il pilotait pour Maserati, avant le retour de Mercedes à la compétition. Les Mercedes profilées engagées à Reims (en haut) sont souvent les voitures les plus rapides sur ce circuit mais leur succès doit également beaucoup au talent d'Alfred Neubauer, omniprésent même pour le panneautage de rentrée au stand lors de la victoire célébrant le retour de son écurie à la compétition (en bas).

The maestro from Argentina

Juan Manuel Fangio (above) was in a class of his own for most of the 1950s, taking five world titles, the first in 1951 then an unmatched four in a row from 1954 to 1957. He was keenly supported by his partner, Andreina (opposite, above left and right), and even in his final championship year he drove his Maserati with undiminished style and aggression, as when winning at Monaco (opposite, below).

Der argentinische Maestro

Fast die gesamten fünfziger Jahre war Juan Manuel Fangio (oben) unangefochten; er errang fünf Weltmeisterschaftstitel, den ersten 1951, dann, bisher unerreicht, viermal hintereinander von 1954 bis 1957. Seine Lebensgefährtin Andreina war immer dabei (gegenüber, oben links und rechts), sein eleganter Stil und seine Angriffslust blieben ungebrochen bis zu seinem letzten Sieg auf Maserati in Monaco (gegenüber, unten).

Le maître argentin

Bénéficiant du soutien de sa compagne Andreina (ci-contre, en haut à gauche et à droite), Juan Manuel Fangio (ci-dessus), un pilote d'une catégorie à part dans les années 1950, remporta cinq titres de champion du monde, le premier en 1951 et les quatre autres de 1954 à 1957. Sa dernière année de compétition, il pilotait encore sa Maserati avec une maestria et une agressivité fantastiques telles qu'il termina vainqueur à Monaco (ci-contre en bas).

The other Berlin wall

The most spectacular feature of the Avus circuit in Berlin was the incredible high banking which linked the long straights at one end of the otherwise fairly uninteresting circuit. The banking, here dotted with Porsches during an early 1950s sports car race, was the steepest and widest anywhere. For some unfortunate drivers, including Jean Behra, who was killed when his Porsche RSK sports car went over the top of the banking in 1959, it was literally a wall of death.

Die andere Berliner Mauer

Der spektakulärste Teil der Berliner Avus war die unglaublich hohe Steilkurve, mit der die beiden langen Geraden der ansonsten wenig anspruchsvollen Strecke an einem Ende verbunden waren. Die Kurve, hier mit einem Aufgebot an Porsche-Sportwagen bei einem Rennen der frühen Fünfziger, war die steilste und breiteste der Welt. Für manch unglücklichen Fahrer, darunter Jean Behra, der 1959 mit seinem Porsche RSK über die Kante hinausgetragen wurde, war es im wahrsten Sinne des Wortes eine Mauer des Todes.

L'autre mur de Berlin

La portion la plus spectaculaire du circuit Avus de Berlin était l'extraordinaire virage relevé qui reliait les deux longues lignes droites à l'une des extrémités d'un tracé par ailleurs assez inintéressant. Ce virage, négocié ici par des Porsche lors d'une épreuve du début des années 1950, était le plus incliné et le plus large du monde. Pour certains pilotes malheureux, dont Jean Behra, tué en 1959 lorsque sa Porsche RSK s'envola à l'extérieur, il s'agissait d'un véritable mur de la mort.

Monza's speedbowl

The Monza Autodrome, in beautiful parkland in the suburbs of Milan, was also once shaped by its famous bankings, until they went out of use as the face of Grand Prix racing changed. This is Behra's Maserati, with streamlined bodywork for this specialised setting, leading Carlos Menditeguy's more conventional Maserati during the 1955 Italian Grand Prix, where they finished fourth and fifth behind Fangio's all-conquering Mercedes, which won at an average speed of 128.4mph.

Tempo in Monza

Das Autodrom von Monza, in einem prachtvollen Park in der Vorstadt von Mailand gelegen, war einst ebenfalls von seinen berühmten Steilkurven geprägt, doch mit neuen Grand-Prix-Anforderungen verschwanden sie aus dem Kurs. Hier sehen wir Behras Maserati, mit Stromlinienverkleidung speziell für diese Art von Rennen versehen, vor Carlos Menditeguys konventionellerer Maserati-Variante beim Großen Preis von Italien 1955, wo sie den vierten und fünften Rang belegten; Sieger war Fangio auf dem unschlagbaren Mercedes, mit dem er eine Durchschnittsgeschwindigkeit von 206,6 km/h erreichte.

Le circuit de Monza

L'Autodrome de Monza, aménagé dans un parc magnifique des environs de Milan, présentait autrefois également de célèbres virages relevés, qui furent abandonnés avec le changement des formules de Grand Prix. La Maserati de Behra, dont l'aérodynamique de la carrosserie a été adaptée à ce circuit particulier, devance la Maserati plus classique de Carlos Menditeguy lors du Grand Prix d'Italie de 1955, où ils finirent quatrième et cinquième derrière l'invincible Mercedes de Fangio, qui remporta la victoire à la moyenne de 206,6 km/h.

The end of one era, the beginning of another
Piero Taruffi leads Wolfgang von Trips across the finish line in Brescia (above) to take first and second places for Ferrari in the 1957 Mille Miglia. It was the final running of the classic Italian road race. At Vienna-Aspern in 1958 (right), Jean Behra leads a field dominated by Porsches, a sight which was becoming increasingly familiar in sports car racing.

Eine Ära geht zu Ende, eine andere beginnt
Piero Taruffi geht knapp vor Wolfgang von Trips über die Ziellinie in Brescia (oben), ein Doppelsieg für Ferrari in der Mille Miglia von 1957. Es war das letzte Mal, dass das klassische italienische Straßenrennen gefahren wurde. In Wien-Aspern (rechts) führt Jean Behra 1958 ein von Porsche beherrschtes Feld an – ein Anblick, an den man sich bei Sportwagenrennen allmählich gewöhnte.

La fin d'une époque au début d'une nouvelle ère
Piero Taruffi bat Wolfgang von Trips sur la ligne d'arrivée de Brescia (ci-dessus) et permet ainsi à Ferrari de prendre les deux premières places du rallye des Mille Miglia de 1957, dernière édition de ce grand classique italien. En 1958, à Vienne-Aspern, Jean Behra précède une meute de voitures dominée par les Porsche (à droite), une vision qui allait devenir de plus en plus fréquente dans la catégorie des voitures de sport.

'Mon Ami Mate'

Mike Hawthorn used to call Peter Collins 'Mon Ami Mate'. Alongside Moss, Collins and Hawthorn were the greatest English drivers of their day, and Collins was widely seen as a future World Champion. In 1956 he took over this Lancia Ferrari from Fon de Portago to finish second to team-mate Fangio in the British Grand Prix. He was third in that year's championship, but was killed at the Nürburgring in 1958.

»Mon Ami Mate«

Mike Hawthorn nannte Peter Collins »Mon Ami Mate«. Neben Moss waren Hawthorn und Collins die größten englischen Fahrer ihrer Zeit, Collins galt als Kandidat für den Weltmeistertitel. 1956 übernahm er von Fon de Portago Lancia Ferrari und wurde beim Großen Preis von England Zweiter hinter seinem Stallgefährten Fangio. In jenem Jahr wurde er Dritter in der Weltmeisterschaftswertung, verunglückte jedoch 1958 auf dem Nürburgring.

« Mon ami Mate »

Hawthorn appelait Collins « Mon Ami Mate ». Collins et Hawthorn étaient, avec Moss, les plus grands pilotes britanniques de leur temps, le premier étant considéré comme le futur champion du monde. En 1956, il prit la succession de Fon de Portago au volant de cette Lancia Ferrari. Il termina 2ᵉ derrière Fangio dans le Grand Prix de Grande-Bretagne et se classa 5ᵉ au championnat du monde des conducteurs. Il se tua au Nürburgring en 1958.

Tragic champion
Mike Hawthorn practising with his Ferrari for the 1958 British
Grand Prix at Silverstone. He was second to team-mate Collins
in the race, and only won one Grand Prix to Moss's four, but
his minor placings gave him the world title by a single point
from Moss. Hawthorn retired at the end of his championship
year, but tragically died in a road accident within months of
walking away from the sport.

Tragischer Champion
Mike Hawthorn mit seinem Ferrari beim Training zum Großen
Preis von England in Silverstone, 1958; beim Rennen belegte er
hinter Collins den zweiten Platz. Anders als Moss, der vier
Rennen gewann, errang er nur einen Grand-Prix-Sieg, doch
die Summe der Platzierungen machte ihn zum Weltmeister.
Anschließend zog sich Hawthorn vom Rennbetrieb zurück,
starb jedoch wenige Monate später bei einem Verkehrsunfall.

Un champion tragique
Mike Hawthorn, ici avec sa Ferrari lors des essais du Grand Prix
de Grande-Bretagne de 1958 à Silverstone, termina 2ᵉ derrière
son coéquipier Collins. Bien qu'il n'ait remporté qu'un seul
Grand Prix cette saison-là, ses places d'honneur régulières lui
permirent cependant d'emporter le titre mondial à un point
devant Moss. Hawthorn mourut dans un accident de la route
quelques mois après avoir abandonné la compétition automobile.

The atmosphere of speed
Reverent crowds watch Ferraris in the paddock at Silverstone in 1956 (opposite, above); mechanics work on Collins's Lancia Ferrari at Monza in 1956 (opposite, left); and two world champions go about their work – Mike Hawthorn during the 1957 Monaco Grand Prix (opposite, right) and Fangio, relaxed and precise in his Maserati (above) while finishing second to Moss's Vanwall at Monza in 1957.

Man spürt das Tempo
Zuschauer betrachten die Ferraris in Silverstone, 1956 (gegenüber, oben); Mechaniker kümmern sich in Monza, 1956, um Collins' Lancia Ferrari (gegenüber, unten links); zwei Weltmeister bei der Arbeit – Mike Hawthorn beim Großen Preis von Monaco, 1957 (gegenüber, unten rechts) und Fangio (oben), entspannt und souverän am Steuer seines Maserati, mit dem er 1957 in Monza hinter Moss' Vanwall als Zweiter ins Ziel ging.

La griserie de la vitesse
La foule des passionnés regarde les Ferrari au paddock de Silverstone en 1956 (ci-contre, en haut) ; des mécaniciens travaillent sur la Lancia Ferrari de Collins à Monza en 1956 (ci-contre, à gauche) ; deux champions du monde vont travailler : Mike Hawthorn lors du Grand Prix de Monaco de 1957 (à gauche) et Fangio, détendu et précis au volant (ci-dessus), qui terminera second derrière la Vanwall de Moss à Monza en 1957.

Starters orders

Drivers sprint to their cars (opposite, above) at the start of the Goodwood 9-Hour sports car race, won by Dennis Poore and Peter Walker for Aston Martin in 1955. The 500cc grid lines up at a dismal Brands Hatch (opposite, below) in 1956. Small capacity sports cars, with Lotuses in the ascendancy (above), leave the start at Silverstone in 1958, showing the new subtlety of ever-improving aerodynamics.

Auf die Plätze ...

Die Fahrer sprinten beim 9-Stunden-Sportwagenrennen von Goodwood, 1955, zu ihren Wagen (gegenüber, oben); Sieger wurden Dennis Poore und Peter Walker auf Aston Martin. Die 500-ccm-Klasse nimmt Aufstellung in Brands Hatch, 1956 (gegenüber, unten). Bei den Sportwagen mit kleinvolumigen Motoren dominierten 1958 die Lotus, hier (oben) in Silverstone 1958; bemerkenswert ist die verbesserte Aerodynamik.

Aux ordres du starter

Les pilotes courent vers leur voiture au départ des 9 Heures de Goodwood (ci-contre, en haut), une épreuve remportée en 1955 par Dennis Poore et Peter Walker sur Aston Martin. La formation de la grille de départ des 500 cm³ lors d'une course à Brands Hatch en 1956 (ci-contre, en bas). Cette image des voitures de sport de petite cylindrée, des Lotus en majorité (ci-dessus), à Silverstone en 1958 témoigne des dernières évolutions de l'aérodynamisme.

Battles in the streets

No other venue has the tradition, setting or special challenges of Monaco – a true street circuit which takes in the town and seafront. Short noses, as on Tony Brooks's Ferrari in 1959 (above), were a Monaco speciality to improve cooling and make a car slightly easier to 'aim', but the track could always be congested, as on the opening lap of the 1958 Grand Prix, won by Maurice Trintignant's Cooper (opposite).

Straßenschlacht

Kein anderer Grand-Prix-Kurs kann es an Tradition, Ambiente und Schwierigkeiten mit der Fahrt durch Monaco aufnehmen. Kurze Nasen, wie 1959 bei Tony Brooks' Ferrari (oben), waren typisch für Monaco – sie ließen mehr Luft an den Kühler und erleichterten das »Zielen«, trotzdem war auf der Strecke oft Gedränge, so in der Eröffnungsrunde des Rennens von 1958 (gegenüber), das Maurice Trintignant auf Cooper gewann.

Des batailles dans les rues

Aucun autre circuit n'offre une telle tradition de sport automobile que le tracé de Monaco. Le choix d'un avant court, comme celui de la Ferrari de Brooks en 1959 (ci-dessus), était réservé à Monaco car il permettait d'améliorer le refroidissement du moteur et rendait la voiture plus facile à « placer ». La piste était souvent l'occasion d'embouteillages, comme lors du 1er tour du Grand Prix 1958, remporté par la Cooper de Trintignant (ci-contre).

Giant-killing genius

In the Monaco Grand Prix of 1959 the agility of the mid-engined Cooper privately entered by Rob Walker, and the brilliance of Stirling Moss, gave the more powerful cars a very hard time. Here Moss hounds Jean Behra's Ferrari through Casino Square, in the days before the circuit was lined with steel barriers and advertising slogans. In 1959, both Moss and Behra retired in Monaco, but a year later Moss drove Walker's Lotus here, and won – scoring a rare Grand Prix victory for a privately entered car in an age of big money teams.

Der Drachentöter

Beim Großen Preis von Monaco im Jahr 1959 machte der von Rob Walker privat gemeldete Mittelmotor-Cooper mit seiner Wendigkeit und dem Geschick von Stirling Moss am Steuer den stärkeren Wagen das Leben schwer. Hier hetzt Moss Jean Behras Ferrari über den Platz vor der Spielbank, zu einer Zeit, bevor die Strecke hinter Stahl-barrieren und Reklametafeln verschwand. 1959 fielen sowohl Moss als auch Behra aus, doch im Jahr darauf trat Moss von neuem in Monaco an, diesmal mit Walkers Lotus, und gewann – einer der seltenen Fälle, in denen ein Privatwagen sich in einem Grand-Prix-Rennen gegen die weitaus finanzkräftigeren Werksmannschaften durchsetzen konnte.

Un génie tueur de géants

Lors du Grand Prix de Monaco de 1959, l'agilité de la Cooper privée à moteur central engagée par Rob Walker et le talentueux pilotage de Stirling Moss ont donné du fil à retordre à des voitures bien plus puissantes. Moss pourchasse ici la Ferrari de Jean Behra au Casino, à une époque où la piste n'est pas encore bordée de barrières en fer et de panneaux publicitaires. Moss, qui a dû abandonner en 1959 avec Behra, remporte la victoire un an plus tard avec la Lotus de Walker et inscrit une victoire en Grand Prix assez rare pour une voiture privée face à de richissimes écuries.

Coming of age

By the end of the 1950s, having returned to Grand Prix racing in 1956, BRM were beginning to show occasional promise, most of it wasted by poor reliability. American Harry Schell (above) drove for BRM at Monza in 1958 and took fifth place, followed by second place in Holland. By the 1950s, the Nürburgring (opposite) had grown into the most challenging of all Grand Prix circuits.

Endlich erwachsen

1956 war BRM auf die Grand-Prix-Pisten zurückgekehrt. Ende der Fünfziger stellten sich erste Erfolge ein, auch wenn mangelnde Zuverlässigkeit noch immer das Hauptproblem war. Der Amerikaner Harry Schell (oben) kam 1958 für BRM in Monza auf den fünften Platz, in Holland sogar auf den zweiten. Der Nürburgring (gegenüber) entwickelte sich in den fünfziger Jahren zur Grand-Prix-Strecke par excellence.

L'époque de la maturité

Revenue aux courses de Grand Prix en 1956, BRM commence à révéler son potentiel, malheureusement souvent gâché par une mauvaise fiabilité, grâce à des pilotes comme l'Américain Harry Schell, qui s'octroie la 5e place à Monza en 1958 (ci-dessus) et termine second en Hollande. Dans les années 1950, le Nürburgring (ci-contre) est devenu l'un des circuits de Grand Prix les plus difficiles de tous.

Flag-to-flag supremacy

By the end of the decade, the mid-engined Coopers were making the front-engined opposition increasingly obsolete, and only the power of Ferrari could seriously challenge their world championship winning ways. At the British Grand Prix at Aintree in 1959, Jack Brabham's Cooper led the grid away in fine style (above), and seventy-five laps later he took the chequered flag (right) ahead of Stirling Moss's BRM. Within a couple of years there would be no more front-engined cars on the Grand Prix grid, as the early years of motor racing gave way to a new modern era.

Von Start bis Ziel die Nase vorn

Als das Jahrzehnt zu Ende ging, hatten die Mittelmotor-Coopers die Konkurrenz mit Frontmotor schon fast verdrängt, und nur Ferrari konnte ihnen noch mit schierer Motorkraft die Weltmeisterschaft streitig machen. Beim 1959er Großen Preis von England in Aintree setzte Jack Brabhams Cooper sich vom Start weg an die Spitze des Feldes (oben), und als fünfundsiebzig Runden später die Zielflagge geschwenkt wurde, ging er auch als Erster über die Linie, gefolgt von Stirling Moss auf BRM. Wenige Jahre darauf waren die Frontmotorwagen von den Grand-Prix-Pisten verschwunden, und eine neue Epoche des Motorsports hatte begonnen.

La suprématie

À la fin de la décennie, les Cooper à moteur central rendent l'opposition des voitures à moteur avant de plus en plus négligeable, seule la puissance des Ferrari pouvant sérieusement contrarier leurs ambitions au championnat du monde. Lors du Grand Prix de Grande-Bretagne, organisé en 1959 à Aintree, la Cooper de Jack Brabham prend magnifiquement la tête dès le départ (ci-dessus) et passe soixante-quinze tours plus tard la première sous le drapeau à damier (à droite) devant la BRM de Stirling Moss. Quelques années plus tard, les voitures à moteur avant auront définitivement disparu de la grille des Grand Prix, laissant la place à l'ère moderne de la course automobile.

gettyimages

This book was created by Getty Images, 21-31 Woodfield Road, London W9 2BA

Over 70 million images and 30,000 hours of film footage are held by the various collections owned by Getty Images.
These cover a vast number of subjects from the earliest photojournalism to current press photography, sports, social history
and geography. Getty Images' conceptual imagery is renowned amongst creative end users.
www.gettyimages.com

Über 70 Millionen Bilder und 30 000 Stunden Film befinden sich in den verschiedenen Archiven von Getty Images.
Sie decken ein breites Spektrum an Themen ab – von den ersten Tagen des Fotojournalismus bis hin zu aktueller
Pressefotografie, Sport, Sozialgeschichte und Geographie. Bei kreativen Anwendern ist das Material von Getty Images
für seine ausdrucksstarke Bildsprache bekannt.
www.gettyimages.com

Plus de 70 millions d'images et 30 000 heures de films sont détenus par les différentes collections dont Getty Images
est le propriétaire. Cela couvre un nombre considérable de sujets – des débuts du photojournalisme aux photographies actuelles de
presse, de sport, d'histoire sociale et de géographie. Le concept photographique de Getty Images est reconnu des créatifs.
www.gettyimages.com

Pictures in this book have been taken exclusively from Getty Images.
Additional acknowledgements:
Cover photograph: Popperfoto
Page 95-6 bottom right: DAS FOTOARCHIV GmbH